SOCIAL ENGLAND

ILLUSTRATED EDITION—Vol. I. Section II.

*FROM THE NORMAN CONQUEST TO THE ACCESSION OF
EDWARD THE FIRST.*

THE ANNUNCIATION

FROM A PSALTER.

SOCIAL ENGLAND

A Record of the Progress of the People

In Religion, Laws, Learning, Arts, Industry, Commerce,
Science, Literature and Manners, from the Earliest
Times to the Present Day

EDITED BY

H. D. TRAILL, D.C.L.

SOMETIME FELLOW OF ST. JOHN'S COLLEGE, OXFORD

AND

J. S. MANN, M.A.

SOMETIME FELLOW OF TRINITY COLLEGE, OXFORD

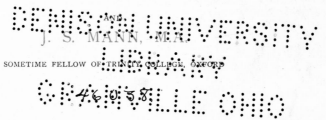

VOLUME I. SECTION II

NEW YORK: G. P. PUTNAM'S SONS
LONDON: CASSELL AND COMPANY, LIMITED
1909

CONTENTS.

CHAPTER III.

FROM THE CONQUEST TO THE CHARTER. 1066–1216.

CHAPTER IV.

FROM CHARTER TO PARLIAMENT. 1216–1273.

CONTENTS.

LIST OF PLATES.

(Brief Notes on some of these will be found with those on the remaining Illustrations.)

NOTES TO ILLUSTRATIONS.

VOLUME I. SECTION II.

———◦•◦———

The minor arts, such as embroidery and the illumination of MSS., flourished in England during the Anglo-Saxon period, and being carried on within the monasteries were not affected by the Norman Conquest. The illustration here reproduced is taken from a Psalter (MS. Roy. 2 A. xxii) written and illuminated in England towards the end of the twelfth century, and shown by internal evidence to have belonged to Westminster Abbey. It contains an illuminated calendar and five miniatures, one of which is here reproduced—the Annunciation, the Visit of Mary to Elizabeth, the Virgin and Child, Our Lord in glory, and David playing on the harp. At the end are five full-page drawings, dating from the second half of the thirteenth century, and representing a king, a knight, Saint Christopher, a bishop, and the face of Christ. Two of these, the knight and the bishop, are respectively shown at Vol. I. p. 688, and Vol. II. p. 35 of this work. This Psalter also contains several beautifully illuminated initial letters, one of which apparently represents Jonah riding on the whale's back towards the land. But it is without that wealth of purely secular and extraneous ornamentation which is found in some Psalters of a later date, such as the Luttrell Psalter and Queen Mary's Psalter, and of which a number of examples are reproduced in this work. Possibly the difference may be due to the fact that these Psalters were made to the order of laymen and for their own use, and that they could not follow the chanting of the Psalms in Latin (*cf.* Vol. II. p. 786, note).

The inscriptions, in hexameter verse, call on the spectator to recognise William the master of the Normans and King of the English.

The first of William I.'s castles at York (rebuilt by Richard III.) was on the left bank of the Ouse, on the present site of Clifford's Tower; the second, on the mound here figured on the right bank, was built in eight days; probably it was either wood or very rough masonry. Both castles were broken down by revolters under Waltheof, but were rebuilt by William. Freeman, *Norman Conquest*, IV.

Obverse, name of king and mint (Ohsnaforda); reverse moneyer's name Bernuald. Keary and Poole, *Catalogue of Coins in the British Museum*, Vol. II., No. 118, and Plate V., No. 9.

PAGE

murder, from the restored drawing of a painting on wood in Canterbury Cathedral. (3) Glass medallion, from window in Canterbury Cathedral, showing the shrine of St. Thomas, from a photograph by the Rev. T. Field, Warden of Radley College, who has kindly permitted its reproduction here: *Journal Arch. Inst.*, XIX., 282. (4) Reliquary in Hereford Cathedral Library, formerly regarded as the shrine of King Ethelbert, patron saint of the cathedral, and representing his murder by order of Offa, King of Mercia. In 1862, however, it was exhibited at South Kensington, and its resemblance to other reliquaries of Becket corrected the mistake. It is composed of oak, covered with copper plates, overlaid in part with coloured Limoges enamel, and partly gilded; it dates from the early part of the thirteenth century.

A RELIC OF THE CULT OF ST. THOMAS 395

Found hidden in a wall of Kewstoke Church, Somersetshire, in 1849; now in the Taunton Museum. In front was a carved figure under a canopy; at the back an arched recess with a door, behind which was the wooden cup containing traces of human blood, presumably that of Becket. It is supposed to have belonged to Woodspring Priory, near Taunton, of which a descendant of one of Becket's murderers was the founder, and a descendant of another a benefactor, and whose prior had a cup or chalice on his seal. It was probably hidden in Henry VIII.'s reign. (*Cf.* Luard, *Materials for the History of Thomas Becket*, Rolls Series, Introduction.)

SCENES FROM THE HISTORY OF ST. HUGH 396, 397

From the modern windows of the Chapterhouse, Lincoln, by Messrs. Clayton and Bell: the funeral scene is a copy of the glass in the rose window of the north transept of Lincoln Cathedral. On the representations of St. Hugh, *see* Canon G. G. Perry, *St. Hugh of Lincoln*, Appendix D.

STATUTES OF WILLIAM I. 399

This record "contains what is probably the sum and substance of all the legal enactments made by the Conqueror, independent of his confirmations of the earlier laws" (Bishop Stubbs). It will be found in Stubbs, *Select Charters*, p. 83. The MS., written by several hands, is of the twelfth and thirteenth centuries.

A PAGE OF DECRETALS, WITH COMMENTARY 407

From a fourteenth-century MS., "written by an English hand for French use," but once belonging to the Monastery of St. Bartholomew, Smithfield, London. The text of the Decretals is enclosed in a border and surrounded by the commentary; the lower and sometimes the side margins contain illuminations of great value.

PAGE FROM BRACTON'S TREATISE 410

The MS. dates from the reign of Edward I.

SITE OF THE FOLK-MOOT, PENNENDEN HEATH 412

Near Maidstone: the "mootstead" of the kingdom of Kent, and the scene of the memorable trial which determined the respective rights of Lanfranc, Archbishop of Canterbury, and Odo, Bishop of Bayeux, in 1076. Until the present century members of Parliament for the county were nominated here, and it was the site of the County Hall.

THE JUDICIAL COMBAT 414

Reproduced and described by Prof. F. W. Maitland, *Pleas of the*

sling, is held down by a catch : when this catch is suddenly let go, the barrel falls, and the missile is discharged with great force. Stones and iron balls were the usual missiles, but mention is also made of hives of bees, with the exit blocked—a primitive form of shell, found especially useful in causing horses to stampede—putrefying quarters of animals, and occasionally human heads. (*Cf.* Oman, *Art of War*, pp. 136–139 and 545–548 ; Kohler, *Kriegswissenschaft ;* A. Schulz, *Hofleben im Mittelalter.*) There appears also to have been a machine intermediate between the mangon and the trébuchet, in which the beam was pulled down by men instead of by the counter-weight. The mangon and balista are derived from ancient Greek and Roman warfare. There is usually much vagueness in the nomencla-ture. After 1200, according to Mr. Oman, "perrière," when used in conjunction with "mangonel," means "trébuchet" ; before that date it probably means the transitional machine mentioned above. A modern trébuchet was constructed by Napoleon III., when Prince President, and is described in his work *De l'Artillerie*, Vol. II. (1851), page 38 *seqq.* With a counterpoise weighing 4,500 kilogrammes, or about $4\frac{1}{2}$ tons, it threw a bullet 21 centimetres ($8\frac{1}{4}$ inches) in diameter nearly 200 feet ; but it seems to have been both cumbrous and dangerous to its manipulators.

E*

See above, note to p. 449. St. Guthlac, during his retirement at Croyland, was much tempted by the devils who haunted the fens. The first medallion represents his castigation of the leader of a band that invaded his oratory, with a whip given him by St. Bartholomew, who had intervened on another occasion to protect him; in the second, he is shown casting out a devil with his girdle from one Egga, whose companions look on in astonishment.

This, alone of extant examples, has the seal appended.

MS. CCC. Camb. 16; probably drawn by Matthew Paris; represents the attack on the "Tower of Damietta," in Egypt, by the Crusaders in 1218.

From a thirteenth-century Bestiary, executed in England (or possibly Flanders), MS. Harl. 4751, containing edifying Latin stories from natural history. The picture is of interest as illustrating details of rigging, etc. The text accompanying this illustration tells how a huge whale sometimes sleeps on the surface of the sea for so long that sand gathers on it and shrubs spring up, and mariners, thinking they have found an island, land on it in order to cook their food. Then the monster, awakened by their fire, suddenly dives, carrying down ship and crew; and thus Satan draws down those who trust him into the bottomless pit.

The name is perhaps suggested by Mark xvi. 7. For its meaning, *see* text, page 470.

The standard account of these is that of the late Mr. C. R. Cockerell, R.A., *Iconography of the West Front of Wells Cathedral,* 1851. Edward the Martyr (murdered at Corfe Castle by his step-mother, and identified by the chalice he holds, the symbol of martyrdom) is on the fourth tier, nearly over the north door. Fulk, Earl of Anjou, is identified by the Oriental character of his dress, he having become King of Jerusalem, 1131. Robert, Duke of Normandy, father of the Conqueror, is next to him. Lindhard, Bishop of Senlis, was brought as her chaplain by Bertha, the Christian Queen of Ethelred of Kent (text, p. 228). These two statues are on the lower tier.

the Gaelic of the Highlands, the "Highland line," as traced by Skene, *Celtic Scotland,* is taken as representing the boundary. *Cf.* that work, Vol. III., p. 22. Orkney and Shetland were still Norse in allegiance as in speech, and Norse was also spoken in the lowlands of Caithness. As to Ireland, Down and Antrim, and in a less degree the districts round Dublin and Wexford, were settled by men of English speech, while there had been Danish settlements in the towns of Wexford and Waterford. The district round Limerick was also settled by English, but no linguistic limits can be very definite, because the English settlers notoriously often became "more Irish than the Irish." Wicklow and the adjacent hill districts certainly remained Celtic. *Cf.* Richey, *History of the Irish People,* p. 137 *seq.* For the boundaries of the English dialects *see* the text; for the northern boundary of Midland, Mr. A. J. Ellis's demarcation, which relates to the present day, has been followed. *See* his *English Dialects*, and Morris and Skeat, *Specimens of Early English.*

MS. Royal 14 C. vii., a thirteenth-century English MS. of Matthew Paris's *Historia Minor,* an abridgment of his larger history, believed by Sir F. Madden, who edited it for the Rolls Series, to have been written and illustrated by the author.

He is prostrate at the feet of the Virgin.

Trinity College, Cambridge : 1, The Riphaeans fighting the Griffins. 2, Alexander and his party. 3, Alexander disembarking.

The date of this famous Latin Psalter is fixed as earlier than 1340 by the statement contained in it that it was caused to be made by Sir Geoffrey Luttrell (of Irnham, Lincolnshire), who died in 1345, and by a miniature representing the knight himself, his wife (who died in 1340), and one of their daughters-in-law. A calendar is prefixed, and this and the margins of the Psalter are adorned with drawings, including many grotesque and fanciful figures. It belonged about 1600 to Lord William Howard. who is commemorated in the *Lay of the Last Minstrel* as "Belted Will," and a hundred years later to Sir Nicolas Shireburn, from whom it eventually passed by inheritance to the family of Weld, of Lulworth Castle, Dorsetshire. It was described by Mr. J. G. Rokewode in *Vetusta Monumenta,* Vol. VI., where some, but by no means all, of its principal illustrations are reproduced. Those given in this work are, it is believed, the first photographed directly from the originals, and the editor and publishers desire to express their gratitude to the Weld trustees for the unrestricted permission accorded them to draw on the stores of this famous MS.

The driver is one of the grotesque figures frequent in this MS.

Made of coarse, greenish earthenware; three feet in height, and about ten feet in circumference; found under several feet of soil in Bucklersbury, in the City of London, in 1865. The finer wines were, doubtless, imported in such jars, which could be closely sealed.

MS. Royal 14 C. vii. (*see* above). The route runs up the left-hand column from London through Rochester—one day's journey—Canterbury, one day from Rochester, and "the chief of the churches of England," near which St. Augustine's monastery is shown, and Dover, "the entrance and key of the rich isle of England," nearly a day's journey from Canterbury. The traveller has then a choice of routes *viâ* Wissant, Calais, or Abbeville. By the first-named, which is most conspicuous, he reaches Paris, or rather St. Denis, in five days, and thence proceeds *viâ* Nogent, Troyes, Bar-sur-Seine, Châtillon-sur-Seine, and Beaune to Lyons in eleven days. Going by Calais or Abbeville he avoids Paris, and joins the main route at Troyes or Beaune respectively. From Lyons he proceeds to Turin by the Mont Cenis in about seven days. In Italy a great variety of routes is given, and most of the great towns are marked, but the indications of time seem to stop just beyond Bologna. The chief aim of the Itinerary is as a guide for pilgrims to the Holy Land, of which, and of the Mediterranean, considerable detail is shown (including a camel), and much information given in notes. Acre appears to have been the usual port of debarkation. The whole occupies seven pages.

These two illustrations, from the MS. of the Alexander Romance at Trinity College, Cambridge, are there given as representing the weaving of silk by the Seres or Chinese; but the artist doubtless found his models at home.

A fine example of the ecclesiastical needlework for which England was noted in the thirteenth century; presented to the Duke of Northumberland by refugee nuns from Portugal, to whose convent it belonged, and whom he sheltered at Syon House during the Continental troubles of the early nineteenth century.

A drawing from the top of a "Roll of the Jews" of 1233, preserved in the Record Office, and recording receipt of sums from various Jews, *e.g.* "Of Rachael, the daughter of David, 11s. 4d., for an aid to marry the king's daughter." *See* Jacobs, *Jews of Angevin England.*

The roll is of 5 Edward I. (1332). The drawing, which is superscribed "Aaron fil diaboli" (Aaron, son of a devil), is set against a record of the proceedings taken against certain Jews of Colchester. In 1267 a gentleman of the neighbourhood was hunting; the deer ran through the town, and the chase was joined by Jews and Christians alike. The deer, in endeavouring to jump a wall, broke its neck, and the townsmen were charged with an offence against the forest laws. The Christians were let off with moderate fines, the Jews sentenced to heavier fines and imprisonment. The drawing is to be regarded as a portrait rather than a caricature, in spite of the superscription, and probably represents one of the offenders who, having fled, came back again ten years after (the entry is dated 1277) and compounded for reversal of sentence of outlawry. The story is effectively told in

CHAPTER III.

FROM THE CONQUEST TO THE CHARTER. 1066–1216.

A. L. SMITH.

THE most striking feature in the history of the land which William of Normandy claimed and won had been the disunion The Norman Conquest. between its rival tribes. This fact, while it decided the immediate victory for him, yet cost him a five years' struggle against rebellions before his conquest was final and complete.

The north had hardly stirred to succour the West Saxon king on his hurried march from Stamford Bridge to Hastings ; but the north was slow to bow to a rule that was more than ever a rule by Wessex over Anglian and Danish districts. England, indeed, which had seemed won at a blow, required to be subdued piecemeal. At one time it appeared as if the great battle had overthrown the champion of Southern England at the hand of the Norman Duke, only that the Norman might in turn fall at the hand of the Dane.

But Senlac was more than a great military victory ; it was a social and moral victory too. Not merely did the English axe and javelin there go down before the Norman sword and bow, the too scanty house-carles and the untrained churls of Harold's following before the disciplined knights and heavy-armed footmen of Northern France, but on that field English kingship and English institutions had no spell to withstand the finer temper of the Norman spirit. The fates of two races hung in the balance ; Anglo-Saxon civilisation had been tried, and found wanting. It was well in the end for England that the victory lay with the race which brought with it the very qualities that England yet lacked—the power of organisation, the sense of law and method, the genius for enterprise. The order and discipline of the Norman host, the story of their devout preparations on the eve of battle, their superior arms and equipment, their skilful stratagems and obedience to one commanding will, are typical of the new forces that were to create a new England.

The slaughter at Senlac made it impossible for the south-eastern shires to prolong resistance. Dover, Canterbury, and

Winchester fell into William's hands; but London was prepared to make a bold stand, till it was left helpless by the selfish desertion of Edwin and Morkere, the incapacity of Edgar the Atheling, and William's march across the Thames at Wallingford to Berkhampstead—a position from which he could bar the way of any reinforcements that might be coming to the city. Hither came many leading men of Wessex, and did him homage; and at last the Witan and the Londoners agreed to accept William, as forty-nine years before they had accepted Canute. On Christmas Day, 1066, only three months from his landing at Pevensey, William was crowned King of England at Westminster. Edgar, chosen king but never crowned, had submitted; the homage of Edwin and Morkere after the coronation seemed to guarantee Mid-England and the north; and if William's authority was but nominal in these districts, at any rate in the eastern and south-eastern shires he was able to begin at once his policy of confiscation and re-grant of lands. That his crown now appeared to him fairly secure seems to be proved by his re-crossing the sea at Easter, 1077, to revisit his Duchy. But he left England in strong hands; for Kent was held by Bishop Odo to ward off any attacks from the Continent, and Herefordshire by Fitzosbern to repel the Welsh; and both Odo and Fitzosbern had Palatine powers in these their earldoms. Moreover, he took with him, for hostages and trophies, Edgar and Waltheof, Edwin and Morkere, and Archbishop Stigand.

Norman Rule.
During William's eight months' absence in Normandy the harsher side of Norman rule showed itself in England. Under the oppression of Bishop Odo and Fitzosbern the men of Kent and of Herefordshire broke into revolt. But such isolated risings were futile. In vain did Kent call over Eustace of Boulogne to its aid, and Edric the Wild summon his Welsh allies to the plunder of Normans in Herefordshire. The revolts were put down, even before William could return.

The nation, which had never taught itself to act in unison, even in the fearful days of Danish ravages, was slow to learn its lesson now. Nothing less than the heavy resistless pressure of the Norman rule, continued for more than a century, could effect this. Thus, the south-west, never yet subdued by William, was in open defiance by the winter of 1067, at the same time as Yorkshire and the north, but acted in no concert with them.

Exeter, where Harold's mother and sons were, offered to yield
and pay taxes if it might in all other respects be independent.
But the fall of Exeter and the ravaging of Dorsetshire carried
the submission of Somerset, Devon and Cornwall, Worcestershire
and Gloucestershire.   It also put into the king's hand a fresh
group of forfeited estates, wherewith to reward his kinsmen and
followers.   Not till the west was thus subdued did the north
rise openly.   By recalling the Atheling from Scotland, the
Northerners made an attempt, by a confederation with Edwin
and Morkere and Edric, and aid promised from Welsh, Scots
and Danes, to set up a separate northern kingdom, and to revive
a division which, alike in the days of Edwy and Edgar, of

SEAL OF WILLIAM I.

Edmund and Canute, and of Godwin and Leofric, had been a
fact either avowed or latent in Anglo-Saxon policy.   But no
crisis could make the Mercian earls loyal allies ; they made their
peace once more, the revolt collapsed, and William entered York
in triumph.   He was now actual ruler of West Saxon, East
Anglian, and most of Mercian England, with the old Deira.
But even over these lands his hold was far from secure ; and
beyond the Tees, the Bernician districts, Durham, Northumberland, and the Lothians were his by the tie of homage only ; and
Cheshire, Shropshire, Staffordshire still held out, and were still
under the influence of Edric.

Yet William appears now to have imagined the hardest part
of his task to .be done.   He allowed many of his Norman
soldiery to depart; he appointed a follower of his own to be

The
Reaction
of the
Conquered.

22

Earl of Northumberland; the long delays of Sweyn seemed to show that the danger from the Danes had passed away. The year 1069 was to bring him a rude awakening. The burghers of Durham massacred the new earl and his men; the burghers of York slew the Norman commandant of the castle; Harold's sons were attacking Devonshire, Edric laying siege to Shrewsbury; the Danish fleet appeared on the south and on the east coasts, finally entering the Humber, and garrisoning York. William had been called away from his vengeance on York to put down another general rising in the south-west. Now, by a hasty return march, he drove the Danes out of Lincolnshire, and again mastered York. Here, by a second coronation, on Christmas Day, 1069, he made a concession to the stubborn sense of independence in the land north of Humber. But he had also been engaged meanwhile in a measure at once of vengeance and of policy which should reduce that independence to a vain memory, and for ever put a stop to the invitation of

The Wasting of the North. Danish fleets. This measure was the famous "Wasting of the ✗ North," the ruin and almost the depopulation of the whole of Yorkshire, a crime which shocked even that age, and one which Englishmen looked on as the chiefest of those three great sins that were to weigh heavy against his soul at the Last Judgment. From York William marched to Durham, and received Waltheof's submission. In February, 1070, he made his winter march from York to Chester, though the wasted land could hardly feed an army, and his starving troops mutinied on the way. With the subjugation of North-Western Mercia his conquest of England was now practically complete. The Danish fleet was bought off by bribes; the resistance of the Fen country, centring about the Isle of Ely and the person of Hereward, was overcome in 1071, after eighteen months of toilsome siege. Edric had before this made his submission; Edwin was dead, and Morkere was now a captive. The five years of gallant but disorganised fighting was over; the verdict of Hastings was ratified; a new race had become the rulers of the land, and not till the bloodless victory of Runnymede in 1215 was it clear that Norman barons had merged into the mass of the English nation. The history of these five years brings into prominence the immense superiority of the Norman mercenaries, not merely in fighting power, but in rapidity of movement and in unity of purpose; in all those points, in fact, which followed from the vigilant and resolute character of their commander. Everywhere his methods are the same—to strike terror by ruthless devastation; to secure the towns by strong Norman garrisons and stone castles; to appoint Norman earls whom he could trust; but to win over the English by pardons and by recognition of native customs

THE BAILE HILL, YORK.
The site of William I.'s second castle.

and ideas. He was anxious from the first to take up the position of a lawful English king. As early as 1070 he had dismissed most of his mercenaries; and as early as 1074 the three rebel earls found that the English had begun to look to the king as their champion against the barons. In him, too, was found, as a later writer puts it, that strong man armed who guards his own house. The Welsh border from this time steadily recedes; the cruel Scottish invasions are punished by William's attack on Scotland in 1072, when Malcolm "bowed to him and became his man." Had William lived two years more, says the English Chronicle, he would have won all Ireland by his wisdom, without any fighting. The long series of Danish ravages and wars, which had hardly known ten years' cessation since

787, ended in the great preparations made by King Canute of Denmark in 1085, but rendered abortive by his murder in 1086.

Nor was the change a less marked one in England's internal condition. "The good order that King William made must not be forgotten," as the contemporary writer of the Peterborough version of the Chronicle admits; "it was such that any man who was himself aught might travel from end to end of the land unharmed; and no man durst kill another, however great the injury which he had received."

The Norman kingship was, indeed, that which the later Anglo-Saxon kingship had come not to be—a real organising power. Nowhere was the effect of the Conquest more immediately apparent than in the military system. The Bayeux tapestry shows us that to the Normans we owe both the mounted knight and the bowman, who displaced the peculiar English fashion of the two-handed axe, and the "shield-wall" of footmen. Already in Domesday Book are signs of that organisation of the feudal levy which is bound up with the definition of knight-service and the development of "knights'-fees." From the policy of William dates that increase of castles which the Crown, though only after a long struggle, kept in its own control, and the survival of that Old English array which did such yeoman service in the conflict against feudalism. Lastly, the connection between England and Normandy kept up the importance of the south coast towns, and produced those French wars which led to the revival of an English navy.

F. YORK POWELL.
Domesday Book. THE great inquest survey, or "Description of all England," which we call Domesday Book, is one of the most precious documents that any nation possesses. It is not so old nor so minute as the wonderful French *Polyptyques;* nor is it so curious and primitive in manner and matter as the Icelandic *Landnámabóc;* but for variety of information, for excellence of plan, for the breadth of land and the space of time it covers, it is probably unrivalled. It is at once a terrier,[1] a rent roll, an assessment register, as well as a book of settlements and a legal record. It is important alike to economist, lawyer, historian,

[1 The roll of a manor, specifying the names, holdings, and obligations of the tenants.]

ethnologist, and philologist. Moreover, it was composed at a
period of transition and change, and enables us, better than any
other writing could, to understand the manner and effects of
the Norman Conquest.

The Peterborough Chronicle, written by one who knew the
Conqueror, gives the best contemporary account of the place,
and meaning of the survey, under the year 1083—

" After midwinter, the King let levy a great geld [or tax] and heavy over
all England that was on each hide two and seventy pence."

[In 1085 King Canute of Denmark, who had to wife Earl Robert's
daughter of Flanders, threatened to invade the land.] " When King William
of England, who was then sitting in Normandy, for he owned both England
and Normandy, got news of this, he fared into England with so great an host
of horsemen and footmen out of France and Brittany as never sought this
land before, so that men wondered how this land might feed all that host.
But the King let divide up this host over all this land among his men, and
they fed the host each according to his land. . . . . But when the King
got news for truth that his foes were hindered, and might not carry out their
journey, then he let some of his host fare to their own land, and some he held
in this land the winter over. Then at midwinter the King was at Gloucester
with his wise men, and held his court there five days, and afterwards the
archbishop and clergy held a three days' synod. . . . After this the
King took much thought and held deep speech with his Wise Men over the
land, how it was settled or established, and with what kind of men. Then
he sent over all England into each shire and had it made out how many
hundred hides there were in the shire, and what the King himself had in
lands, and of live-stock on the land, and what rights he ought to have every
twelve months off the shire. Also, he had written how much land his archbishops had, and his suffragan bishops, and his abbots and earls, and, though
I tell it at length, what or how much each man that owned land in England
had in land and live-stock, and how much money it might be worth. So very
narrowly he had it inquired into that there was not one single hide nor one
yard of land, nor even—it is shame to be telling of, but he did not think it
shame to be doing it—one ox nor one cow nor one swine was left out that was
not set down in his record, and all the records were afterwards brought to
him." [The instructions for taking the survey ran thus :—

" The King's barons [the Commissioners] enquire by oath of the sheriff
of the shire and of all the barons [free tenants] and of the French-born of
them and of the whole hundred, of the priest, the reeve, and six villeins
[copyholders] from each manor " . . . " the name of the manor, who held it
T.R.E. [*tempore Regis Edwardi*, in the time of King Edward Confessor]
and who held it now [1086], how many hides there were in each manor, how
many ploughs on the domain, how many men, how many villeins, how many
cottars, how many bondsmen, how many freemen, how many socmen,[1] how

[[1] Freeholders, but liable to pay fixed rent or service to the lord.⌐

much wood, how much meadow, how much pasture; what mills, what fish-ponds; what had been added or taken away, what it was worth T.R.E. and how much it was worth now [1086]; how much each freeholder held; and whether more could be got out of it than now."

Rights and claims were registered, as well as holdings and premiums. There were several sets of Commissioners, each with a separate circuit—*e.g.* Bishop Remigius of Fécamp, Henry of Ferrieres (Lord of Tutbury), Walter Giffard (afterwards Earl of Buckingham), and Adam Fitz Hubert took the circuit in which Worcester lay; the south-western counties formed a circuit, and Oxford, Warwick, and Stafford shires were grouped together. Northumberland and Durham were not surveyed, probably because much of the north was wasted and empty Cumberland, Westmorland, and North Lancashire were not yet parts of England. Rutland was surveyed under parts of Northants and Lincolnshire, South Lancashire under parts of Yorkshire and Cheshire. We have in the Exon Domesday and in Vol. II. of the great Domesday Book examples of the draft returns for the five south-western and three eastern counties (Norfolk, Suffolk, Essex) respectively. A transcript of the original Cambridgeshire returns also exists. In the rest of the surveyed districts the draft returns were not only arranged, but abridged, as in the first volume of the great Domesday.

The record being on oath was a regular verdict, and could not be disregarded, contradicted, or disallowed as evidence.

How the Survey was taken. In compiling the draft returns each county was taken hundred by hundred, each hundred manor by manor, and a numbered index of the tenants-in-chief (immediate crown-tenants) was affixed to each county; the king coming first, the rest following according to rank.

The Commissioners, in putting down the returns of their local inquests, did not attempt to alter the local reckoning; hence in different parts of the country we find, as Mr. Round has lately shown—

The English reckoning :—1 hide = 4 virgates or yard-lands.
The Kentish reckoning :—1 suling = 4 yokes.
The Dano-Norman reckoning :—1 ploughland or carucate = 8 ox-gangs or bovates.

In each case this reckoning applied only to the arable, and to land which was geldable (liable for the King's land-tax), at so much per unit; the unit, whether called suling, hide, or carucate, being always an ideal of 120 acres, whether the manor was worked on a two- or three-field system. After stating the geldable area, the non-geldable area is put down : this is sometimes land fresh tilled since the days of Ethelred when this land-tax or geld was first taken (probably on a local county assessment). For in the year 991 on a proposal (borrowed from Frankish and Roman expedients) of Archbishop Sigric, the first great payment of £10,000 was made by the nation as tribute to the Danes; but whether this first Danegeld was raised, as later payments in this reign probably were, by taxation on the hide, we do not know. Sometimes the non-geldable land is land that has received for some reason exception from this tax by the king's favour. After the return as to hidage and acres come the other returns called for by the king. The following specimen of a rural manor will show the way the returns were finally registered :—

"THE LAND OF WILLIAM OF BRAIOSE. In REDINGES hundred.

"William of Braiose holdeth of the king SUDCOTE. Brictward held it of K. Edward. [William the Norman has displaced Brictward the Englishman as royal tenant.]

"The land defended itself for two hides, now for one hide. [The old assessment for land tax on this manor was for two hides, but for some satisfactory reason it is now assessed for one hide.]

"The land is of three ploughs. [The whole extent of arable is three ploughlands, though it was only assessed at two hides.]

"There is one in the domain [William manages one ploughland himself] and five villeins [copyhold tenants] and bordars [cottiers] with two ploughs [there are two teams in the domain].

"There is a mill of 18 shillings-worth and a fishery of 50 pence-worth.

"It [the estate] was worth £4; now [it is worth] 100 shillings."

A notable bit of record is that touching Oxford, a new town come into note as the resting-place of a saint, a place of coinage under Alfred, a stronghold against the Danes under Edward, and a convenient meeting-place for great moots under Egar and Ethelred It embraces, as will be seen, not only taxation but amercements and rents and other dues.

COIN OF ALFRED, STRUCK AT OXFORD.

"In the time of King Edward OXFORD used to pay for toll and gafol and all other customs yearly to the king £20 and 6 sestiers [apparently pints] of honey. To Earl Elfgar £10, besides a mill which he had inside the city. When the king went to war 20 burgesses used to go with him in place of all the others, or they used to give £20 to the king that all might be free. Now Oxford pays £60 by tale [not by weight, which would be unfavourable to the payer] of 20d. to the *ora* [a Danish money of account, twelve to the £]. In this said town, both within the wall and without, there are 243 houses paying geld, and beside these there are 500, less 22, so waste and destroyed that they cannot pay geld. . . . All the mansions which are called mural, T.R.E., were free from all custom save going to war and wall repair. . . . And if the wall, when there be need, be not restored by him who ought so to do, he shall either pay 40s. to the king or lose his mansion. All the burgesses of Oxford have in common outside the town a meadow paying 6s. 8d." They still have it, and it is called Port-Meadow.

Among Oxfordshire customs are these :—" If any man break the king's peace given by hand or seal, so that he slay the man to whom the peace was given, both his life and lands shall be in the king's power if he be taken, and if he cannot be taken he shall be held an outlaw by all, and if anyone shall be able to slay him he shall have his spoils by law. If any stranger wishing to stay in Oxford and having a house without kin shall finish his life there, the king shall have what he leaves. If anyone by force break or enter any man's court or house to slay or wound or assault a man, he shall pay 100s. to the king as fine. Likewise he that is warned to go on service and goeth not shall give 100s. to the king. If anyone slay a man within his court or his house, himself and all his substance are at the king's will, save the dower of his wife if he have endowed her."

The general results of the survey may be summed up thus : There were about 5,000,000 acres tilled each year, and about 300,000 families, *i.e.* about 2,000,000 souls. This population was thus divided as to tenure :—

(a)	1,400 tenants-in-chief 7,900 under-tenants	gentry and clergy.		
(b)	12,000 liberi hommes	freeholders	N. of Watling St.	
	23,000 socmen	yeomen	S. of Yorks.	
(c)	109,000 villeins	copyholders	W. of Lincoln and Essex. E. of Cheshire.	
	90,000 cottars and bordars	small copyholders	S. of Thames mostly.	
(d)	25,000 bondsmen	landless labourers	S. of Midlands and S.W.	

The burgesses and many of the clergy are not reckoned, so that any estimate of their number must be drawn from other sources.

A PAGE FROM DOMESDAY BOOK; OXFORD.
(*Record Office.*)

Change of Owner-ship.

Of the tenants-in-chief the greater part were "Frenchmen" —soldiers who had come over to fight with William, or church-men who had come over to pray for him; and the greater part of the under-tenants of good estate were "Frenchmen" too. Thus in Oxfordshire only a few thanes (such as Lefwine, Osmund, Sawold, Siward the huntsman) and the ecclesias-tical foundations and priests remained as before the Conquest. The king, besides the royal manors, had got the forfeited lands of Earls Harold and Edwin; Queen Edith's land had been parted among Norman barons; the Norman bishops of Bayeux and Lisieux, the transmarine Abbey des Preaux, and William's new foundation of Battle got possessions in the country at the expense of English owners. Earls Hugh of Chester, Albery of Northumberland, Robert of Mortain, William of Hereford, Eustace of Boulogne, William of Evreux, and barons of the houses of Ivri, Todeni, Gifard, Pevrel, Hesding, and Ansculf became the king's tenants, while English landowners such as Archbishop Stigand, Earl Tosti, Turgot, Alfric, Hacon, Godric, and their heirs were ousted. Robert d'Oily married Ealdgyth, the daughter of a great English landowner, Wigod of Walling-ford, and got about half of his father-in-law's estates in the shire. In fact, one may sum up the change in England by saying that some 20,000 foreigners replaced some 20,000 Englishmen; and that these newcomers got the throne, the earldoms, the bishoprics, the abbacies, and far the greater portion of the big estates, mediate and immediate, and many of the burgess holdings in the chief towns. The English owners had either fallen in battle or fled into exile, or, if they remained, they had forfeited their estates by armed or avowed resistance to the new and crowned king. In some cases the new landowner married the former landowner's daughter, as in the instance given above, or his widow, but this was not by any means the usual case; and the accounts we have of English nobles and barons flying to Scotland and to East Europe show that the newcomers mostly ousted the former owners and their heirs. William had to pay his fellow-con-querors and to keep up an army. This could only be done in a regular way by endowing them; and, both to reward men who had risked much in his quarrel and to enable him to hold what he had, he had to parcel out the forfeited lands bit by bit, as he won them. We need not suppose any settled policy of dividing the great barons' estates (a policy for which we have not any good ancient authority). The fact of the Conquest occurring piecemeal will account for the fact of many great Norman landowners holding lands in many counties. Thus Hugh of Chester seems to have held lands in Stafford, which were afterwards exchanged for possessions elsewhere; but he retained land in twenty-one several counties, Robert of Mortain in twenty, Odo of Bayeux in seventeen, Eustace of Boulogne in twelve. There were forty-one great vassals with estates in more than six counties—laymen all. Nor was William afraid of handsomely rewarding his fellow-venturers, especially those of his own blood. Thus, Robert of Mortain, his brother, got 793 manors; Odo of Bayeux, another brother, 439; Alan of Brittany, a kinsman, 442. Some of William's shrievalties became hereditary, some of his earldoms were palatine, but he took care not to make many new earls; and the condition of regular military service—so many armed knights to be supplied for so much land (as Mr. Round has shown)—whereby the irregular and varied thegn-services were replaced by more regular requirements, told probably in favour of the Crown.

The new landowners, though they might have made a little different bargain with the king than their forerunners, yet had not a whit more power or less over their tenants by law or custom; and the old folk-moots, courts of hundred, and hall-moots, subsisted as before with the old fines, fees, and forfeitures. Every free unlanded man still had to find a responsible patron, and every free landed man to be in a local peace-pledge society; every freeman had to take oath of allegiance to the king as before. The king's rents were still largely paid in kind, and the first scale of commutation (remembered a century later) was an ox 1s., sheep 4d., fodder for twenty horses 4d., bread for 100 men 1s. The statutes of William the Conqueror are mostly re-enactments of former kings' laws, and his chief innovations are his substitution, out of piety, of mutilation for capital punishment; his arrangements to prevent the murder of the Frenchmen that came with him by strengthening the police regulations as to fines, etc.; and his ordinance separating the temporal

and spiritual pleas, confining the latter to the bishops' jurisdiction.

The New-comers.

It is well here to remember (as Bishop Stubbs points out)
that the new aristocracy was largely akin to the Norman
duke. Thus, of the ducal house came the Earls of Brionne,
Evreux, Eu, Mortain, Kent; while from marriage-kinship there
was a close connection with the Beaumonts of Mellent, and
the houses of Montgomery, Warenne, Giffard, and Breteuil.
The other three great Norman families came from Yves of
Belesme, Bernard the Dane, and Osmond of Coutville, also
allies of the ducal house, as the Court legends sufficiently
attest. The old list of ships, though by no means authoritative or complete, shows the kind of help given by Norman
barons to the king :—

	Ships.	Knights.		Ships.	Knights.
William FitzOsbern	60	—	Remi, Bishop of Lincoln	1	20
Hugh, Earl of Chester ...	60	—	Nicholas, Abbot of St.		
Robert, Earl of Eu	60	—	Owen	20	100
Robert, Earl of Mortain ...	120	—	Hugh of Montfort Con-		
Roger of Beaumont	60	—	stable	50	—
Roger of Montgomery ...	60	—	Gerald the Steward ...	40	—
Walter Giffard	30	100	Fulk the Lame	40	—
Odo, Bishop of Bayeux ...	100	—	William, Earl of Evreux	80	—

Other Normans that brought good help were Ralf of
Conches, William of Warenne, Hugh of Grantmesnil, Roger
of Mowbray, Baldwin and Richard of Brionne, Hugh the
Butler, and Aimery of Thouars. William's allies "his good
neighbours [1] Bretons, Mancels [men of Maine], Angevins, men
of Ponthieu and Boulogne"[2] and French, "to whom he promised land if he could conquer England, rich pay and good
bounties" (though neither the King of France nor the Earl of
Flanders would aid his enterprise), saw to it that his promises were carried out. Only one knight and one churchman
out of the great host that sailed in "three thousand ships
and three" to maintain William's claim to the Crown are
recorded to have refused to take other men's goods and estates.
Even the cooks, the huntsmen, and other body-servants of

[1] Alan of Brittany, William's son-in-law, and Ralf Guader, Earl of Norfolk,
were the chief among the Bretons, a very powerful contingent.

[2] Eustace III., Earl of Boulogne, a kinsman of Edward the Confessor, led
these.

the king got their share of the land, though he took care to
settle no mercenaries after the first conquest, and preferred
to raise a heavy tax rather than make unjust confiscations.
William I., like Edward I., was a law-abiding king, and in face
of even great temptations he seldom broke his own rules,
and never violated the oath he had sworn and the promise he
had made to rule as his predecessor had ruled, according to
the laws and customs of the land, putting down evil and
maintaining mercy and righteousness.

The Conquest meant, indeed, that the executive, the central
administration and the local government, temporal and spiritual,
had been taken over by a new set of men—better managers,
keener, more unscrupulous, less drunken and less quarrel-
some, better trained, harder, thriftier, more in sympathy with the
general European movements, more adventurous, more temperate. The result was, inevitably, better organisation, quicker
progress, great exactions and oppressions in Church and State;
for the under-tenants were not in sympathy with their new
lords, and both sides stood on the letter of the law (which
necessarily favoured the lord); a new and vigorous foreign
policy, and extension of the English king's domains and claims
within and without these islands. But (contrary to a venerable belief) the English tongue and the English law held
their own throughout this realm, and within a century the
French baron had become an English lord.

Outwardly the greatest changes were the building of many
great keeps and baileys by the king and his richest barons,
and the continuance of the movement that had already begun
of raising churches and large minsters in stone. Agriculture
must have been rather checked by the exactions of the lords
(who seem to have set up their courts *or* hall-moots wherever
they could), by the heavy taxes, and by the devastations of civil
war. But though the towns suffered grievously by war and
by the clearances of sites for castles, commerce grew and
flourished. Besides the questionable benefit of the arrival
of the Jews who followed the Conquest, as they had followed
the Northmen in Gaul two centuries earlier, many Norman
merchants settled in London and other market towns and
seaports.

**The Effects
of the
Conquest.**

A. L.
SMITH.
The Reign
of William
Rufus.
1087–1100.
THE accession of William Rufus against the support given to
Robert by the Norman barons was a victory for the English
people. It was to the people that he promised good govern-
ment and their own old customs, to win their aid and that of
the Church, already beginning to act as the people's champion.
It was the levy of the people that enabled him to drive
off Duke Robert's fleet at Pevensey, and to take Rochester
Castle and with it his uncle, Bishop Odo, the head of the
Norman revolt. It was the same levy that he summoned in
1094 to Hastings to the number of 20,000 to repel a threatened

SEAL OF WILLIAM II.

invasion from France.   His very tyranny and greed fell less
on the mass of the people than on the great feudatories. It
is true he was merciless in his fines and savagely jealous of
his forest rights, and he used the local courts as mere engines
of extortion, while his shameless life and blasphemous sayings
deeply shocked the best feelings of his age. But at least he
allowed no tyranny in England but his own.   He crushed
another feudal rising in 1095, and confiscated the lands of
Mowbray of Northumberland and others for taking part in
it. He repulsed an invasion of Malcolm, King of Scots, in
1091, forced him to renew his homage, wrested from him the
district of Carlisle, and colonised it with English settlers. By
his grants—as, for instance, to Montgomery and Lacy—the
English border advanced rapidly westwards at the expense of
the Welsh, despite the check caused by a raid upon Anglesey

TOMB OF WILLIAM II., WINCHESTER CATHEDRAL.

by Magnus of Norway, who defeated Hugh, Earl of Chester, there. His reign, almost in spite of himself, fostered that alliance between Crown and people which, begun almost at the Norman Conquest in their common interest against feudal anarchy, has ever since been so characteristic of English history. In the wars, too, against Scots and Welsh, and even against the French, the English took up their Norman rulers' quarrel as their own. Only when he set himself against the new Archbishop Anselm did he take up a position in which the nation would be against him (p. 364). And the popular demonstrations

SEAL OF HENRY I.

in favour of the prelate both during the contest and upon his victory were an omen of the course of those future struggles in which the kings were to find that the nation, loyal as it was to the Crown, owned a higher loyalty still to the Church.

Henry I.
1100-1135

Alliance between Crown and people had been the mark of William II.'s reign ; but in a much more intimate sense it becomes the guiding principle of Henry I.'s policy. His accession he owed to his being an Atheling, the English-born son of a king ; to his own promptitude and use of his treasures ; to his immediate recall of Anselm ; but above all to the Charter which he published. This promised not merely a relaxation of the feudal rules which his brother had strained to the uttermost against his tenants-in-chief, but also ordered that the barons should in their turn give the same relaxation in dealing with their vassals. The Charter promised also that "the laws of Edward"—that is, the Old English offices and institutions—

should be preserved.   When he married Edith, daughter of Malcolm, and niece of Edgar Atheling, the people felt they had again an English king; he was identified with "the Lion of Justice" of Merlin's prophecies.   When the leading barons joined Robert of Normandy in his claim of the English throne, the English people so heartily aided their king that he was able to attack and reduce in succession the four castles of Robert of Belesme, who, as representative of the great house of Montgomery, and lord of two earldoms in England and two in Normandy,

EFFIGIES OF HENRY I. AND EDITH ("QUEEN MAUD"), ROCHESTER CATHEDRAL.

was the acknowledged head of the feudal party.   This man was of the worse type of feudal lord, and with his overthrow, said the exulting English, the king had now become a king indeed. From 1104 Henry's chief activity was in France.   Indeed, the long struggle of the royal power against the baronage was fought out in these fields from 1104 to 1118.   The battle of Tenchebrai, 1106, made him master of Normandy, and consigned Duke Robert to a life-long captivity.   With Anjou and Brittany he formed alliances, and married his daughter Matilda to the Emperor Henry V.   But he was harassed by intrigues in favour of Duke Robert's son, William Clito, till the latter's death in

23

1126. Meanwhile the strength of Henry's position in England had been shown by the reception of his own son William in 1115 as future king; and he was even able, after his son's tragical death at the wreck of the White Ship in 1120, to have the same oaths taken to his daughter Matilda in 1126. The process of the subjugation of Wales, despite frequent Welsh revolts, was continued by the energy of Earl Strongbow, the building of castles in the country, and the planting of colonies of Flemings in Pembrokeshire.

Internal Reform.

The internal history of the reign is a history of steady advance in good government. The local courts of hundred and shire were revived; the local customs of the towns were recognised and recorded in charters; the Central Exchequer system was being steadily developed; itinerant justices (p. 402) were sent

COIN OF HENRY I.

on circuits; the coinage was amended, the abuses of purveyance were restrained, the old payments in kind were replaced by money taxes. A new nobility was raised up from Englishmen and from Normans of lesser rank. These men served the king as ministers in Exchequer and in the Council, and were rewarded with the confiscated lands of the older baronage of the north. The line of great Justiciars, the king's lieutenants in military and judicial powers, begins 1107 with Roger the Poor, Bishop of Salisbury, and his family (p. 367). The feudal Council begins to show a division into greater and lesser barons, the line of division destined to grow into the deeper demarcation between House of Lords and House of Commons. The native chronicles are full, indeed, of lamentations over plague, and famine, and murrain, and "the heavy taxes which never slackened." But the same chroniclers are emphatic in their acknowledgment of the prompt and stern justice which began to make England, after the incorrigible anarchy and violence of Anglo-Saxon times, a land of unwonted order and peace. "A good man he was, and all men stood in awe of him. No man durst misdo against another in his time. He made peace for man and beast." Men came to

THE CHURCH AND THE CONQUEST.

speak of the laws of King Henry's days as they had hitherto spoken of the laws of King Edward, and with much better reason ; for Henry I. laid the foundations on which his greater grandson built up the enduring fabric of the English Constitution —a Norman superstructure upon an English basis. Even the greatest of all the medieval problems, the relation of Church and State, was brought at least to a temporary solution by the mingled firmness and moderation of the king. A compromise was made (1107) which would be sure to work well for the Crown. The bishop-elect was to do homage to the king, and only then receive his spiritual insignia—the ring and pastoral staff—from spiritual hands. This settlement emphasised better the spiritual character of the episcopate : but the bishops were also great barons, and over them, as over other barons, the Crown kept its hold by the ceremony of homage. The best tribute to the work and character of Henry I. is the outburst of feudalism in its most hateful form which followed as soon as the strong hand of the last real Norman ruler was removed.

THE Conquest had a great and immediate effect on the English Church. The invasion itself had been from the first made to bear something of the character of a religious work. It was at once a mission, the claiming of a lawful heritage filched by a perjured usurper, and a Crusade before the Crusaders. The invaders, coming to a conquest that was blessed by the Pope, were pledged of necessity to change in Church as in State. We have seen that the condition of the Church warranted, if it did not necessitate, a change. It was one of the great aims of the Conqueror to carry it through.

W. H.
HUTTON.
The
Church
and the
Conquest.

The first four years of the reign were fully occupied with material and physical contest. The ecclesiastical reformation had perforce to wait till the land was fully conquered by the sword. When that was done, in 1070 William turned to work which he had had in mind from the first. In the Easter feast at Winchester, with Papal legates by his side, he began to provide for the governance of the English Church.

Ealdred of York, who had anointed him king, was dead. Stigand of Canterbury, who had received his pallium from the anti-Pope, Benedict X., was with ease deposed as uncanonical.

With him fell his brother Ethelmer, Bishop of the East Angles, a married man. Bishops and abbots fled or were deprived. Their places were filled generally, but not always, by men of foreign race. The great prize of all, the Primacy of all England, was conferred on one than whom there was no man in **Lanfranc.** Europe worthier to fill it. Lanfranc, the law-student of Pavia, then Prior of Bec, now abbot of William's own great Church of St. Stephen at Caen, the scholar, statesman, administrator, friend of the stern Conqueror, was consecrated in the metropolitan church to be what the Worcester annalist of the time calls "the English Pope." There is in this phrase —a phrase repeated when Pope Urban greeted Anselm as Apostolic or "Pope of a second world"—a real meaning. **England** Just as the old English kings, when the Welsh and Scots **and the** had submitted to their sway, began to take to themselves **Papacy.** Imperial titles and the badges of Imperial authority—thus claiming to be apart from the great Roman Empire, and to rule a little empire of their own—so the English Primates, who had exercised spiritual supremacy over many kingdoms before England yet was one, had felt themselves, and were recognised to be, patriarchs of the nations beyond the sea. That William was determined such should be the position of those who ruled the English Church we see clearly enough from the letters that passed between him and that greatest of medieval Popes, the Hildebrand of Clugny and Canossa, Pope Gregory VII. Nothing so clearly brings back the life of those times as the letters— now cautious, now familiar—which passed between the clear-sighted statesmen who ruled over peoples so different and lands so far separate, each with a clear, keen purpose and a stern unbending will. To Gregory, William is the "dearest king," the "unique and precious son of the holy Roman Church," whom he has ever in his prayers ; but whom he must at times admonish, lest he fall into great condemnation. To William, Gregory was his Father and Pontiff, whose prayers he craved, and whose "Romescot"[1] he would pay. But when it came to a question between them that the English king should profess himself the Pope's man — and this the Pope asked — then the answer was clear and brief. No fealty had William ever promised ; none had his predecessors paid. As they did, so

---

[1] Annual gift to the Papal see.

CHURCH OF ST. STEPHEN (ABBAYE AUX HOMMES), CAEN.

would he: he was the rightful successor of the good King Edward.

Such relation between king and Pope could not be maintained if the first man in England after the Sovereign, the chief bishop of the English Church, were himself in league with the Roman Pontiff. It seems certain that no question ever arose between William and Lanfranc; their agreement had been confirmed, we may be sure, years before it was carried out on English soil. But though no division arose between king and archbishop, it was clear to all men what were the rules of the king's dealings with Rome. These rules seemed to the historian a novelty; but the circumstances and the men were also new. " He would not suffer," says Eadmer, " that anyone in all his dominions should receive the Pontiff of the City of Rome as apostolic Pope "— there were then many contests on vacancies in the Holy See— " except at his command, or should on any condition receive his letters if they had not been first shown to himself. He did not suffer the primate of his kingdom, the Archbishop of Canterbury, if he had called together under his primacy an assembly of bishops, to enact or prohibit anything but what was agreeable to his will and had been first ordained by him. He did not allow any of his bishops publicly to implead, excommunicate, or constrain by penalty of ecclesiastical rigour any of his barons or servants who was informed against for adultery or any capital crime, except by his own command." And, further, he exercised —so Henry I. claimed—a control upon the reception of Papal legates by the English Church.

These customs, though it does not appear that it ever came to a question of enforcing them, formed a precedent for later sovereigns, and often a battle-ground between the rulers in Church and State. But they created at least as many difficulties as they solved. It might be necessary to limit the power of Church assemblies, and to restrain the exercise of spiritual power by which the king in consorting with his own men might become, as it were by a by-blow, excommunicate. When so much of the foreign policy of the country was conducted through the Papal Curia, where the strings of all international relations were held, it was undoubtedly wise to control such recognition of a Supreme Pontiff, when two opponents claimed the Chair of St. Peter, as might commit the English king, against his will, to a warfare with the emperor and the emperor's nominee. But no concordat on the lines of the historic maxim " Cujus regio ejus religio " [1] has ever been wholly satisfactory or successful. It may work well where Church and State, as under Lanfranc and William, are agreed ; but a bad king, or an archbishop with a policy of his own, must soon upset the arrangement.

It might seem that by these rules William intended to tie the hands of the Church ; but if he fettered her action in one direction, he enlarged her freedom in another. The Church courts, under the old English kings, though they retained jurisdiction over moral questions and the doctrine and discipline of the clergy, had become assimilated in procedure, in time of session, and even in the persons attending them, to the local courts of hundred and shire. The bishop sat in the shire-moot, and there, without adjourning to his own court, he would hear suits which to the strict lawyers and canonists of Normandy seemed wholly apart from lay jurisdiction. William and Lanfranc, though they were no obedient vassals of the Pope, were thoroughly imbued with the spirit of order and love of distinction and definition which animated the legal mind of Gregory VII. It was intolerable to them, as it would have been to him, that any branch of law should be carried on, as it were, at haphazard. Thus, an edict was issued by the king with the object of putting an end to confusion, and making Church and lay courts separate in action as they were in idea. No longer were bishops and archdeacons to hear ecclesiastical cases in the hundred-courts. They were to try their causes in their own courts, and "secundum episcopales leges et sanctorum canonum praecepta," [2] not by customary law. They were to allow no spiritual questions to come before lay judges. Laymen, too, were forbidden to intrude themselves into ecclesiastical causes. The king would, through the sheriff, enforce the sentence of excommunication when issued by the bishop. While William thus placed the Church courts in a position of considerable freedom and independence, he gave to the clergy also an important part in the ordinary criminal jurisdiction. The last resort in criminal cases was the ordeal, the solemn appeal to the

The Church and the State.

[1 " Whose is the land, his is the religion " : *i.e.* the sovereign controls the faith of his subjects.]

[2 "According to the episcopal laws and the precepts of the holy canons."]

'judgment of God.   This was now definitely placed under the control of the bishops, and was to be held only in their cathedral cities or in other places chosen by them.

The importance of these changes of the Conqueror can hardly be overrated.   The clergy, placed under a government which became more centralised every year, found themselves in possession of new powers and expected to show a class interest separate and independent of the rest of their country-men.   This interest was contended for hotly during the next two centuries, and the contest was a means of securing national freedom through the assertion of class privilege.   But the growth of canon law, combined with the action of the Church courts and the revived study of the civil law, had a very natural result in the recognition of the Papal Court as a tribunal of appeal.

Church Reform. These measures of William and of Lanfranc cannot be taken by themselves ; they were part of a general scheme for the purification and elevation of the Church.   Not only were the bishoprics now filled by foreigners, but the sees themselves were removed from the country villages or small towns to cities. Thus Sherborne was deserted for the hill fortress of Old Sarum, Dorchester [1] for Lincoln, Thetford for Norwich, Wells for Bath, Selsey [2] for Chichester, Lichfield for Chester ; and the bishops found themselves in the society of the warrior and the burgher rather than the monk and the hind.   Great efforts, too, were made to check the marriage of the clergy and the growth of a hereditary ecclesiastical caste.   Social evils were combated with zeal.   Lanfranc and the good English bishop Wulfstan, whom no envy or avarice was strong enough to dislodge from the see of Worcester, which he served with such sagacity and holiness, made crusade against the kid-napping and slave-trade in the port of Bristol.   All through we can see that the king's aim was to bring peace to the land and to the Church.   He was not always successful.   At St. Albans the tombs of the English abbots were destroyed by their Norman successor.   At Glastonbury, Thurstan, in his unwisdom, called in his archers against the monks who loved their old Gregorian chants more than the new singing of

[1 The Oxfordshire Dorchester, situated on the Thames, near Wallingford.]
[2 In the extreme south-west of Sussex.]

THE HILL FORTRESS OF OLD SARUM.

William of Fécamp. "Then were the monks sore afeard of
them, and wist not what to do, and fled hither and thither.
. . . . And a rueful thing there happened that day, for the
Frenchmen brake into the choir, and shot towards the altar
where the monks were, and some of the knights went up to
the up-floor (the triforium) and shot downwards towards the
halidom (sanctuary), so that on the rood that stood above the
altar stuck on many arrows.   And the wretched monks lay
about the altar, and some crept under it, and cried with
yearning to God, craving his mildness for that they could get
no mildness from men.   What may we say but that they shot
sorely, and that others brake down the doors there and went
in and slew some of the monks to death, and many wounded
therein, so that the blood came from the altar upon the graden
(steps), and from the graden upon the floor." [1]   But such
strife was rare, and this was sternly punished.   In most parts
French and English were soon knit together by the bonds
of the Church.   Seven monasteries under St. Wulfstan joined
themselves together—humble monks of English birth and
rulers of the conquering race—as one heart and one soul.
A pleasant illustration of the good-fellowship into which the
two peoples soon entered comes to us from St. Albans.   There
even the insolent abbot Paul, who swept away the tombs of
his predecessors, received from the English Ligulf and his
wife two bells for the minster.   "How sweetly bleat my goats
and my sheep," said the worthy Englishman when he heard
the new bells ring.

The
Church
under
William
Rufus.

Such in the main was the result of the Conqueror's reign:
the bells of peace sounded above the chance local frays.   So
long as Lanfranc lived the peace continued; even the wild
Rufus held his hand for fear of the wise man whom his father
had loved.   But when he died there began the carrying out of
what seems to have been a deliberate policy of despiritualising
the Church.   The sees were kept vacant and their revenues
appropriated.   The appointments that were made were a matter
of sale and barter; and men were placed in the most sacred
offices whose merit was only their assistance to the king in
his tyranny and vice.   Ranulf Flambard, who "drave the
gemots throughout all England," was given the bishopric of

[[1] Old English Chronicle, under the year 1083.]

ST. WULFSTAN'S CRYPT, WORCESTER CATHEDRAL.

Anselm.

Durham, a palatine see like those of the great German prince-bishops, which made its possessor a petty sovereign.   At length, in 1093, a seemingly mortal illness brought the Red King to a fit of superstitious remorse, in which he filled up the see of Canterbury by the appointment of Anselm.   No better choice could have been made.   Spiritual where Lanfranc was only statesmanlike, Anselm combined in rare perfection the virtues of the philosopher and the saint.   A Burgundian of Aosta, he had ruled the famous abbey of Bec with a gentle reasonableness more effective than severity.   He was tender-hearted but resolute, high-minded yet childlike, and about the absolute purity of his devotion no slightest breath of doubt could cling.   In the simple cell at Bec he thought out the remarkable books, the "Monologion"[1] and the "Proslogion,"[2] which show the Christian Platonism of the Middle Ages in one of its most fascinating aspects, and in the "Cur Deus Homo"[3] he elaborated an argument which has profoundly influenced theology down to our own time.

Anselm accepted the archbishopric only on compulsion, but when at last he did so he had no intention of placing his conduct under the direction of any temporal prince.   He was not to be terrified by the ferocity of the king, or entrapped into concession by the guile of treacherous bishops.   From the moment of the king's recovery difficulties arose.   There was the question of English acknowledgment of a Pope; and Anselm finally induced William to recognise Urban II. There was the question about the pallium, the badge of the primacy, made from the white wool of the lambs of St. Agnes and sent by the Pope to the archbishop; and Anselm stoutly resisted the claim of the king to place it on his shoulders, and at last, by one of those prudent compromises to which his wise humility inclined him, took it himself from the altar at Canterbury, on which it was laid.   There was the accusation of supplying for the Welsh war a contingent insufficient

[1 "Solitary discourse," a treatise "meant to represent a person discoursing secretly with himself on the ground of his belief in God" (Dean Church).]

[2 "Address" (*i.e.* to God); an appeal to God to enable us to understand the reason of our faith.   This work anticipates Descartes' attempt to prove the existence of God from the idea we have of a most perfect Being, by the argument that existence is part of such an idea.]

[3 "Why God is Man:" a treatise on the Incarnation.]

for his feudal obligations. There were the ceaseless exactions of the king and distresses of the Church; and these at last led to Anselm's departure, in 1097, to seek the counsel of the Pope.

Three years later the new king, Henry I., called the archbishop back again with expressions of reverence :—"Myself and the people of the whole land I commit to your counsel and that of those who ought with you to counsel me." Anselm returned as the first constitutional adviser of the Crown, and became in 1101 the means of uniting clergy and people in support of the king against the invasion of his brother Robert and the faithless barons. For a time it seemed as though the days of the Conqueror were returned. Church and State were in firm alliance. But it was impossible for England to keep out of the European contest. Henry claimed, as did the monarchs of the Continent, that it was his to appoint bishops and abbots, and to invest them with the ring and pastoral staff, the symbols of the prelacy. Before the significance of this had been seen the claim had been tacitly assented to ; Anselm himself had received investiture at the hands of Rufus. But the Church, in a Lateran Council, at which Anselm was himself present, had now decided that it must be a question of principle to preserve the spiritual character of the appointments, and to protest against "the shame and mischief of allowing great Church offices to be disposed of by the kings and princes of the time without an effort to assert their meaning and sacredness." This was a point at which there could be no concession. Appeals for the guidance of the Pope only

The Church under Henry I.

SEAL OF ANSELM.

confirmed Anselm in his steadfastness. Henry persisted in his demands, Anselm in his refusals; and at length the archbishop set out for Rome " in the king's peace, invested with all that belonged to him," to win a settlement at the

EFFIGY OF ROGER THE POOR, SALISBURY CATHEDRAL.

Papal Court. This settlement, due largely to his own tact and tolerance, and an anticipation by sixteen years of the Concordat of Worms, which ended the investiture dispute abroad, gave to the king the right of bestowing the temporalities alone, and of receiving the homage and fealty of the bishop-elect before consecration, while " the king granted and decreed that from that time forth for ever no one should be invested in England with bishopric or abbey, by staff or ring, either by the king or by any lay hand."

So the chief point of dispute was ended, and, as it seemed, in favour of the Church. But Henry still treated the ecclesiastical offices as a means of rewarding his ministers, and during his reign the character of the episcopate underwent a complete change. William the Conqueror, though he had appointed foreigners to the sees which he had made vacant for them, had preferred men who would serve the Church. Henry sought and rewarded those who were already ministers of the State. That the chapters had a right to elect their superiors he allowed; but the election must be held in his court, and his candidates, without compulsion, must be chosen. With such canonical election was Roger, a poor priest, who had first attracted the king's attention by the rapidity with which he could say mass "fitly for hunting men," and had proved himself as steward and as chancellor to be *magnus in secularibus*,[1] chosen Bishop of Salisbury. He became justiciar, and the offices of State were in time filled by his kinsfolk as they were organised by his hand. Under him grew up the great system of financial centralisation depending on the Exchequer, of which his great-nephew[2] has left a curious account.

THE nineteen years which are known as the reign of Stephen are more truly to be regarded as an interval of mere anarchy between the reigns of two great rulers and organisers. But this brief period, given over, as it seems to be, to blank confusion, to utter turmoil and misery, is yet a period which in

A. L. SMITH. The Anarchy. 1135–1154.

SEAL OF STEPHEN.

several ways has a unique place and interest in the story of the English race. These nineteen years determined how and where the two component elements of that race should be blended into one. They taught to the stubborn English spirit

[1 "Great in the affairs of this world."]
[2 Richard Fitzneale, in the "Dialogue on the Exchequer" (*Dialogus de Scaccario*).]

of local independence that essential lesson, the need of submission to centralisation, which even the dreadful years of
Danish invasions and the dark hour of Norman conquest
had failed effectually to teach. By allowing for once a real
reign of feudalism, they made it for ever afterwards impossible
in England. Finally, in these years of chaos, the two centres
of hope and progress in the medieval world—that is, the
Church and the town—made a decided advance in power
and in claims.

On the death of Henry I. the feudal party refused to abide
by the oaths which the late king
had made them swear to his
daughter Matilda. Their Norman
pride could not endure to be
ruled by the wife of a Count of
Anjou. Stephen, son of William
the Conqueror's daughter, already
endowed with English estates and
allied by marriage to one of the
baronial families, and himself a
man of gallant and generous spirit,
was regarded by them as one of
themselves. London supported
him, to avoid what seemed a
foreign rule; the aid of his
brother, the Bishop of Winchester,
and his own absolute submission
to clerical demands, won the
Church to his side.

SEAL OF MATILDA.

But the inherent weakness of his position forced him to
call in mercenaries from abroad, and to lavish on his partisans
titles and pensions and, above all, the fatal permission to raise
new castles. In three years the new king had quarrelled
with Robert, Earl of Gloucester, Matilda's half-brother; had
been attacked by David, King of Scotland, her uncle; and
had even thrown his own brother the bishop into the ranks
of his foes by quarrelling with the powerful family group of
ecclesiastics who had held the chief State offices since 1101.
The landing of Matilda in 1139 was the signal for the open
outbreak of civil war. In the course of this war Stephen was

captured at Lincoln and imprisoned, but exchanged for Earl Robert; Henry of Winchester, now Papal Legate, changed

COIN OF ROBERT, EARL OF GLOUCESTER.

sides once more; London revolted again; and Matilda, who owed to her rival's unpopularity a brief success, owed its loss to her own imperious folly.

With her withdrawal to Normandy in 1146, and the death of her half-brother Robert, her cause languished till 1148. In that year her son Henry, now aged fifteen, arrived in Scotland, and began to attack England from that side. In 1150 he was made Duke of Normandy, and soon succeeded to Maine and Anjou. But after his marriage in 1152 to Eleanor of Aquitaine had made him lord of two-thirds of modern France, his mere advent in England was enough to force his rival to the compromise called the Treaty of Wallingford. Stephen was to retain the crown for life; and

COIN OF ELEANOR OF AQUITAINE.

Henry was to be adopted as his son and to succeed him.

During this long conflict the nobles had made hardly a pretence of even party loyalty; it was a greedy scramble for

COIN OF STEPHEN.

power, and that of the worst feudal kind. "In olden days" (says the chronicler, William of Newburgh) "there was no king in Israel, and everyone did that which was right in his own eyes; but in England now it was worse; for there was a king, but impotent, and every man did what was wrong in his own eyes." The Peterborough continuation of the English Chronicle[1] sums

[1 Under the year 1137.]

24

up all in words with which in their pregnant simplicity no modern description can possibly vie :—" They filled the land full of castles, and filled the castles with devils. They took all those that they deemed had any goods, men and women, and tortured them with tortures unspeakable ; never were martyrs so tortured as they were. . . . Many thousand they slew with hunger . . . they robbed and burned all the villages, so that thou mightest fare a day's journey nor ever find a man dwelling in a village nor land tilled. Corn, meat, and cheese, there was none in the land. The bishops were ever cursing them, but they cared nought therefor, for they were all forcursed and forsworn and forlorn. . . . Men said openly that Christ slept and His

COIN OF EUSTACE.

saints. Such and more than we can say we suffered nineteen winters for our sins."

Without such grim experience of what feudalism unmastered would be, the education of the English race would have been incomplete. Unlicensed castles, private wars, private coinage, seigniorial jurisdiction, these outward signs of the feudal spirit are written at large on this page alone of our history. But meanwhile the silent unwritten processes of growth were working all for good. The boroughs—as a comparison shows of their charters under Henry I. with those won under Henry II. —were advancing steadily, and no doubt served as havens from the disorders outside. The Church itself was as a strong city of refuge. As Becket reminded Henry II., it was the Church that transferred the crown from Stephen to him. It was the Church that at the crisis of Henry I.'s death claimed the right " to elect and to ordain the king," that rejected the succession of Stephen's son Eustace, " the child of a perjured man " ; that declared that the God of Battles had decided the ordeal against Stephen ; and that, when at length peace was made, blessed it with the blessing of Isaiah's prophecies.

In that other important but almost hidden process, the fusion of Norman with English blood, the Church again plays its part ; for the best evidence of this fusion lies in two events which are both under clerical direction. These are the Crusading expedition of 1138, which took Lisbon from the Moors; and the Battle of the Standard, a defeat of the Scots at Northallerton, 1138, by the militia of the northern shires, accompanied by their parish priests, bearing as standard a crucifix. On each of these occasions English yeomen obey Norman leaders; English and Normans are called "the sons of one mother"; English and Norman traditions are alike invoked. We are prepared for the

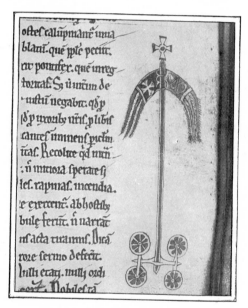

THE STANDARD.
(*Corpus Christi College, Cambridge.*)

official testimony a few years later that owing to intermarriages it had become impossible to distinguish English from Norman, except in the case of serfs.

The wheel had come round; the evil of the day of Senlac was worked out; its good effects—the vivifying and widening of Anglo-Saxon life and character by the keener, loftier Norman temper, the defining and concentrating of Anglo-Saxon institutions by the Norman genius for organisation, the stimulating and awakening of Anglo-Saxon patriotism by the Norman tyranny—were by this time incorporated and absorbed. From this period of fierce trial there emerges as from a furnace a new product—the English national character; and to its fusion of Norman fire with Saxon earnestness we owe the noblest scenes in our "rough island story" and the most imaginative creations of our unrivalled literature.

A. L. SMITH.
The Early Plantagenets:
Henry II.

THE Plantagenet family, who began with Henry II. — an occupation of the throne that was to last for more than three hundred years—were a family of characters so remarkable that contemporaries accounted for them by tracing their descent back to a demon ancestress. Of them all, perhaps Henry II.

SEAL OF HENRY II.

was the most remarkable. Strong man as he was, all his capacities of mind and body, all his organising genius and clearness of purpose, his fiery energy and harsh, stubborn will were needed for the task before him. That was, to build up a lasting fabric of centralised power. This meant that he must finally crush feudalism, call in the conquered race to co-operate in political work, and weld together English local institutions with Norman principles of centralisation.

His first measures were drastic enough, but were facilitated by the exhaustion of the land after the civil wars and the withdrawal of many barons to the Holy Land for the Crusade of 1147. "Those ravening wolves, the Flemish hirelings, were driven forth; the new castles razed; the Crown demesnes and revenues recovered; and justice set to work again." Here and

EFFIGIES OF HENRY II. AND ISABELLA, WIFE OF KING JOHN, FONTEVRAULT.

there a Mortimer or a Bigod showed fight for a brief while,
but as a whole the feudal party looked on and made no sign
while for nineteen years the unresting king was founding
deep and strong his administrative and judicial system, on
which, when at last the barons awoke, their forces dashed
themselves in vain.

This result, demonstrated thus in 1173, was already a fore-
gone conclusion when in 1159 the barons accepted the king's
offer to commute for a money payment the military service due
for their fiefs.   By this institution of scutage[1] the king at one
stroke destroyed the military strength of feudalism and supplied
himself with a far more convenient mercenary force for his
war abroad.

For Henry II., though wise enough to feel that England was
the real key of his dominions, yet, being lord in his own and his
wife's right of two-thirds of France, was more often abroad than
not, and was rarely free from war with his neighbour the King
of France.   In 1158 he had betrothed his son Geoffrey to the
heiress of Brittany, and himself became guardian of the Duchy
on the Duke's death in 1165.   In 1159 he laid claim to the
county of Toulouse, and was embroiled in constant, if rather
uneventful, warfare with King Louis VII.   This became an
important fact when Louis offered shelter to Thomas Becket
in 1167.   The conflict between Henry and Becket will be
dealt with on a later page (p. 390).   But Becket's murder
in Canterbury Cathedral was the fatal blunder of Henry II.'s
life, and the dividing-point of the prosperous from the
disastrous period of his reign.   Its first effect was to raise

**Relations
with
Ireland
and Wales.**
such an outburst of religious feeling that he had to escape
from it by an expedition to Ireland.   A Bull of Adrian IV.
in 1156 had already assumed to annex Ireland to the English
crown, and in 1170 Richard de Clare (Strongbow) had taken
Dublin, married the heiress of Dermot, King of Leinster, and
succeeded to that province.   Henry now marched through
Ireland, receiving homage from all the native chiefs, and left
Strongbow as his deputy to govern the whole island.   Thus a
step was taken in the great design of a union of all the British
Isles under one crown; for Wales now contained but   two
small independent kingdoms, Gwynedd and Debenborth (p. 353).

[1 Literally "shield-money."]

Though Henry II. thrice attacked the former with little success, yet until Stephen's reign the other Welsh princes appear at the English Court as vassals. The connection of Wales with England

MURDER OF THOMAS BECKET (MS. Jul. A. xi.).

had hitherto been slight. There were two brief invasions by Harold, in 1055 and 1063, a long series of piecemeal annexations by the Norman Marcher barons, and the settlement by Henry I. of a colony of Flemings in Pembrokeshire.

Scotland in 1157 had been forced to relinquish that hold on

Relations with Scotland. the three northern counties of England which, despite the Battle of the Standard, had been maintained throughout Stephen's reign. Now in 1173 the Scottish king eagerly seconded the powerful league against Henry II. which was headed by Henry's own sons and joined by the King of France, the Count of Flanders, and the barons of Normandy, England, Brittany, Gascony. The connection of all this with the murder of Becket was shown by Henry when, as he saw the disasters thickening

around him, he hastened to the tomb of " the blessed martyr," and was scourged in penance before the shrine. That very day, men noted with awe, the invading host of William the Lion was utterly routed at Alnwick and the King of Scots captured. Even before Henry's arrival in England the Justiciar had defeated the rebel Earls of Norfolk, Leicester, and Derby.

By the Treaty of Falaise the King of Scots surrendered castles to Henry, did him homage at York, and acknowledged the English overlordship.

PENANCE OF HENRY II. AT BECKET'S SHRINE, FROM A PAINTING ON GLASS.

The crisis had shown the precariousness of the accidental tie which bound together dominions reaching from the Cheviots to the Pyrenees, and embracing so many different races. But it had also shown the complete confidence of the English nation in the Crown; it had revealed the existence of a strong group of loyal northern barons, descendants of Henry I.'s ministers and ancestors of the men who were forty years later to take the initiative in the movement of Magna Charta; and it had tested and approved the strength of that administrative

system which this great king had been putting together
with rare insight since his very accession.

"Henceforth," proudly writes the royal treasurer, "let any
one, however great a lord, learn that it is no light task to
wrest the club from the hands of Hercules."

There was one cause which besides the sacrilege of 1170 **Henry II.**
opened the way for the peril of 1173. This was the king's **and his**
relations with his own sons. He intended, doubtless, to divide **Sons.**
out territories which he must have felt it hopeless to keep
together. To secure the succession in England, Normandy,
and Anjou to his eldest
son Henry, he had the
coronation performed by
the Archbishop of York
in 1170. Geoffrey would
be Duke of Brittany.
Richard was to rule
Poitou and Aquitaine.
John was appointed lord
of Ireland in 1177. But
the sons were not content
to wait for their father's
death. The three eldest
joined the rebellion of
1173 against him; and
when, during Richard's
successful revolt against
him in 1188, the old king

SEAL OF HENRY, SON OF HENRY II.

discovered that John, his youngest and best-loved child,
had long been intriguing against him, the shock of this
news, coming close upon the seizure of Anjou and Touraine
by his despised and hated rival, Philip of France, and
his humiliation before that rival and his own unnatural
son, killed him in two days. The domestic history of his
later days is a tragical one. A treacherous and revengeful
wife; sons who made war on each other and on him, and
brought the darkest accusations against him; the death
of his eldest and third sons—in all this men traced a
divine vengeance for "the saint martyr of Canterbury," for
Henry's own illicit amours, and for his ungovernable and

blaspheming temper. But despite the failure of his foreign policy, the years from 1173 to 1189 continued the great series of measures by which the fabric of our Constitution was being

IRISH HALFPENNY OF JOHN.

built up. The "Assizes" united indissolubly the royal and the popular elements of justice, replaced judicial combat by something not far from our trial by jury, encouraged the principle of elective representation, revived and reorganised the national militia. In 1170 a clean sweep was made of the corrupt local sheriffs, and royal officials were substituted. In 1178 we begin to discern the appellate jurisdiction of the King's Council, the germ of our Chancery courts. In 1188 two important advances are made in taxation, whereby the clergy are put under contribution, and personal property henceforth shares the burden with land. Few have been the kings whose career and experience were more varied; very few who could show such many-sided abilities and so strong and remarkable a personality; perhaps none who did more lasting good to their people, than Henry Plantagenet.

Richard I.   Under Richard I., a king who could hardly speak a word of English, whose whole stay in the country amounted only to a few months, who treated all English offices and royal possessions as so much saleable property, it would seem as if there must come a check to the constitutional progress which had been the direct fruit of alliance between the people

AQUITANIAN COIN OF RICHARD I.

COIN OF HENRY II.

and the Crown. But the royal ministers carried on the great work as thoroughly as before; they enlarged the self-governing powers of the local courts of hundreds and shires; they had the grand

juries for the assizes elected ; they made assessment by elected
representatives the regular rule for taxation both of personalty
and of land, and thus left but one step to be taken towards the
creation of representative Parliaments ; they augmented the
rights given in charters to boroughs ; and when they let London
organise itself under an elective mayor, they were permitting
an advance in municipal independence such as (says Richard
of Devizes) "neither Richard himself nor his father, Henry,
would have allowed for a thousand times a thousand marks."

SEAL OF RICHARD I.

Most of this wise policy, however, came after the downfall of
William Longchamp, the Bishop of Ely. This man, a Norman
by birth, and insolently contemptuous of the English, was left
by Richard in 1189 to govern the kingdom. As Justiciar and
Chancellor and Papal Legate his power was so great that only
the most foolish arrogance in exercising it can explain his
failure. He had bitterly offended not only his colleagues, but
also the prelates, the barons, the Londoners, the mass of the
nation, when in 1191 John, released from the oath of three
years' residence abroad that Richard had imposed upon him,
headed the movement against the "upstart" which ended in
his dismissal and exile. Thus for the first time in our history
had expression, however imperfect, been given to that most
fruitful of all constitutional ideas—the responsibility of the
king's ministers, not to the king alone, but to the nation also.
But bully and braggart as Longchamp had been, he was at

least loyal to his absent master.   John—who in position, if
not in official title, held the first place in England through
1192 to 1193—spent all his energies in plotting to wrest the
crown from his brother, who was now, to the scandal of
Christendom, held a captive on German soil.   When the
passionate remonstrances of Queen Eleanor, his mother, and
the loyal generosity of the whole English nation in raising the
enormous ransom, freed Richard in the spring of 1194, John
was warned by his accomplice, Philip of France, with the significant notice, "Take care of yourself; the devil is loose."
John, who was at the time openly warring against the Justiciar,
was treated better than his deserts.   In a brief stay of two
months Richard settled the kingdom to his mind, and handed
it over to Hubert Walter, Archbishop of Canterbury, Papal
Legate, who now became Justiciar as well.   He was nephew of
Ranulf Glanvil, who had succeeded in 1180 to the Justiciarship
after Richard de Luci, and who had spent his life in Henry II.'s
service.   Nor was he unworthy to stand in this great line.
It is true that, pressed himself by Richard's insatiable demands
for money, he had to press hard upon the people; but to him
was due most of the constitutional progress of the reign.   His
position of taskmaster encouraged at once the growth of ministerial responsibility and ministerial freedom of action.   In 1198
the Great Council, led by St. Hugh, Bishop of Lincoln, flatly
refused a royal demand for money : the sole precedent for such
refusal was Becket's action in 1163.   The Justiciar took the
opportunity to resign, and Geoffrey FitzPeter, a great baron,
succeeded him.   During these last four and a half years of
his career Richard was frittering away, in a petty warfare of
vengeance against Philip, the powers of organisation and the
fiery energy that, when exerted in Palestine, had almost availed
to achieve the impossible, and restore life to the dead bones
of the Frankish Settlement in the East.

   It is characteristic of the man that he received his death
wound in trying to wrest treasure-trove from a recalcitrant
vassal, and that on his death-bed he displayed a noble generosity and a sincere penitence.   He was hardly in any sense an
Englishman, but he had done much for England, by his exploits, by his choice of ministers, and indirectly by his absences
and his very extortions.

1216]

Richard had at one time intended to make Arthur of Brittany his heir; but in the end he accepted John, whose election shows that the feudal rule of descent had not yet superseded the Old English practice of choosing for king

IMPRISONMENT AND WOUNDING OF RICHARD I. (MS. Vitell. A. xiii.)

whoever of the royal house seemed most suitable. Arthur, for whom no single voice was raised in England, had a strong party abroad, and, besides Brittany, held for a while Anjou, Maine, and Touraine. But he was used as a cat's-paw by Philip, was taken prisoner by John, and disappeared—

382 FROM THE CONQUEST TO THE CHARTER.

being no doubt murdered—in 1203.   Upon this, Philip renewed the sentence of forfeiture which he had passed against John in the Court of Peers of France.   By the end of 1204 the vast domains of Henry II., comprising three-fifths of modern France, were all lost, with the exception of Gascony and part of Guienne.   Thus was England severed from Normandy; the tie, which had lasted 140 years, was broken.   By it England had suffered much, but had gained even more—had gained a wider horizon, a European interest, and a breath of the daring, life-giving Norman spirit.   Now that England had got all it could get, a continuance of the connection would have become a misalliance, a Mezentian union of the dead and the living.   That this was so is shown by the striking fact that when the two countries now parted, only a handful of families were found who had lands in both.   That is, the baronage on the two sides of the Channel had already become distinct.   In fact, Henry I. had repeatedly confiscated the English estates of the most turbulent Norman barons.   The feudal element had learned its lesson in 1174, and had now been drilled by fifty years of strict order; Henry II.'s scutage turned military feudatories into country gentlemen; families like the Beaumonts and the Montforts divided up their estates, the Norman to the elder branch, the English to the younger.   From all these causes the baronage had become genuinely English.   That this was so is proved above all by the confidence which the people began to repose in them, a confidence which makes the chief feature in constitutional history for the next two hundred and fifty years, and which is nobly displayed and nobly justified on the page of Magna Charta.

Loss of Normandy

The barons had felt a keen humiliation at the loss of the French provinces—less, perhaps, at the actual loss than at the contemptible manner of it.   When first the danger arose, John had insolently demanded their feudal service, though he had carried out none of the solemn promises made at his coronation, but had seized their castles, and in several cases dishonoured their families in the foulest way.   When the forces did assemble, thrice he plundered and dismissed them; or only took them across the sea to look on idly while the Norman fortresses fell.   The conduct that was really due to

King, Barons, and Pope.

EFFIGIES OF RICHARD I. AND QUEEN ELEANOR, FONTEVRAULT.

Photo: Daveau, Rouen.

suspicion and consciousness of inadequate means could in the barons' eyes show only as cowardice and imbecility. In 1213 they flatly refused to send a force abroad at all; now that Normandy was gone, Poitou was nothing to them. But the decisive factor in the sum of the events which issued in Magna Charta was John's quarrel with the Church. On the very day of Hubert Walter's death in 1205, the younger monks of Christ Church, Canterbury, elected their sub-prior, and sent him off at once to Rome for Papal confirmation. But the king got wind of it, and promptly installed his own candidate in the estates of the see; and at the same time the bishops insisted that the right to elect an Archbishop of Canterbury was theirs. The Pope, the great Innocent III., saw his chance. He overrode the claims of all three parties, and appointed a member of his own Court, an English **Stephen Langton.** Cardinal resident at Rome, Stephen Langton. No better man could have been chosen. It was natural, therefore, that John should refuse to receive him, and, when punished by an Interdict in 1208 being laid on the kingdom, should retaliate by outlawing the bishops and confiscating Church property. The next step was the solemn excommunication of the king; and the final one, a Bull of deposition. The closing of the churches, the hushing of the bells and services, the cessation of the sacraments, the severance of himself from the Church like a leper, the absolving of his subjects from their allegiance, the commission to King Philip to invade England and wrest the kingdom from " a son of perdition "—against all these John only hardened his heart. But when a crazy fanatic prophesied that on Ascension Day, 1213, John would have lost the crown, the king showed all the cowardice of a tyrant and the superstitiousness of a blasphemer, and grovelled in abject submission before Pandulf, the very Papal Legate who, in 1208, had been met only with a threat that " he should dance upon air" if he entered the royal presence again. John now gave up his kingdom to the Pope, to receive it back as a tributary and a vassal, and accepted Langton as archbishop. Langton entered England, and the key to the whole situation was found. John had outraged the barons, had desecrated the Church, had despoiled and oppressed the people. But the barons had looked on while the Church had suffered;

and the barons had based their own resistance upon technicalities of feudal tenure, not on broad and national grounds.
To bring out a mutual confidence between the three classes,
and to fix this on a constitutional basis, was the mission of
the new archbishop. At a Council in St. Paul's, 25th of
August, 1213, he produced the Charter of Henry I., of which
the Great Charter itself is but an expanded copy.

Under this banner the rebellion was organised while John

SEAL OF JOHN.

was abroad in Poitou, and in November, 1214, a month after
he returned, the baronage had met at St. Edmunds and taken
a solemn oath to exact from him a Charter on such a model.
In vain John struggled to break up their party, to buy over
the Church, to invoke the protection of the Pope. The toils
closed around him. At the following Easter an armed host
of some 10,000 men met at Stamford; on 24th May they
entered London amid rejoicings. Hereupon the few barons
who still adhered to the king—mostly members of the old
feudal group, men like Earl Warenne and Ranulf, Earl of
Chester—deserted him; and John, with rage and treachery
in his heart, had to yield at last. The Great Charter was **Magna**
sealed at Runnymede, 15th June, 1215. It is a misunderstand- **Charta.**
ing to regard the Charter either as containing new principles
or as terminating a struggle. On the contrary, its character is
eminently conservative, setting up "the laws of Henry I." as
its standard. At the same time "confirmation of the Charter"

25

becomes the rallying-cry of the next three generations, and the constitutional progress up to 1340 is little more than the working out of the Charter's main clauses.

John survived by sixteen months this day of his humiliation. In that brief space were crowded events well worthy to form the last scenes of Shakespeare's play—the fiery energy of the king, his victories over his enemies in detail, the Pope's excommunication of the rebels and suspension of the archbishop, the barons' desperate transfer of the Crown to Prince Louis of France, the blind and savage vengeance exercised by John's foreign soldiers, who swept to and fro through the land, and whose marches were a track of flames and blood, till the sands of the Wash ruined John's army, and

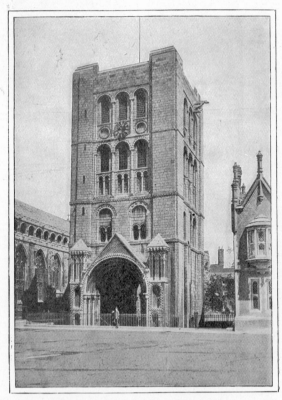

BURY ST. EDMUNDS—NORMAN TOWER.

THE MONK OF SWINESHEAD OFFERING JOHN THE POISONED CUP.
(MS. Vitell. A. xiii.)

the monk of Swineshead—so ran the popular account—
sacrificed himself to become the instrument of God's wrath
upon the tyrant.

AT the accession of Stephen the Church presented the
appearance of a great secular corporation. Roger of Salisbury
was still justiciar, his son Roger chancellor, his nephew Nigel
treasurer and Bishop of Ely, and another nephew, Alexander,
was Bishop of Lincoln. It was to Roger that Stephen
chiefly owed his crown, and the support of the clergy was
acknowledged in the new king's early charters. When the

W. H.
HUTTON.
The Con-
flicts of
Church
and
Crown.

civil war broke out, it was the foolish arrest of the great
prelates that threw the country into confusion, suspended
all legal and constitutional administration, and gave Matilda
her little day of triumph.   The Church held the balance
between parties, and the pendulum swung as she directed.
Individual churchmen stood out among the chaos of those
"nineteen winters" as directors and guides, though often
blind leaders of the blind.   Henry of Blois, Stephen's
brother and Bishop of Winchester, a stern Cistercian of
unbending fidelity to the independent interests of the Church,
endeavoured to be an arbitrator, but was little more than
a changeable partisan.   Theobald, Archbishop of Canterbury,
was a consistent supporter of Matilda, but his influence was
overshadowed by the great Bishop of Winchester.   He
gathered round him, nevertheless, a circle of students and
thinkers who gave England fame in Europe, even in the
midst of her darkest gloom at home.   And the reign of

Growth of Monasticism.
Stephen witnessed an extraordinary extension of monasticism
which was to change the whole features of Northern England.
The northern shires had not recovered from their harrying
by the Conqueror; even to 1130 the land lay waste round
York for a breadth of sixty miles.   It was the monks, and
chiefly the Cistercians, who turned the wilderness into a
fruitful field.   "In the short time Stephen bore the title
of king," says William, the Augustinian Canon of Newburgh,
"there arose in England many more dwellings of the servants
and handmaids of God than had risen in the whole century
past."   Twenty religious houses in Yorkshire, nineteen in
Lincolnshire, many more in other shires, were founded in
the midst of the anarchy—"God's castles," says the chronicler,
"in which the servants of the true anointed King do keep
watch, and His young are exercised in war against spiritual
wickedness."   At the same time, too, the one distinctively
English order was created.   Gilbert of Sempringham, a Lincolnshire man, established a society to which both men and
women were admitted, and which spread over England with
great rapidity.   His work was educational as well as spiritual,
and William of Newburgh says "he bears away the palm from
all who have applied their religious labours to the teaching
and training of women."

EFFIGY OF KING JOHN, WORCESTER CATHEDRAL.

Extension of Ecclesiastical Jurisdiction.

While the work of the Church was thus progressing, and the terror and confusion of the times had suspended the sessions of the ordinary courts of the realm, it was natural that the Church courts, administered by men more and more trained in canonical and civil law, should encroach upon the province of the secular jurisdiction. Suits between clerk and layman concerning land, matters of criminal issue in which a clerk was interested as criminal or as injured, debts in which there was a pledging by oath, and the like, fell wholly into the hands of the ecclesiastical courts. Thus, when the land was again at peace, and Henry the Angevin sat on the throne of his grandfather with a settled aim to make all men equal before one system of law and government, a conflict between Church and State was inevitable. Foremost among the scholars of Archbishop Theobald had been one

Thomas Becket.

Thomas of London, the son of Gilbert surnamed Becket, a merchant of Rouen who had settled in London and become sheriff. A bright lad, of keen wit and pure life, he had risen to be Archdeacon of Canterbury several years before Stephen died, and he was commended to his successor as "companion of his counsels," and became chancellor in 1154. The two young men became fast friends ; "when business was over they would play together like boys of an age; in hall, in church, they sat together, or rode out. . . . . Sometimes the king rode on horseback into the hall where the chancellor sat at meat ; sometimes, bow in hand, returning from hunting or on his way to the chase ; sometimes he would drink and depart when he had seen the chancellor. Sometimes, jumping over the table, he would sit down and eat with him. Never in Christian times were there two men more of a mind or better friends." So writes the friend and biographer of Thomas, William Fitzstephen, who was with him to the end of his chequered life. Thomas aided, if he did not guide, the great law reforms by which Henry inaugurated his reign ; he went on embassies, he heard causes, he led knights in the field. But when Theobald died, and the king insisted that the man he knew and loved best should sit on the throne of Augustine, he "put off the deacon," and became, at a step, the champion of the rights and the claims of the Church. In October, 1163, at a council at Westminster, the king demanded that clerks accused of great crimes should be tried in his courts. He was not without the support of canonists

Photo: Green Bros., Grasmere.

CISTERCIAN ABBEY, FURNESS.

Photo: Hudson.

CISTERCIAN ABBEY, KIRKSTALL.

and civilians, and before long he won to his side the majority of the timid and time-serving bishops. In the Constitutions of Clarendon, January, 1164, he set out the claim at length, with added restraints on appeals to Rome, and on the trial of civil suits concerning lands and debts. The archbishop stood firm.

Photo: Paul Robert, Paris.

THOMAS BECKET'S VESTMENTS, SENS.

He was already engaged in a purification of the Church; in his own diocese "he plucked up, pulled down, scattered, and rooted out whatever he found planted amiss in the garden of the Lord." He was anxious, like the king, to purge the Church of abuses; but it was an internal reformation that he designed, and he would not call in the secular arm. Nine months passed, and there was no prospect of agreement. The king then caused Becket to be tried in a council of North-ampton on charges bearing only indirectly on the questions in dispute. After a stormy scene the archbishop appealed to Rome, and in a few days left England. For the next six years he resided in France, and one attempt after another to make peace between Church and State failed. Henry perse-cuted and banished Becket's kinsfolk and supporters. Becket excommunicated those who invaded and plundered his see. Pope and Antipope bid for the English king's support, and Alexander III. now censured and now praised the vehemence of the Church's champion. As the years went on Becket, at Pontigny and at Sens, gathered round him a circle like that of an exiled monarch: the learned men of Europe corresponded with him, and the Church in all lands

Thomas Becket's Grace Cup.
(By permission of the Duke of Norfolk.)

Painting of Becket's Murder.
(By permission of the Dean of Canterbury).

Glass Medallion showing Shrine.
(By permission of the Warden of Radley College.)

Enamelled Reliquary of St. Thomas.
(By permission of the Dean of Hereford.)

MEMORIALS OF BECKET.

watched him as a gladiator in the arena. At last Henry yielded, promised to annul the Constitutions and receive the archbishop to the kiss of peace. On December 1, 1170, Becket landed at Sandwich; on the 29th he was murdered in his own cathedral. Though he had been everywhere received by the acclamations of the people, the bishops who had been of the king's party had still refused to submit to his authority, and their complaints had drawn from the king the passionate cry, too hastily interpreted, " I have nourished and promoted in my realm sluggish and wretched knaves who are faithless to their lord, and suffer him to be tricked thus infamously by a low clerk." Thomas of Canterbury met his death at the hands of four reckless knights with a fortitude that astonished the timid monks who surrounded him. " I am ready," he said, " to die for my Lord, that in my blood the Church may obtain liberty and peace. But in the name of Almighty God I forbid you to hurt my people, whether clerk or lay." The result of his death was the complete submission of the king. The " customs " were entirely given up, and clerks and offenders against them were left to ecclesiastical tribunals. No other issue was possible. The king was involved in the horror which thrilled through Europe at the murder.

St. Thomas of Canterbury. Becket all through his years of struggle had been adored by the people of England ; his praises were sung by Garnier, the poet of the poor ; his fellow-citizens of London made him their patron ; obscure writers in distant lands told of his fight for the Church ; crusading knights founded a new order in his honour, and in Iceland a saga embodied the story of his life. More than this : himself the first man born on English soil who had worn the mitre of metropolitan since William's Conquest, he stood out for centuries as the great national hero. He was canonised in 1173. No saint was so popular an object of veneration ; his memory was closely embedded in the very heart of the national life.

It must always be remembered that the forces at the back of St. Thomas represented not only the respect which men feel for a bold fight for principle, but also that blind struggle against the hideous punishments of the age, of which the assertion of ecclesiastical privilege, covering widows and orphans as well as clerks and those who injured them, was a natural expression.

The reformation that Becket and Henry designed was far from being accomplished. Satirists pointed to the babies whose

promotion in the Church was secured before they could speak.
Infants in cradles, they complain, are made archdeacons, that
out of the mouths of babes and sucklings may be perfected
praise. Children at the
breast are set to dispense
the sacraments. Boys are
made bishops at the age
when an apple is dearer
to them than a dozen
churches. Their training
is only in the things of
this world. They are sent
to Paris, where they learn
every vice: and they return
to England only to hawk
and to hunt. The bishops
who won their sees by
secular work or mean in-
trigue make it no care to
labour in the Lord's vine-
yard. "What bishop,"
says Giraldus, the shrewd
Welsh archdeacon, "fulfils
the canonical description

A RELIC OF THE CULT OF ST. THOMAS.
*(By permission of the Somersetshire Archæological and
Natural History Society)*

of the true pastor even in small things ? " Much of this must be
set down to literary exaggeration : it was a common recreation
of ecclesiastical satirists to throw stones at bishops, and little did
the bishops mind it. But there are more than enough instances
in the works of the baldest of annalists to show that the Church
was in far from wholesome condition. It is recorded among the
virtues of St. Thomas that he would actually descend from his
horse to minister the sacrament of confirmation. It was a
wonder to the beholders when St. Hugh of Avalon, Bishop of
Lincoln, washed with his own hands the sores of lepers. Quarrels
for precedence took up much of the time of those whose hearts
should have been set on things above. The primates contended
for the dignity of their sees. "Verily," says William of Newburgh, " that apostolic rule 'in honour preferring one another'
is so disregarded by the bishops of our time that they, laying
aside pastoral solicitude, contend with one another for dignity

both in obstinacy and emptiness." Thus in 1176, when a Papal Legate held council in London, "The Archbishop of York, being arrived the earlier, took possession of the chief seat, claiming the same as his own. The Archbishop of Canterbury, however, like a man who has sustained an injury, refused to take the lower room, and solemnly proclaimed his grievance in the matter of the seat that had been taken ; but his attendants, being more fiercely jealous of his dignity, proceeded from a simple strife of words to a brawl. The Archbishop of York (for the contrary party was the stronger) was driven with shame from the place he had so prematurely taken, and showed to the Legate his torn cope as a mark of the violence used towards him ; and he declared that he would summon the Archbishop of Canterbury with his gang before the Holy See. Thus, while the metropolitans battled, all business was thrown athwart, and the council was not celebrated, but dispersed ; and all those who had been summoned, and had come together to hold council, returned to their own homes."

ST. HUGH AND THE LEPERS.
(*Chapter House, Lincoln.*)

The Church under Richard and John was at once contentious and secularised. Hubert Walter, Archbishop of Canterbury, was a shrewd financier and an honourable conscientious statesman, but as a prelate he is noted chiefly for his quarrels with his chapter. Quarrels such as his, and those of Hugh of Nunant at Coventry, Savaric of Wells, and Geoffrey of York are, however, not always proof of the secular arrogance of bishops. They show, more often, the claims of the great monastic houses to be exempt from all

[[1] William of Newburgh, Book III., c. i.]

episcopal governance, and to be subject only to the Roman Curia. These claims, striven for with varying success during the next century, were slowly but surely won, and the greatest difficulty of the Church in England came to be, before the House of Anjou had ceased to rule, that independence of monasteries which made firm governance impossible, and arrayed monks and bishops in opposite camps, till the bishops themselves yielded to the tide, and handed themselves over, in the fifteenth century, as subservient vassals of the Papacy.

THE FUNERAL OF ST. HUGH.
(Chapter House, Lincoln.)

But it is easy to paint too dark a picture. There is light here, as elsewhere, if we will look for it. It may be that the crusades are fruitless; but the preaching of them at least held up before men a high standard of sacrifice and devotion. And few prelates but at one time or another gave their substance, if not their hearts, to the Holy War. Nor is there anything more touching in the history of the Middle Ages than the fervour with which bishop and priest, clerk and layman, threw away their lives to succour their brethren in the East. And at home men like St. Hugh stand out as models of sagacity, clear-sightedness, genuine piety. The man who could dare such kings as Henry II. and Richard I., and beat them with their own weapons, could shock the dignitaries of the Church by fixing his teeth in a precious relic. Yet no man more gentle or more reverend ever breathed. Later, when England fell under the rule of the vilest of her kings, an Englishman and an English Primate could lead the barons and the people to the freedom that was won for all time.

True Church Reformers.

Of the struggle between John and the Church (p. 384) the most significant result was the way in which the Church was now brought forward as the champion of the people. When king and barons plunged again into war, it was Stephen Langton, patriot as well as prelate, who produced to the constitutionalists the Charter of Henry I., on which their demands should be based, and from which Magna Charta sprang. "Quod Ecclesia Anglicana libera sit"[1] is the first article of the Great Charter, and the freedom which allowed the chapters to choose their own bishops was the type and pattern of the liberty asserted for the whole land.

F.W.MAIT-LAND. English Law under Norman and Angevin. THE Normans when they invaded England were in one important particular a less civilised race than were those English whom they came to subjugate. We may say with some certainty that they had no written laws. A century and a half ago a king of the Franks had been compelled to cede a large province to a horde of Scandinavian pirates. The pirates had settled down as lords of a conquered people; they had gradually adopted the religion, the language, and the civilisation (such as it was) of the vanquished; they had become Frenchmen. They may have paid some reverence to the written laws of the Frankish race, to the very ancient Lex Salica and the capitularies[2] of Merovingian and Carlovingian kings. But these were fast becoming obsolete, and neither the dukes of the Normans nor their nominal overlords, the kings of the Franks or French, could issue written dooms such as those which Canute was publishing in England. Some excellent traditions of a far-off past, of the rule of Charles the Great, the invaders could bring with them to England; and these transplanted into the soil of a subject kingdom, could burst into new life and bear new fruit—the great record that we call "Domesday Book" is a splendid firstfruit—but written laws they had none.

To all seeming, the Conqueror meant that his English subjects should keep their own old laws. Merely duke of the Normans, he was going to be king in England, and he was

[1 "That the Church of England is free."]
[2 Collections of ordinances.]

affirmeo. qd infra & ext anglia willo regi fideles
ee uoluer seruit & honore illius oma fidelitate cu eo ser
uare. 7 aut cu conte inimicos defende. Volo aut rex omis
hoies qs mecu adduxi. aut p me uenerossio in pace
mea. 7 gere. Et si qs de ill occisus fuer edus ei hat
infra einqz dies homicida ei si pocueste Sin aut iterp
se psoluere in. xLvi. marcas argenti qmdiu sub
stantia illi diu peruraint. Vbi u substancia defecer
cot hundredul in q occisio facta e commut redditae
qd remaner. Et omis franagena q tpe regis eduar
di qping mei fuerut in anglia. participes consuetudinu
anglor. qd ipi dicunt onhlote 7 anscote. psoluatur
secdm legem anglor. Hoc decretu sanctu e in autem
claudia.

Iterdicimi eria. ut nulla uina pecunia uedas ure
emat n infra ciuitares. 7 si aut tres fideles testes n
aliqu de uerista. sine sedicissioe. 7 guarantess si
alit fecerit soluat 7 psoluat. 7 pea forisfactam.

Decerni e eria. ubi ut si francigena appellauit angli
de puirio. aut morteo. furto. homicidio. ran. qd an
gli dicut apta rapina. q negaui n p anglus se de
sendat p qd meluis noluerit. aut uidras feren. aut
duello. Et aut anglus infirmus fuir. uincuat aliu q
p eo faciat Si qs cor uico fuer euideo. ul solid regi.
Si anglus francigene appellauit. 7 pbare noluerit.
uidico aut duello. uolo ut francigena purgare se
sacrmento n francco.

Hoc q sapio 7 uolo. ut omi haut 7 ueneat lege e
dimuard regis. in cirt 7 in omibz rebz adaucis ul q
Sctrui ad utilitate popli anglos.

Omis ho q uoluerit se ceu 7 libero sic in plegio. ut

not dissatisfied with those royal rights which, according to
his version of the story, had descended to him from King
Edward. About a few points he legislated. For example,
the lives of his followers were to be protected by the famous
murder-fine. If a Frenchman was found slain, and the slayer
was not produced, a heavy sum was to be exacted from the
district in which the crime was done. The establishment of
a presumption that every murdered man is a Frenchman until
the contrary is proved—a presumption highly advantageous to
the king's exchequer—gave rise in later days to the curious
process known as " the presentment of Englishry." The hundred had to pay the fine unless the kinsfolk of the dead man
would testify to his English birth. But this by the way.
William had also to regulate the scope of that trial by battle
which the Normans brought with them, and in so doing he
tried to deal equitably with both Normans and English. Also
it was necessary that he who had come hither as in some sort
the champion of Roman orthodoxy should mark off the sphere
of spiritual from that of temporal law by stricter lines than
had yet been drawn in England. Much, again—though by
no general law—he altered in the old military system, which
had lately shown itself to be miserably ineffectual. Dealing
out the forfeited lands amongst his barons, he could stipulate
for a force of armoured and mounted knights. Some other
changes he would make ; but in the main he was content that
the English should live under their old law, the law that now
bore the blessed Edward's name.

**Law under
Henry I.**
    And so again when on the death of Rufus—from Rufus
himself we get and we expect no laws—Henry seized the
crown, and was compelled to purchase adherents by granting
a charter full of all manner of promises, made to all manner
of people—the promise by which he hoped to win the hearts
of Englishmen was that he would restore them to Edward's
law with those amendments that the Conqueror had made in it.
Henry himself, great as a governor, was no great legislator.
A powerful central tribunal, which is also an exacting financial
bureau, an " exchequer," began to take definite shape under
the management of his expert ministers; but very few new
laws were published. The most characteristic legal exploits
of the Norman period are the attempts made by various

private persons to reconstruct "the law of St. Edward." They translate some of the old English dooms into Latin as best they can—a difficult task, for the English language is rapidly taking a new shape. They modify the old dooms to suit a new age. They borrow from foreign sources—from the canon law of the Catholic Church, from Frankish capitularies, now and again from the Roman law-books. But in Henry I.'s reign they still regarded the Old English dooms, the law of King Edward, as the core of the law that prevails in England. They leave us wondering how much practical truth there is in what they say; whether the ancient criminal tariffs that they transcribe are really observed; whether the Frenchmen who preside in court pay much attention to the words of Canute, even when those words have been turned into Latin or into French. Still, their efforts assure us that there has been rather a dislocation than a complete break in the legal history of England; also that the Frenchmen have not introduced much new law of a sufficiently definite kind to be set down in writing.

As yet the great bulk of all the justice that was done, was done by local courts, by those shire-moots and hundred-moots which the Conqueror and Henry I. had maintained as part of the ancient order, and by the newer seigniorial courts which were springing up in every village. The king's own court was but a court for the protection of royal rights, a court for the causes of the king's barons, and an ultimate tribunal at which a persistent litigant might perhaps arrive when justice had failed him everywhere else. Had it continued to be no more than this, the old English law, slowly adapting itself to changed circumstances, might have cast off its archaisms and become the law for after-times, law to be written and spoken in English words. Far more probably "St. Edward's law" would have split into a myriad local customs, and then at some future time Englishmen must have found relief from intolerable confusion in the eternal law of Rome. Neither of these two things happened, because under Henry II. the king's own court flung open its doors to all manner of people, ceased to be for judicial purposes an occasional assembly of warlike barons, became a bench of professional justices, appeared periodically in all the counties of England under the

26

guise of the Justices in Eyre.[1]   Then begins the process which makes the custom of the king's court the common law of England.   Ever since the Conquest the king's court had been in a very true sense a French court.   It had been a French-speaking court, a court whose members had been of French race, and had but slowly been learning to think of themselves as Englishmen.   Its hands had been very free.   It could not, if it would, have administered the Old English written laws in their native purity: for one thing they were unintelligible; for another thing in the twelfth century they had become barbarous—they dealt with crime in a hopelessly old-fashioned way.   On the other part, there was, happily, no written Norman code, and the king did not mean to be in England the mere duke he had been in Normandy.   And so the hands of his court were very free; it could be a law unto itself.   Many old English institutions it preserved, in particular those institutions of public law which were advantageous to the king —the king, for instance, could insist that the sheriffs were sheriffs, and not hereditary *vicomtes*—but the private law, law of land tenure, law of possession, of contract, of procedure, which the court develops in the course of the twelfth century, is exceedingly like a *coutume* from Northern France. Hundreds of years will elapse before anyone tries to write about it in English; and when at length this is done, the English will be an English in which every important noun, every accurate term, is of French origin.

Legal language.   We may say a little more about the language of our law, for it is not an uninteresting topic.   From the Conquest onwards until the year 1731 the solemnest language of our law was neither French nor English, but Latin.   Even in the Anglo-Saxon time, though English was the language in which laws were published and causes were pleaded, Latin was the language in which the kings, with Italian models before them, made grants of land to the churches and the thegns.   In 1066 the learned men of both races could write and speak to each other in Latin.   We shall be pretty safe in saying that anyone who could read and write at all could read and write Latin.

[1 Eyre is from Lat. *iter*, a journey.   These were travelling members of, or delegates from, the king's high court, sent on circuit under the Act 22 Hen. II., 1186, and the forerunners of the present circuit system.]

As to French, it was as yet little better than a vulgar dialect of Latin, a language in which men might speak, but not a language in which they would write anything except perhaps a few songs.   The two tongues which the Conqueror used for laws, charters and writs were Latin and English.   But Latin soon gets the upper hand, and becomes for a while the one written language of the law.   In the king's Chancery they write nothing but Latin, and it is in Latin that the judgments of the king's courts are recorded.   This, as already said, is so until the year 1731 ; to substitute English for Latin as the language in which the king's writs and patents and charters shall be expressed, and the doings of the law-courts shall be preserved, requires a statute of George II.'s day.

Meanwhile there had been many and great changes.   Late in the twelfth or early in the thirteenth century French was beginning to make itself a language in which not only songs and stories but legal documents could be written.   About the middle of the thirteenth century ordinances and statutes that are written in French began to appear.   Just for one moment England puts in a claim to equality.   Henry III. " þurȝ Godes fultume king on Engleneloande "[1] issued one proclamation in English.   But this claim was either belated or premature. Under Edward I. French, though it cannot expel Latin from the records of litigation, becomes the language in which laws are published and law-books are written.   It continues to be the language of the statute-book until the end of the Middle Ages. Under Henry VII. English at length becomes the speech in which English lawgivers address their subjects, though some two hundred and fifty years must yet pass away before it will win that field in which Latin is securely entrenched.

As the oral speech of litigants and their advisers, French has won a splendid victory.   In the king's own court it must prevail from the Conquest onwards, but in the local courts a great deal of English must long have been spoken.   Then, however, under Henry II. began that centralising movement which we have already noticed.   The jurisprudence of a French-speaking court became the common law, the measure of all rights and duties, and it was carried throughout the land by

[" [1] Through God's support king in England," the opening words of the proclamation in question.]

the journeying justices. In the thirteenth century men when they plead or when they talk about law, speak French; the professional lawyer writes in French and thinks in French. Some power of speaking a decent French seems to have been common among all classes of men, save the very poorest; men spoke it who had few, if any, drops of foreign blood in their veins. Then in 1362, when the prolonged wars between England and France had begun, a patriotic statute endeavoured to make English instead of French the spoken tongue of the law-courts. But this came too late; we have good reason for thinking that it was but tardily obeyed, and at any rate, lawyers went on writing about law in French. Gradually in the sixteenth century their French went to the bad, and they began to write in English; for a long time past they had been thinking and speaking in English. But it was an English in which almost all the technical terms were of French origin. And so it is at the present day. How shall one write a single sentence about law without using some such word as " debt," " contract," " heir," " trespass," " pay," " money," " court," " judge," " jury " ? But all these words have come to us from the French. In all the world-wide lands where English law prevails, homage is done daily to William of Normandy and Henry of Anjou.

Henry II.'s Legal Reforms.   What Henry did in the middle of the twelfth century was of the utmost importance, though we might find ourselves in the midst of obsolete technicalities were we to endeavour to describe it at length. Speaking briefly, we may say that he concentrated the whole system of English justice round a court of judges professionally expert in the law. He could thus win money—in the Middle Ages no one did justice for nothing—and he could thus win power; he could control, and he could starve, the courts of the feudatories. In offering the nation his royal justice, he offered a strong and sound commodity. Very soon we find very small people—yeomen, peasants—giving the go-by to the old local courts and making their way to Westminster Hall, to plead there about their petty affairs. We may allow that in course of time this con-centrating process went much too far. In Edward I.'s day the competence of the local courts in civil causes was hemmed within a limit of forty shillings, a limit which at first was fairly wide, but became ever narrower as the value of money fell, until in the last century no one could exact any debt that was not of trifling amount without bringing a costly action in one of the courts at Westminster. But the first stages of the process did unmixed good—they gave us a common law.

King Henry and his able ministers came just in time— a little later would have been too late: English law would have been unified, but it would have been Romanised. We have been wont to boast, perhaps too loudly, of the pure "Englishry" of our common law. This has not been all pure gain. Had we "received" the Roman jurisprudence as our neighbours received it, we should have kept out of many a bad mess through which we have plunged. But to say nothing of the political side of the matter, of the absolute monarchy which Roman law has been apt to bring in its train, it is probably well for us and for the world at large that we have stumbled forwards in our empirical fashion, blundering into wisdom. The moral glow known to the virtuous schoolboy who has not used the "crib" that was ready to his hand, we may allow ourselves to feel; and we may hope for the blessing which awaits all those who have honestly taught themselves anything.

In a few words we must try to tell a long story. On the continent of Europe Roman law had never perished. After the barbarian invasions it was still the "personal law" of the conquered provincials. The Franks, Lombards, and other victorious tribes lived under their old Germanic customs, while the vanquished lived under the Roman law. In course of time the personal law of the bulk of the inhabitants became the territorial law of the country where they lived. The Roman law became once more the general law of Italy and of Southern France; but in so doing it lost its purity, it became a debased and vulgarised Roman law, to be found rather in traditional custom than in the classical texts, of which very little was known. Then, at the beginning of the twelfth century, came a great change. A law-school at Bologna began to study and to teach that Digest in which Justinian had preserved the wisdom of the great jurists of the golden age. A new science spread outwards from Bologna. At least wherever the power of the emperor extended, Roman law

Roman Law in Mediæval Europe.

had—so men thought—a claim to rule. The emperors, though now of German race, were still the Roman emperors, and the laws of their ancestors were to be found in Justinian's books. But further, the newly discovered system—for we may without much untruth say that it was newly discovered —seemed so reasonable that it could not but affect the development of law in countries such as France and England, which paid no obedience to the emperors.

Canon
Law. And just at this time a second great system of cosmopolitan jurisprudence was taking shape. For centuries past the Catholic Church had been slowly acquiring a field of jurisdiction that was to be all her own, and for the use of the ecclesiastical tribunals a large body of law had come into being, consisting of the canons published by Church Councils and the decretal [1] epistles—genuine and forged—of the Popes. Various collections of these were current, but in the middle of the twelfth century they were superseded by the work of Gratian, a monk of Bologna. He called it " The Concordance of Discordant Canons," but it soon became known everywhere as the Decretum. And by this time the Popes were ever busy in pouring out decretal letters, sending them into all corners of the western world. Authoritative collections of these " decretals " were published, and the ecclesiastical lawyer (the " canonist " or " decretist ") soon had at his command a large mass of written law comparable to that which the Roman lawyer (the " civilian " or " legist ") was studying. A Corpus Juris Canonici begins to take its place beside the Corpus Juris Civilis. Very often the same man had studied both ; he was a " doctor of both laws " ; and, indeed, the newer system had borrowed largely from the older ; it had borrowed its form, its spirit, and a good deal of its matter also.

The canonical jurisprudence of the Italian doctors became the ecclesiastical law of the western world. From all local courts, wherever they might be, there was an appeal to the ultimate tribunal at Rome. But the temporal law of every country felt the influence of the new learning. Apparently we might lay down some such rule as this—that where the attack is longest postponed, it is most severe. In the thirteenth century the Parliament of Paris began the work of harmonising

[1 *i.e.* containing decrees, or having the force of law. Part of the canon law is known as " Decretals," having been codified from such epistles.]

A PAGE OF DECRETALS, WITH COMMENTARY   (MS. Roy. 10, E. iv.).

and rationalising the provincial customs of Northern France, and this it did by Romanising them. In the sixteenth century, after " the revival of letters," the Italian jurisprudence took hold of Germany, and swept large portions of the old national law before it. Wherever it finds a weak, because an uncentralised, system of justice, it wins an easy triumph. To Scotland it came late; but it came to stay.

Roman
Law in
England. To England it came early. Very few are the universities which can boast of a school of Roman law so old as that of Oxford. In the troubled days of our King Stephen, when the Church was urging new claims against the feeble State, Archbishop Theobald imported from Italy one Vacarius, a Lombard lawyer, who lectured here on Roman law, and wrote a big book that may still be read. Very soon after this Oxford had a flourishing school of civil and canon law. Ever since William the Conqueror had solemnly sanctioned the institution of special ecclesiastical courts, it had been plain that in those courts the law of a Catholic Church, not of a merely English Church, must prevail; also that this law would be in the main Italian law. In the next century, as all know, Henry and Becket fell out as to the definition of the province that was to be left to the ecclesiastical courts. The battle was drawn; neither combatant had gained all that he wanted. Thenceforward until the Protestant Reformation, and indeed until later than that, a border warfare between the two sets of courts was always simmering. Victory naturally inclined to those tribunals which had an immediate control of physical force, but still the sphere that was left to the canonists will seem to our eyes very ample. It comprehended not only the enforcement of ecclesiastical discipline, and the punishment—by spiritual censure, and, in the last resort, by excommunication—of sins left unpunished by temporal law, but also the whole topic of marriage and divorce, those last dying wills and testaments which were closely connected with dying confessions, and the administration of the goods of intestates. Why to this day do we couple " Probate " with " Divorce " ? Because in the Middle Ages both of these matters belonged to " the courts Christian." Why to " Probate " and " Divorce " do we add " Admiralty " ? Because the civilians—and in England the same man was usually both canonist and civilian—succeeded, though at a comparatively late time, in taking to themselves the litigation that concerned things done on the high seas, those high seas whence no jury could be summoned. So for the canonist there was plenty of room in England; and there was some room for the civilian: he was very useful as a diplomatist.

But we were speaking of our English common law, the law of our ordinary temporal courts, and of the influence upon it of the new Italian but cosmopolitan jurisprudence; and we must confess that for a short while, from the middle of the twelfth to the middle of the thirteenth century, this influence was powerful. The amount of foreign law that was actually borrowed has been underrated and overrated; we could not estimate it without descending to details. Some great maxims and a few more concrete rules were appropriated, but on the whole what was taken was logic, method, spirit rather than matter. We may see the effect of this influence very plainly in a treatise on the Laws of England which comes to us from the last years of Henry II. It has been ascribed to Henry's Chief Justiciar—Viceroy, we may say—Ranulf Glanvill; and whether or no it comes from his pen   **Glanvill.** (he was a layman and a warrior), it describes the practice of the court over which he presided. There are very few sentences in it which we can trace to any Roman book, and yet in a sense the whole book is Roman. We look back from it to a law-book written in Henry I.'s time, and we can hardly believe that only some seventy years divide the two. The one can at this moment be read and understood by anyone who knows a little of mediæval Latin and a little of English law; the other will always be dark to the most learned scholars. The gulf between them looks like that between logic and caprice, between reason and unreason. And then from the middle of the thirteenth century we have a much greater and better book than Glanvill's. Its author we   **Bracton.** know as Bracton, though his name really was Henry of Bratton. He was an ecclesiastic, an archdeacon, but for many years he was one of the king's justices. He had read a great deal of the Italian jurisprudence, chiefly in the works of that famous doctor, Azo of Bologna. Thence he had obtained his idea of what a law-book should be, of how law should be arranged and stated; thence also he borrowed maxims and some concrete rules; with these he can fill up the gaps in our English system. But he lets us see that not much more can now be done in the way of Romanisation. Ever since Henry II.'s time the king's court has

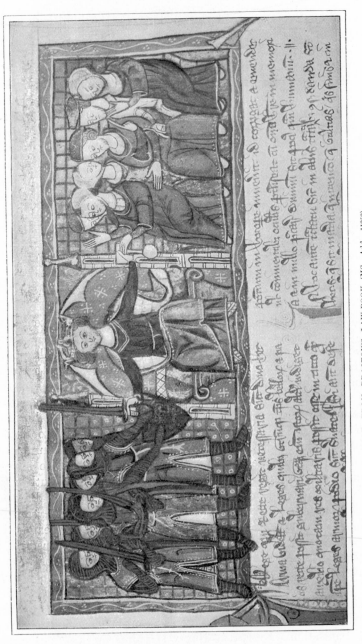

PAGE FROM BRACTON'S LAW-BOOK (MS. Add. 11353).

been hard at work amassing precedents, devising writs, and commenting upon them. Bracton himself has laboriously collected five hundred decisions from the mile-long Rolls of the Court and uses them as his authorities. For him English law is already "case law"; a judgment is a precedent. While as yet the science of the civilians was a somewhat unpractical science, while as yet they had not succeeded in bringing the old classical texts into close contact with the facts of mediæval life, the king's court of professional justices—the like of which was hardly to be found in any foreign land, in any unconquered land—had been rapidly evolving a common law for England, establishing a strict and formal routine of procedure, and tying the hands of all subsequent judges. From Bracton's day onwards Roman law exercises but the slightest influence on the English common law, and such influence as it exercises is rather by way of repulsion than by way of attraction. English law at this early period had absorbed so much Romanism that it could withstand all future attacks, and pass scathless even through the critical sixteenth century.

It may be convenient, however, to pause at this point in the development of our judicial institutions, in order to trace the history of our legal procedure.

For a long time past Englishmen have been proud of their trial by jury, and proud to see the nations of Europe imitating as best they might this "palladium of English liberties," this "bulwark of the British Constitution." Their pride, if in other respects it be reasonable, need not be diminished by any modern discoveries of ancient facts, even though they may have to learn that in its origin trial by jury was rather French than English, rather royal than popular, rather the livery of conquest than a badge of freedom. They have made it what it is; and what it is is very different from what it was. The story is a long and a curious one. *Trial by Jury.*

Let us try to put before our eyes a court of the twelfth century; it may be a county court or a hundred-court, or a court held by some great baron for his tenants. It is held in the open air—perhaps upon some ancient moot-hill, which ever since the times of heathenry has been the scene of justice. An officer presides over it—the sheriff, the sheriff's bailiff, the lord's steward. But all or many of the free landowners *Legal Forms in the Twelfth Century.*

of the district are bound to attend it; they owe "suit" to it, they are its suitors, they are its doomsmen; it is for them, and not for the president, "to find the dooms." He controls the procedure, he issues the mandates, he pronounces the sentence; but when the question is what the judgment shall

SITE OF THE FOLK-MOOT, PENNENDEN HEATH.
(By permission of J. Arcoll, Esq., Foley House, near Maidstone.)

be, he bids the suitors find the doom.   All this is very ancient, and look where we will in Western Europe we may find it.   But as yet we have not found the germ of trial by jury. These doomsmen are not "judges of fact."   There is no room for any judges of fact. If of two litigants the one contradicts the other flatly, if the plain "You did" of the one is met by the straightforward "You lie" of the other, here is a problem that man cannot solve. He is unable as yet to weigh testimony against testimony, to cross-examine witnesses, to piece together the truth out of little bits of evidence. He has recourse to the supernatural. He adjudges that one or other of the two parties is to prove his case by an appeal to God.

The judgment precedes the proof. The proof consists, **The Oath.** not in a successful attempt to convince your judges of the truth of your assertion, but in the performance of a task that they have imposed upon you: if you perform it, God is on your side. The modes of proof are two, oaths and ordeals. In some cases we may see a defendant allowed to swear away a charge by his own oath. More frequently he will have to bring with him oath-helpers—in later days they are called "com-purgators"[1]—and when he has sworn successfully, each of these oath-helpers in turn will swear "By God that oath is clean and true." The doomsmen have decreed how many oath-helpers, and of what quality, he must bring. A great deal of their traditional legal lore consists in rules about this matter; queer arithmetical rules will teach how the oath of one thegn is as weighty as the oath of six ceorls, and the like. Sometimes they require that the oath-helpers shall be kins-men of the chief swearer, and so warn us against any ration-alism which would turn these oath-helpers into "witnesses to character," and probably tell us of the time when the bond of blood was so strong that a man's kinsfolk were answerable for his misdeeds. A very easy task this oath with oath-helpers may seem in our eyes. It is not so easy as it looks. Ceremonial rules must be strictly observed; a set form of words must be pronounced; a slip, a stammer, will spoil all, and the adversary will win his cause. Besides, it is common knowledge that those who perjure themselves are often struck dead, or reduced to the stature of dwarfs, or find that they cannot remove their hands from the relics they have profaned.

But when crime is laid to a man's charge he will not **The** always be allowed to escape with oaths. Very likely he **Ordeal.** will be sent to the ordeal. The ordeal is conceived as "the

[1 "Co-purgers," helping him to cleanse himself from the charge.]

judgment of God." Of heathen origin it well may be, but long ago the Christian Church has made it her own, has prescribed a solemn ritual for the consecration of those instruments—the fire, the water—which will reveal the truth. The water in the pit is adjured to receive the innocent and to reject the guilty. He who sinks is safe, he who floats is lost. The red-hot iron one pound in weight must be lifted and carried three paces. The hand that held it is then sealed up in a cloth. Three days afterwards the seal is broken. Is the hand clean or is it foul? that is the dread question. A

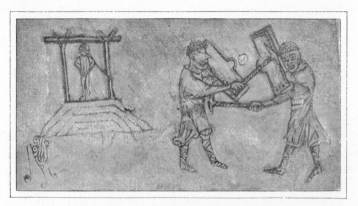

THE JUDICIAL COMBAT (Curia Regis Roll No. 216).
(*Record Office.*)

blister "as large as half a walnut" is fatal. How these tests worked in practice we do not know. We seldom get stories about them save when, as now and again will happen, the local saint interferes and performs a miracle. We cannot but guess that it was well to be good friends with the priest when one went to the ordeal.

Trial by Battle.

Then the Norman conquerors brought with them another ordeal—the judicial combat. An ordeal it is, for though the Church has looked askance at it, it is no appeal to mere brute force; it is an appeal to the God of Battles. Very solemnly does each combatant swear to the truth of his cause; very solemnly does he swear that he has eaten nothing, drunk nothing "whereby the law of God may be debased or the devil's law exalted." When a criminal charge is made

—"an appeal of felony"—
the accuser and the ac-
cused, if they be not
maimed, nor too young,
nor too old, will have to
fight in person. When a
claim for land is made,
the plaintiff has to offer
battle, not in his own
person, but in the person
of one of his men. This
man is in theory a witness
who will swear to the
justice of his lord's cause.
In theory he ought not to
be, but in practice he often
is, a hired champion who
makes a profession of
fighting other people's
battles. If the hireling be
exposed, he may have his
hand struck off; but as a
matter of fact there were
champions in a large way
of business. At least in
some cases the arms that
are used are very curious:
they are made of wood
and horn, and look (for
we have pictures of them)
like short pickaxes. Pos-
sibly they have been in
use for this sacral purpose
—a sacral purpose it is—
ever since an age which
knew not iron. Also we
know that the champion's
head is shaved, but are
left to guess why this is
done. The battle may

BISHOP WYVILLE AND HIS CHAMPION.
(From a brass-rubbing by E. Doran Webb, Esq.)

last the livelong day until the stars appear. The accuser has undertaken that in the course of a day he will "prove by his body" the truth of his charge; and if he cannot do this before the twilight falls, he has failed and is a perjurer. The object of each party in the fight is not so much to kill his adversary — this perhaps he is hardly likely to do with the archaic weapon that he wields—but to make him pronounce "the loathsome word," to make him cry "craven." In a criminal case the accused, if vanquished, was forthwith hanged or mutilated; but in any case the craven had to pay a fine of sixty shillings, the old "king's ban" of the Frankish laws, and, having in effect confessed himself a perjurer, he was thenceforth infamous.

Growth of the King's Courts. But long ago the Frankish kings had placed themselves outside the sphere of this ancient formal and sacral procedure. They were standing in the shoes of Roman governors, even of Roman emperors. For themselves and their own affairs they had a prerogatival procedure. If their rights were in question, they would direct their officers to call together the best and oldest men of the neighbourhood to swear about the relevant facts. The royal officers would **The Inquest.** make an inquisition, hold an inquest, force men to swear that they would return true answers to whatever questions might be addressed to them in the king's name. They may be asked whether or no this piece of land belongs to the king; they may be asked in a general way what lands the king has in their district; they may be asked (for the king is beginning to see that he has a great interest in the suppression of violent crime) to tell tales of their neighbours, to report the names of all who are suspected of murder or robbery, and then these men can be sent to the ordeal. This privilege that the king has he can concede to others; he can grant to his favourite churches that their lands shall stand outside the scope of the clumsy and hazardous procedure of the common courts; if their title to those lands be challenged, a royal officer will call upon the neighbours to declare the truth—in other words, to give a verdict. It is here that we see the germ of the jury.

The Norman duke in his conquered kingdom was able to use the inquest with a free hand and on a grand scale.

Domesday Book was compiled out of the verdicts returned by the men of the various hundreds and townships of England in answer to a string of questions put to them by royal commissioners. We have read how the stern king thought it no shame to do what the English monk thought it shame to write, how he numbered every ox, every cow, every pig in England (p. 341). Thenceforward the inquest was part of the machinery of government; it could be employed for many different purposes whenever the king desired information. He could use it in his own litigation, he could place it at the service of other litigants who were fortunate enough or rich enough to obtain this favour from him. But throughout the reigns of our Norman kings it keeps its prerogatival character.

Then Henry II., bent upon making his justice supreme throughout his realm, put this royal remedy at the disposal of all his subjects. This he did not by one general law, but piecemeal, by a series of ordinances known as " assizes," [1] some of which we may yet read, while others have perished. For example, when there was litigation about the ownership of land, the defendant, instead of accepting the plaintiff's challenge to fight, was allowed to " put himself upon the king's grand assize." Thereupon the action, which had been begun in some feudal court, was removed into the king's court; and twelve knights, chosen from the district in which the land lay, gave a verdict as to whether the plaintiff or the defendant had the better right. In other cases—for example, when the dispute was about the possession, not the ownership, of land—less solemn forms of the inquest were employed; twelve free and lawful men, not necessarily knights, were charged to say whether the defendant had ejected the plaintiff. Before the twelfth century was at an end, the inquest in one form or another—sometimes it was called an assize, sometimes a jury—had become part of the normal procedure in almost every kind of civil action. Still there long remained many cases in which a defendant could, if he chose, reject the new-fangled mode of trial, and claim the ancient right of purging himself with oath-helpers, or of picking up the glove that the plaintiff had thrown down as a gage of battle. Even a prelate of the Church would sometimes rely rather upon the

The King's Assizes.

[1 From the "assises" or "sittings" of the council which passed them.]

27

strong arm of a professional pugilist than upon the testimony of his neighbours. Within the walls of the chartered boroughs men were conservative of all that would favour the free burgher at the cost of the despised outsider. The Londoners thought that trial by jury was good enough for those who were not citizens, but the citizen must be allowed to swear away charges of debt or trespass by the oaths of his friends. In the old communal courts, too, the county and hundred courts, where the landowners of the district sat as doomsmen, trial by jury never struck root, for only by virtue of a royal writ could a jury be summoned: this is one of the reasons why those old courts languished, decayed, and became useless. However, before the Middle Ages were over, trial by jury had become the only form of trial for civil actions that had any vitality. So late as 1824 a lucky litigant, taking advantage of his adversary's slip, presented himself at the bar of the King's Bench, prepared to swear away a debt—"to make his law" was the technical phrase—with the aid of eleven oath-helpers, and not until 1833 was this world-old procedure abolished by statute ; but long before this, if the plaintiff was well advised, he could always prevent his opponent from escaping in this easy fashion.

The Earliest Jury Trial. We have spoken of "trial by jury." That term naturally calls up before our minds a set of twelve men called into court in order that they may listen to the testimony of witnesses, give a true verdict "according to the evidence," and, in short, act as judges of those questions of fact that are in dispute. But it is very long after Henry II.'s day before trial by jury takes this form. Originally the jurors are called in, not in order that they may hear, but in order that they may give, evidence. They are witnesses. They are neighbours of the parties ; they are presumed to know before they come into court the facts about which they are to testify. They are chosen by the sheriff to represent the neighbourhood—indeed, they are spoken of as being "the neighbourhood," "the country"—and the neighbourhood, the country, will know the facts. In the twelfth century population was sparse, and men really knew far more of the doings of their neighbours than we know nowadays. It was expected that all legal transactions would take place in public ; the conveyance of land was made in open court, the wife was endowed at the church-door, the man who bought cattle in secret ran a great but just risk of being treated as a thief; every three weeks a court was held in the village, and all the affairs of every villager were discussed. The verdict, then, was the sworn testimony of the countryside; and if the twelve jurors perjured themselves, the verdict of another jury of twenty-four might send them to prison and render them infamous for ever. In course of time, and by slow degrees—degrees so slow that we can hardly detect them—the jury put off its old and acquired a new character. Sometimes, when the jurors knew nothing of the facts, witnesses who did know the facts would be called in to supply the requisite information. As human affairs grew more complex, the neighbours whom the sheriff summoned became less and less able to perform their original duty, more and more dependent upon the evidence given in their presence by those witnesses who were summoned by the parties. In the fifteenth century the change had taken place, though in yet later days a man who had been summoned as a juror, and who sought to escape on the ground that he already knew something of the facts in question, would be told that he had given a very good reason for his being placed in the jury-box. We may well say, therefore, that trial by jury, though it has its roots in the Frankish inquest, grew up on English soil; and until recent times it was distinctive of England and Scotland, for on the continent of Europe all other forms of legal procedure had been gradually supplanted by that which canonists and civilians had constructed out of ancient Roman elements.

We have yet to speak of the employment of the inquest in criminal cases. The Frankish kings had employed it for the purpose of detecting crime. Do you suspect any of murder, robbery, larceny, or the like? This question was addressed by royal officers to selected representatives of every neighbourhood, and answered upon oath, and the suspected persons were sent to " the judgment of God." The Church borrowed this procedure; the bishop could detect ecclesiastical offences as the king detected crimes. It is not impossible that this particular form of the inquest had made its way into England some half-century before the Norman Conquest; but we hear very little about it until the days of Henry II. He ordained that it should be used upon a very large scale and as a matter of ordinary practice, both by the justices whom he sent to visit the counties and by

Criminal Procedure.

the sheriffs.   From his time onward a statement made upon oath by a set of jurors representing a hundred, to the effect that such an one is suspected of such a crime, is sufficient to put a man upon his trial.   It is known as an indictment.   It takes its place beside the old accusation, or " appeal," urged by the person who has been wronged, by the man whose goods have been stolen or the nearest kinsman of the murdered man.   It is but an accusation, however, and in Henry's days the indicted person takes his chance at the hot iron or the cold water ; God may be for him, though man be against him.   But already some suspicion is shown of the so-called judgment of God ; for though he comes clean from the ordeal, he has to leave the country, swearing never to return.   At last, in 1215, the Fourth Lateran Council forbade the clergy to take part in this superstitious rite. After this we hear no more in England of the ordeal as a legal process, though in much later days the popular belief that witches will swim died hard, and many an old woman was put in the pond.   The judges of the thirteenth century had no substitute ready to take the place of that supernatural test of which an enlightened Pope had deprived them.   Of course, if the indicted person will agree to accept the verdict of his neighbours, will " put himself upon his country "—that is, upon the neighbourhood—for good and ill, all is easy.   Those who have indicted him as a suspicious character can now be asked whether he is guilty or no ; and if they say that he is guilty, there will be no harm in hanging him, for he consented to the trial, and he must abide the consequences.   To make the trial yet fairer, one may call in a second jury different from that which indicted him. Here is the origin of those two juries which we see employed in our own days—the grand jury that indicts, and the petty jury that tries.   But suppose that he will not give his consent ; it is by no means obvious that the testimony of his neighbours ought to be treated as conclusive.   Hitherto he has been able to invoke the judgment of God, and can we now deprive him of this ancient, this natural right ?   No, no one can be tried by jury who does not consent to be so tried.   But what we can do is this—we can compel him to give his consent, we can starve him into giving his consent, and, again, we can quicken the slow action of starvation by laying him out naked on the floor of the dungeon and heaping weights upon his chest until he says that he will abide by the verdict of his fellows. And so we are brought to the pedantic cruelty of the "peine forte et dure." Even in the seventeenth century there were men who would endure the agony of being pressed to death rather than utter the few words which would have subjected them to a trial by jury. They had a reason for their fortitude. Had they been hanged as felons their property would have been confiscated, their children would have been penniless; while, as it was, they left

"Peine Forte et Dure."

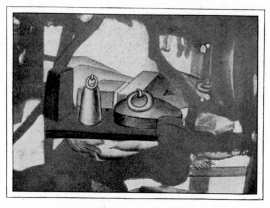

PRESSING TO DEATH.
(From a painted glass medallion in the Election Hall, Eton College.
By permission of the Provost of Eton College.)

the world obstinate, indeed, but unconvicted. All this—and until 1772 men might still be pressed to death—takes us back to a time when the ordeal seems the fair and natural mode of ascertaining guilt and innocence, when the jury is still a new-fangled institution.

The indictment, we have said, took its place beside the "appeal"—the old private accusation. The owner of the stolen goods, the kinsman of the murdered man, might still prosecute his suit in the old manner, and offer to prove his assertions by his body. The Church had not abolished, and could not abolish, the judicial combat, for though in truth it was an ordeal, no priestly benediction of the instruments that were to be used was necessary. By slow degrees in the thirteenth century the accused acquired the right of refusing his accuser's challenge and of putting himself upon a jury. What is more, the judges began to favour the "indictment" and to discourage the "appeal" by all possible means. They required of the accuser a punctilious observance of ancient formalities, and would quash his accusation if he were guilty of the smallest blunder. Still, throughout the Middle Ages we occasionally hear of battles being fought over criminal cases. In particular a convicted felon would sometimes turn "approver"—that is to say, he would obtain a pardon conditional on his ridding the world, by means of his appeals, of some three or four other felons. If he failed in his endeavour, he was forthwith hanged. But those who were not antiquarians must have long ago ceased to believe that such a barbarism as trial by battle **A Survival: Abraham Thornton's Case, 1818.** was possible, when in 1818 a case arose which showed them that they had inadequately gauged the dense conservatism of the laws of their country. One Mary Ashford was found drowned; one Abraham Thornton was indicted for murdering her; a jury acquitted him. But the verdict did not satisfy the public mind, and the brother of the dead girl had recourse to an "appeal": to this accusation the previous acquittal was no answer. Thornton declared himself ready to defend his innocence by his body, and threw down, in Westminster Hall, as his gage of battle, an antique gauntlet, "without either fingers or thumb, made of white tanned skin, ornamented with sewn tracery and silk fringes, crossed by a narrow band of red leather, with leathern tags and thongs for fastening." The judges did their best to discover some slip in his procedure; but he had been careful and well advised; even his glove was of the true medieval pattern. So there was nothing for it but to declare that he was within his rights, and could not be compelled to submit to a jury if he preferred to fight. His adversary had no mind to fight, and so let the glove alone. After this crowning scandal Parliament at last bestirred itself, and in the year of grace 1819 completed the work of Pope Innocent III. by abolishing the last of the ordeals.

The Working of Trial by Jury. If we regard it as an engine for the discovery of truth and for the punishment of malefactors, the medieval jury was a clumsy thing. Too often its verdicts must have represented guess-work and the tittle-tattle of the countryside. Sometimes a man must have gone to the gallows, not because anyone had seen him commit a crime, not because guilt had been brought home to him by a carefully tested chain of proved facts, but because it was notorious that he was just the man from whom a murder or a robbery might be expected. Only by slow degrees did the judges insist that the jurors ought to listen to evidence given by witnesses in open court, and rely only upon the evidence that was there given. Even when this step had been taken, it was long before our modern law of evidence took shape, long before the judges laid down such rules as that "hearsay is not evidence," and that testimony which might show that the prisoner had committed other crimes was not relevant to the question whether he had perpetrated the particular offence of which he stood indicted.

But whatever may have been the case in the days of the ordeal —and about this we know very little—we may be fairly certain that in the later Middle Ages the escape of the guilty was far commoner than the punishment of the guiltless. After some hesitation our law had adopted its well-known rule that a jury can give no verdict unless the twelve men are all of one mind. To obtain a condemnatory unanimity was not easy if the accused was a man of good family; one out of every twelve of his neighbours that might be taken at random would stand out loyally for his innocence. Bribery could do much; seigniorial influence could do more; the sheriff, who was not incorruptible, and had his own likes and dislikes, could do all, since it was for him to find the jury. It is easy for us to denounce as unconstitutional the practice which prevailed under Tudors and Stuarts of making jurors answer for their verdicts before the King's Council; it is not so easy for us to make certain that the jury system would have lived through the sixteenth century had it not been for the action of this somewhat irregular check. For the rest, we may notice that the jury of the Middle Ages, if it is to be called a democratic institution, can be called so only in a medieval sense. The jurors were freeholders. The great mass of Englishmen were not freeholders. The peasant who was charged with a crime was acquitted or convicted by the word of his neighbours, but by the word of neighbours who considered themselves very much his superiors.

If, however, we look back to those old days, we shall find ourselves deploring not so much that some men of whose guilt we are by no means satisfied are sent to the gallows, as that many men whose guilt is but too obvious escape scot-free. We take up a roll upon which the presentments of the jurors are recorded. Everywhere the same tale meets our eye. " Malefactors came by night to the house of such an one at such a place; they slew him and his wife and his sons and his daughters, and robbed his house; we do not know who they were; we suspect no one." Such organisation as there was

Marauders.
for the pursuit of these marauders was utterly inefficient. Every good and lawful man is bound to follow the hue and cry when it is raised, and the village reeve, or in later days the village constable, ought to put himself at the head of this improvised and unprofessional police force. But it was improvised and unprofessional. Outside the walls of the boroughs there was no regular plan of watch and ward, no one whose business it was to keep an eye on men of suspicious habits, or to weave the stray threads of evidence into a halter. The neighbours who had followed the trail of the stolen cattle to the county boundary were apt to turn back, every man to his plough. " Let Gloucestershire folk mind Gloucestershire rogues." They would be fined, when the justices came round, for neglect of their duties—for the sheriff, or the coroner, or someone else, would tell tales of them—but meanwhile their hay was about, and the weather was rainy. Even when the jurors know the criminal's name, the chances seem to be quite ten to one that he has not been captured. Nothing could then be done but outlaw him. At four successive county courts—the county court was held month by month—a proclamation calling upon him to present himself, "to come in to the king's peace," would be made, and at the fifth court he would be declared an outlaw. If after this he were caught, then, unless he could obtain some favour from the king, he would be condemned to death without any investigation being made of his guilt or innocence; the mere fact of his outlawry being proved, sentence followed as a matter of course. But the old law had been severer than this: to slay the outlaw wherever he may be found was not only the right but the duty of every true man, and even in the middle of the thirteenth century this was still the

customary law of the Welsh marches. The outlaw of real life was not the picturesque figure that we have seen upon the stage; if he and his men were really "merry" in the greenwood, they were merry in creditable circumstances. Still, it is not to be denied that he attracted at times a good deal of romantic sympathy, even in the ages which really knew him. This probably had its origin in the brutal stringency of the forest laws, which must be charged with the stupid blunder of punishing small offences with a rigour which should have been reserved for the worst crimes.

The worst crimes were common enough. Every now and then the king and the nation would be alarmed, nor needlessly alarmed, by the prevalence of murder and highway robbery. A new ordinance would be issued, new instructions would be given to the judges, sheriffs would be active, and jurors would be eager to convict; a good deal of hanging would be done, perhaps too indiscriminately. But so soon as the panic was over, Justice would settle down into her old sluggish habits. Throughout the Middle Ages life was very insecure; there was a great deal of nocturnal marauding, and the knife that every Englishman wore was apt to stab upon slight provocation.

The Church had not mended matters by sanctifying places and persons. In very-old days when the blood-feud raged, when punishment and vengeance were very much one, it was a good thing that there should be holy places to which a man might flee when the avenger of blood was behind—places where no drop of blood might be spilt without sacrilege. They afforded an opportunity for the peacemaker. The bishop or priest would not yield up the fugitive who lay panting at the foot of the altar until terms had been made between him and his pursuers. But at a later time when the State was endeavouring to punish criminals, and there would be no punishment until after trial, the sanctuary was a public nuisance. The law was this:—If a criminal entered a church he was safe from pursuit; the neighbours who were pursuing him were bound to beset the church, prevent his escape, and send for the coroner. Sometimes they would remain encamped round the church for many days. At last the coroner would come, and parley with the fugitive. If he confessed his crime, then he

might " abjure the realm "—that is, swear to leave England
within a certain number of days (he was allowed days enough
to enable him to reach the nearest seaport), and never to
return. If he strayed from the straight road which led to the
haven, or if he came back to the realm, then he could at once
be sentenced to death. For a man to take sanctuary, confess
his crime and abjure the realm, was an everyday event,
and we must have thus shipped off many a malefactor to
plunder our neighbours in France and Flanders. If the man
who had taken sanctuary would neither confess to a crime,
nor submit to a trial, the State could do no more against him.
It tried to teach the clergy that their duty was to starve him
into submission; but the clergy resented this interference
with holy things. A bad element of caprice was introduced
into the administration of justice. The strong, the swift, the
premeditating murderer cheated the gallows. Especially in
the towns he might fairly complain of bad luck if he could
not slip into one of the numerous churches before he was
caught. On the other hand, the man who had not plotted his
crime would get hanged.

Benefit of Clergy.   And then the clergy stood outside the criminal law. If a
clerk in holy orders committed a crime—this was the law of the
thirteenth century—he could not be tried for it in a lay court.
He could be accused there, and the judges might ask a jury
whether he was guilty or no; but even though they found him
guilty, this was no trial. At the request of his bishop—and
the bishops made such requests as a matter of course—he
was handed over for trial in an ecclesiastical court. Such a
court had power to inflict very heavy punishments. It might
draw no drop of blood, but it could imprison for life, besides
being able to degrade the clerk from his orders. As a matter
of fact, however, we hear very little of any punishment save
that of degradation. What is more, the criminal procedure of
the ecclesiastical courts in England was of an absurdly old-
fashioned and clumsy kind. They held by compurgation. If
the accused clerk could but get some eleven or twelve friends
of his own profession to swear that they believed him
innocent, he was acquitted; he might resume his criminal
career. Church and State are both to blame for this sad
story. The Church would yield no jot of the claims that

Photo: W. M. Dodson, Bettws-y-Coed.
Knocker on St. Nicholas' Church, Gloucester.   Knocker on Sanctuary Door, Durham Cathedral.

The Sanctuary Entrance, Durham Cathedral.   The Frydstool, Beverley Minster.

RELICS OF SANCTUARIES.

were sanctified by the blood of St. Thomas; the lay courts would not suffer the bishops to do criminal justice in a really serious fashion. There can be no doubt that many of the worst criminals—men who had been found guilty by a jury of brutal murders and rapes—escaped scot-free, because they had about them some slight savour of professional holiness. It should be understood that this immunity was shared with the bishops, priests, and deacons by a vast multitude of men who were in "minor orders." They might have no ecclesi- astical duties to perform; they might be married; they might be living the same life which laymen lived; but they stood outside the ordinary criminal law. One of the worst evils of the later Middle Ages was this "benefit of clergy." The king's justices, who never loved it, at length reduced it to an illogical absurdity. They would not be at pains to require any real proof of a prisoner's sacred character. If he could read a line in a book, this would do; indeed, it is even said that the same verse of the Psalms was set before the eyes of every prisoner, so that even the illiterate might escape if he could repeat by heart those saving words. Criminal law had been rough and rude, and sometimes cruel; it had used the gallows too readily; it had punished with death thefts which, owing to a great fall in the value of money, were becoming petty thefts. Still, cruelty in such matters is better than caprice, and the "benefit of clergy" had made the law capricious without making it less cruel.

C. W. C. OMAN. The Art of War. IT was at Hastings that the last trial of the old military system of the English was made. There the house-carles of King Harold, backed by the thegnhood of all Southern England and the disorderly masses of the levy of the home counties, drew themselves out on the hillside of Senlac to face an enemy of a different sort from any that had yet been seen north of the Channel. When Dane had fought Englishman, the battle had generally been between serried bodies of foot-soldiery, meeting fairly face to face in dense masses, each with its shield-wall of warriors standing elbow to elbow, and hewing at each other over the "wall of war-lindens" till one side or other had the mastery. But the Normans of Duke William had learnt from their

NORMAN HORSE AND BOWMEN.

(*Bayeux Tapestry.*)

Frankish neighbours the new method of fighting, which in the tenth century had superseded on the Continent the array of the ancient tribal hosts. While the Anglo-Danes of Harold stood on foot, behind their wattled palisades, forming a compact shield-wall like their ancestors who had fought under Alfred and Guthrum, the Normans and mercenary French of William came out in a 'triple line armed in three divers manners. First stood the archery, then the heavy-armed foot, who still represented the ancient method of armament, then the great bodies of mailed horse-men, to whom the English had nothing to oppose. A few years before, Earl Ralph of Hereford had tried to teach the English thegnhood the art of fighting on horse-back; but they did not take kindly to it. When he led them against the Welsh, disaster had followed, and the disaster had been universally ascribed to the fact that "Anglos contra morem in equos pugnare jussit."[1] If only the experiment had been successful, Hastings might have seen a very different end to its battle.

Cavalry.   William the Bastard knew only too well how to deal with the antiquated array of the English army. His archers, if unsupported by cavalry, might have been driven off the field by a single charge; his cavalry, if unsupported by archers, might have surged for ever against the formidable shield-wall of the English. But by combining the two arms, with perfect skill, he won his crowning victory. The English could not stand for ever unmoved under the deadly hail of the Norman arrows. After long endurance the undisciplined masses of the "fyrd" sprang out from behind their defences and burst down from the heights to sweep away the archery that galled them so. Then, when the compact shield-wall was broken, William thrust his horsemen into the gaps, and the steadfast house-carles of Harold, though they stood their ground to the last man, were slowly hewn down.

> " So Harold Godwinson was laid
> Across his broken banner cold
> Upon the blood-soaked Sussex mould,
> And o'er the wrack of Senlac field
> Full-fed the grey-nebbed raven wheeled."

[1 "He ordered the English to fight on horseback, contrary to their custom."]

The Norman Conquest produced a complete change in the military organisation of England—the system of raising the armed force, the tactics that it employed, and the weapons that it used, being all alike new. For the next two hundred and fifty years the mailed feudal horseman was to be the main

STORMING A STRONGHOLD (from a MS. Bible).
(*Corpus Christi College, Cambridge.*)

power in war. The Anglo-Norman kings continued to call out the Old English "fyrd" on occasion, but never trusted to it as their chief strength; infantry had become of secondary importance in the field. It was the mounted followers of the Norman knights and earls, among whom William had distributed the lands of the English on the tenure of military service, that were the really important element in his army. Clad in the long mail shirt and peaked helmet with nasal, bearing the kite-shaped Danish shield, and using the lance as their chief weapon, the Norman horse were the flower of the chivalry of Europe, as they showed not only on English soil, but in far-off fights like Civitella, Durazzo, or Antioch.

Castles.

Besides introducing the supremacy of cavalry, the Normans developed to a hitherto unexampled importance the building of castles and fortresses. Saxon and Dane had been contented to surround themselves with a moat and palisade, except when (as at London or Chester) they could patch up and utilise an old Roman town wall. The Normans commenced a new era in military building, just as they did in ecclesiastical building. Conquered England was held down by dozens of castles, square keeps with walls of enormous thickness built of solid stone, and often relying solely on their own strength without being surrounded by any outworks. The English, in their revolts, could never storm one of the new castles, and the Norman kings themselves had always the greatest difficulty in reducing the stronghold of a revolted vassal. In the eleventh century the art of defence had quite outgrown the art of attack; siege engines were few and primitive; to undermine a corner of the castle, or strive to set it on fire, was the most that a besieger could do Starvation was the only sure and certain way of reducing it. and unless the castellan had been caught unawares and unprovisioned, the process of starvation took many months.

The two centuries during which feudal cavalry was supreme in England were more notable for their sieges than for their great battles in the open field. To take the defensive behind strong walls was so far more profitable a policy for the weaker party than to try the fortune of war in the pitched battle, that campaigns were generally nothing more than a series of successful or unsuccessful sieges. William Rufus's war with his revolted vassals, Henry I.'s struggle with Robert de Belesme, the long duel between Stephen and Queen Maud, produced sieges by the dozen; but only two really important battles, that of the Standard, in 1138, and Lincoln, in 1141. Tenchebrai and Bremûle, the two Continental fights of Henry I., were mere cavalry skirmishes. The details of the fight of Lincoln show the all-importance of cavalry. The king had his infantry massed in the centre, and his horse on the flanks ; the Earls of Chester and Gloucester, his adversaries, had three bodies of horse as their main line, flanked by some Welsh light infantry on the wings. The battle was settled by the king's horse being driven off the field by that of the barons, when the mass of infantry in the centre, where Stephen himself stood, was surrounded and gradually broken up by charges of the victorious cavalry of the two earls.

ATTACK ON A STRONGHOLD, SHOWING USE OF CROSS-BOW.
(*Trinity College, Cambridge.*)

The Battle of the Standard (1138; p. 371) differed from the other engagements of the time in being mainly fought between infantry. The army of David of Scotland was composed of wild tribal levies of Highland and Galwegian footmen, with only two hundred mailed knights who served about the king's person. The English army which opposed him was the levy of Yorkshire, with a comparatively small body of fully armed knights to back it. Hence the fighting consisted of a series of dashes made by the undisciplined Scots against the level front of spears and axes which the Yorkshiremen opposed to them. Archery mainly

The Battle of the Standard.

28

settled the day; for the English—for the first time on record—had brought many bowmen into the field, to whom the Scots had nothing to oppose. The only cavalry charge of the day occurred when Prince Henry of Scotland broke for a moment the English left wing by a desperate onslaught at the head of his little squadron of two hundred knights. But this success was not followed up: they were scattered and hewn down, and finally only "eight took their harness safely back to Scotland."

The Cross Bow.

From the days of Stephen to those of Edward I. there is not much to record in the way of change in the tactics of English armies. The cavalry still remained the greater power, while infantry was only treated as an auxiliary. Richard I., the greatest soldier of his day, whose tactics in Palestine were the admiration of all his contemporaries, only leaves his mark on our military annals in virtue of his introduction of the cross-bow, and his systematic castle-building. That the cross-bow passed as a decisive and important weapon shows how little the archery of England had yet developed; the long-bow was still in its infancy, and in the assize of arms of Henry II. (1181), no class of subjects of the realm is required to come to war with bow and arrows: the yeomen, who in after generations formed the invincible archery of England, were bidden to equip themselves with hauberk and spear. The cross-bow was mainly in the hands of foreign mercenaries: Richard and John both kept bands of Continental cross-bowmen in pay, and the second battle of Lincoln (1216) was mainly won by the strong shooting of the mercenary cross-bowmen of Fawkes de Bréauté, John's French captain of adventurers.

The Professional Soldier.

The second half of the twelfth century has one point of interest which must be noted—the supplementing of the feudal levies by the hiring of professional soldiers of fortune. Kings who, like Henry II. and Richard I., waged long wars far from home, felt the gravest inconvenience from the character of the armies which they led. A feudal host could only be kept in the field for a short time; it was untrained, undisciplined, and disorderly. Long service away from home it would not brook. So the kings were driven to the expedient of employing large bodies of mercenaries, who would keep the field for any space of time, and would serve as long as they were paid. Henry II. made habitual the institution of scutage,

CHÂTEAU GAILLARD.

an invention of his grandfather Henry I., by which every one was allowed to compound for personal service with the king, by paying a fixed sum for every shield that he was feudally bound to bring to the host. The device was accepted with content, and for distant expeditions the king in future raised large bodies of mercenaries, paid with the funds which the scutage brought him in. For expeditions nearer home, against Welsh, or Scots, or native rebels, both the feudal levy and the national "fyrd" were still employed. It was, for example, mainly the native levy-en-masse which routed the Earl of Leicester's mercenaries at Fornham in 1174, and took Bedford from the rebellious Fawkes de Bréauté in 1224.

The Art of Defence.

While the art of war still remained almost stationary as to war in the open field, the improvements in the art of fortification never ceased to progress. The old Norman castle, with its square and massive keep, was, in the twelfth century, surrounded by outer defences, which grew more and more complicated. First outer walls were added to the towers, then these outer walls were strengthened with gate-towers, and other towers were inserted in the *enceinte* to provide a cross-fire from the flank against any attacks made on the long stretches of "curtain." Machicolation [1] and projecting brattices (galleries standing out from the face of the wall) were added to enable the garrison to command the ditch and the foot of the walls better than could be done from the rampart itself. At last a well-built castle, like Richard I.'s great masterpiece the Château Gaillard, became a complicated mass of fortification, with concentric lines of defence, which could be held one after another in succession even when the besiegers had forced the outer wall. Meanwhile in the art of attack, though siege engines—catapults, mangonels, and perriers of all sorts—were increased in number and efficiency, they were still quite unable to cope with the new obstacles which the improved fortification threw in their way. Sieges lasted for month after month, and starvation was still the only absolutely certain method of attack. A persevering general would build a line of circumvallation round the enemy's walls, and leave hunger to do its work. The only

[1 Openings in the floor of a projecting gallery, through which missiles could be discharged on an enemy underneath.]

way of hastening a protracted but hopeless defence was to threaten to hang the garrison if they resisted after all chance of succour was gone—a threat occasionally carried into execution—as, for example, by Hubert de Burgh at Bedford, in 1224.

It is with the second half of the thirteenth century that we find the military art begin to show signs of rapid development in England, and Warfare under the Angevin Kings. that the tactics which made the English name so great in war in the fourteenth century begin to appear. The habitual use of the long-bow, a weapon in every respect superior to the cross-bow, first appears as established in the Assize of Arms of 1252, when all holders of forty shillings in land or nine marks in chattels are desired to provide themselves with "a sword, dagger, bow and arrows." Whence the English got their long-bow is not quite easy to decide; the Normans at Hastings—as the

MEDIEVAL SIEGE ENGINE (MS. Harl. 3281).

Bayeux Tapestry clearly shows—still used the short four-foot bow, not the great six-foot weapon with its cloth-yard arrow. It was the short-bow, too, that won the Battle of the Standard. Probably the Anglo-Norman learnt to use the long-bow from the south Welsh, whose enormous bows and heavy arrows are celebrated by Giraldus Cambrensis in the last quarter of the twelfth century. Giraldus had seen the archers of Gwent send a shaft into a four-inch door so that the point stood out on the farther side. At any rate, the long-bow was well known by the second half of the thirteenth century though it was reserved for Edward I. to exalt it as the great national weapon. But in the French wars of

Henry III., and even as late as the Welsh war of 1281, we find the cross-bow still held in high esteem, perhaps even in higher esteem than the rival that was ere long to supersede it.

W. LAIRD CLOWES. Maritime Warfare and Commerce.

VERY little is known concerning the fleet which carried William and his army to England. The contemporary chroniclers were not men possessed of special naval knowledge, and the accounts given by them differ considerably one from another. One historian gives the number of vessels as four hundred ships, each with a large mast and sail, and more than a thousand transport boats; another tells us that there were three thousand craft carrying sails; a third speaks of nine hundred and seven great ships; and William of Poitiers says that, although Agamemnon conquered Troy with a thousand vessels, William needed more to conquer England. Nor can we be certain as to the sizes and types of ships engaged. The chief source of information upon these points is the Bayeux Tapestry. There is some doubt as to the exact destination and intent of this tapestry, though its age is certainly not remote from the date of the events it depicts; it has even been conjectured to be the work of English ladies at the Norman Court. In no age have women, especially those of gentle birth, had more than a very imperfect acquaintance with ships and ship-life. They cannot, moreover, be expected to appreciate the importance of a block, the significance of a rope or stay, or the force of the laws which govern a ship's stability and seaworthiness. It cannot, therefore, be supposed that the workers of the Bayeux Tapestry have left us an exact and trustworthy representation of the details of such vessels as they may have seen and voyaged in. Indeed, there is specific as well as presumptive evidence that the needlework disdains accuracy, and aims only at general effects. In the Tapestry, for example, William's own ship is shown, with its stern decorated with the effigy of a boy blowing a horn and holding in his left hand a gonfalon,[1] and with its bow bearing a lion's head as a figurehead, but a contemporary MS. in the Bodleian Library says that on the bow of William's ship, the *Mora*, Matilda, who had ordered

[¹ A pennon with several streamers, on either a lance or a revolving frame.]

THE "MORA" AND OTHER NORMAN SHIPS.
(Bayeux Tapestry.)

the vessel to be built, caused to be placed a golden boy, with his right index finger pointing to England, and with his left hand pressing an ivory horn to his lips; and Wace corroborates this account of the position of the boy.

Norman Ships.

None of the ships of the period were large; and it seems probable that few, if any, of them were of more than about thirty tons burthen. They were clincher-built, or, in other words, their planks were laid on so that each one overlapped the upper edge of the one immediately below it, and they were constructed on the beach and launched bows foremost. Both bow and stern were raised, and, in the case of the larger vessels, both bore some kind of ornament. There was never more than one mast, which was stepped amidships, and which could be struck by being lowered down forward. It carried a single yard, and a lug-sail which was often parti-coloured, and which was sometimes covered with a decorative design. At the mast-head there was neither truck nor vane, except in the chief vessel of a squadron or fleet. The Tapestry represents the *Mora* to have carried, at the masthead, a sort of square white banner charged with a gold upright cross within a blue border, the whole surmounted by a gold cross. Wace describes the mast-head as having borne a lantern and a gilt brass vane. The steersman sat in the stern, holding in his left hand the sheet, and in his right the steering-paddle, or *clavus*. It is not likely that the largest ships carried more than forty or fifty men. The freeboard of all the vessels was low, and it was no doubt with the object of heightening it, and so keeping out a certain amount of spray, that the soldiers who were on board disposed their shields around the gunwale. There is no evidence that any of William's ships were decked, and it may be safely assumed that in bad weather they were exceedingly unsafe and terribly uncomfortable. Before the expedition started, and while it was lying off Saint-Valery-en-Caux, several of the vessels foundered at their anchors; and, seeing how long the fleet was delayed, it is only surprising that there were not many more losses of this kind. The vessels, it is interesting to note, appear to have been always carefully painted, generally with horizontal stripes of different colours. They were not, it must be supposed, very costly to build, for William, after landing at

Pevensey, destroyed the whole of his flotilla; and this, had it been difficult to replace them, he would scarcely have done merely in order to impress his followers with the fact that there was for them no retreat.

The only fittings of the Norman vessels consisted, apparently, of the mast and its stays, the sail, the oars, the steering-paddle, a cable, and an anchor, which was carried inboard, and dropped, as now, over the bows. Some of William's

The Fittings.

LANDING THE CONQUEROR'S HORSES.
(*Bayeux Tapestry.*)

ships carried horses—to the number of from three to eight—as well as men; but there are no signs that any special provision was made for the comfort of the animals; and the Tapestry represents them as being landed by the simple expedient of being driven overboard and allowed to walk or swim ashore. How the yard was connected with the mast we do not know, nor is it possible to say whether or not blocks were used. The Normans, were, however, acquainted with blocks, for they employed them in launching, if not in rigging and working, their vessels.

The crews that manned the war-fleets in those days were made up of several elements. There were a few professional seamen, there were large numbers of soldiers, and there were

The Crews.

a great many adventurers, scoundrels, and cut-throats. The discipline both in England and in Normandy was lax. Harold, immediately before the invasion, found himself unable, owing to the withdrawal of his men, to keep his ships in commission, and his commanders were, in consequence, deprived of the power of meeting William at sea. William, for his part, experienced great difficulty, first in collecting, and then in keeping together, his forces. He bribed his great nobles and the clergy to assist him, promising them money, land, or slaves. As an inducement to Remi, priest of Fécamp, he held out an English bishopric in exchange for a ship and a score of men-at-arms; and, when his followers became depressed and apprehensive, William revived their spirits not only by reminding them of the high favour with which the Church regarded the undertaking, but also by keeping them well supplied with strong drink. The professional seamen were probably not numerous enough to leaven the whole mass of the fleet. It had never been the policy of the Normans to foster a commercial navy; and where there is no commercial navy there cannot be many seamen. But even among the Normans there seems to have been already a small class of men who followed the sea as a calling, and who made their descendants seamen also. Stephen Fitz-Erard, captain of the *Mora*, apparently belonged to this class; and it was Thomas, his son, or grandson, who, in 1120, was captain of the *Blanche* or "White Ship" upon the unhappy occasion when William, son of Henry I., and many of his noble relatives and friends, were drowned among the rocks in the Race of Catteville.

Harold's Navy.

In England, on the other hand, trade had been encouraged and had flourished amazingly. The River Thames was always full of shipping, English and foreign; and the tolls must have amounted to large sums. There can be no question that the merchant navy, under Edward the Confessor and Harold, was very considerable; neither is there any doubt that there was also a regular war-navy. There had, indeed, been one ever since the days of Ethelred. It had, moreover, been called out for exercise every year immediately after Easter. We do not know exactly how it was raised and paid; but it is certain that at least part of it was furnished and manned by the leading maritime ports. Dover and Sandwich, if not all the places which later became known as the Cinque Ports, and many other havens, were, long before the Conquest, severally obliged to furnish the king with twenty ships for fifteen days, once in every year, each vessel having a crew of twenty-one persons. And some of the inland towns contributed in men, in money, or in kind. There were also, from time to time, special levies for ships, and there was the permanent tax called Danegeld, which developed into a fund for national defence. There was thus, in England, a school of seamen of old standing and a respectable navy, when William started upon his expedition, and everything points to the conclusion that if Harold's men had not been allowed too literally to interpret the law which permitted them, after their annual service, to go to their homes on the Feast of the Nativity of St. Mary, William, who sailed three weeks later, might have been easily defeated at sea. The men would probably have been willing to remain had the danger of the kingdom been properly represented to them ; for many of them seem to have spontaneously rejoined immediately after William had landed. They rejoined too late, however, to be of any practical use. Godwine and Edmund, the sons of Harold, put themselves at the head of the fleet and carried it to Ireland, whence for several years they conducted a series of semipiratical depredations on the coast of the West of England ; but these operations were no more effective than were the very similar operations of Prince Rupert against the Commonwealth nearly six hundred years afterwards ; and the ships of the princes were, one by one, fruitlessly expended. Thus England was, for a time, left without a war-navy ; and so absolutely unable was she, three or four years after William had destroyed his fleet, to make her power felt upon the sea, that, in 1070, the Conqueror found himself obliged to buy off the Danes, who for four months had lain unmolested in the Humber, and had used their ships as a centre whence to ravage and plunder from York to Ely. But William recreated an English fleet ere he had been long upon the throne. As early as 1071 he was able to operate by sea against the rebellious Earl Morkere ; and in 1072 he despatched a force of ships against Scotland. These ships were obtained in part from the coast towns under the stipulations of their tenures; in part from the Danegeld; and in part from private owners, who exchanged their ships for grants of land.

Maritime Affairs, 1087-1100. It would be idle to deny that the maritime population of England was at this period wild and lawless in the extreme; and that the coasts, even in times of nominal peace, were generally unsafe for honest people. The king was supposed to protect the narrow seas from the depredations of pirates and robbers, and in part return he received certain dues and tolls, and all the fish known as "great," or "royal," that were caught or stranded within his dominions. "Of sturgeon caught on our lands," runs the ordinance as quoted by Nicolas from Bracton, "we will that it shall be ours, saving to the finder his costs and expenses. And of whales so found we will that the head shall be ours, and the tail our consort's, agreeable to ancient usage." Whether the early Norman sovereigns also arrogated to themselves the dominion of the seas is doubtful. It was the object of Selden, Prynne, and the learned jurists of their day to make it appear that our kings had done so almost from time immemorial; but it is more than suspected that some of these lawyers strained, if they did not invent, facts to substantiate their conclusions; and there is little ground for belief that the dominion of the seas was ever formally claimed for this country before the days of John. It is certain, in any case, that the seas and coasts were very badly policed, and that, if pretensions to maritime sovereignty were cherished, the kings did little or nothing towards the practical assertion of them. The narrow seas swarmed with freebooters of several nationalities; and the shores, unlighted and unbuoyed, were rendered the more dangerous by the fact that those who lived upon them were pirates and wreckers. Only in a few of the larger ports were the laws observed. Elsewhere might was right.

The expedition which, in 1098, was fitted out by the Earls of Chester and Shrewsbury against Anglesey provides illustration of the state of affairs in the reign of William II. Like the buccaneers of the Spanish Main in a later age, they landed, plundered and massacred the inhabitants, and had collected, ready for shipment, an enormous booty, when Magnus,

King of Norway, descended upon them from the sea, defeated them, killed the Earl of Shrewsbury, and carried off all the spoils (pp. 4, 351).

The lack of system and subordination that had rendered the fleet of Harold useless against the invasion of William the Conqueror did not disappear in the immediately succeeding reigns; and to ill discipline and insubordination there was added, in the reign of Henry I., disloyalty. In 1101, when Robert, Duke of Normandy, was threatening invasion, Henry had little difficulty in collecting a large squadron; but he

Henry I.'s Navy, 1100-1134.

SEAL OF PEVENSEY.

could not retain it. No sooner had it sailed than great part of it deserted to the enemy; and, had not a timely peace been arranged between the royal brothers, Henry would have probably lost his crown, for, in the history of England, the dominion of the soil has usually lain with him who has enjoyed command of the sea. The disloyalty of the seamen and coast population wore away, however, as the reign grew older, and as Henry won opportunity for making his true nature known to them. His modification of the law of wreck was no doubt a measure that gained him much popularity as well with the maritime as with the great commercial classes. Up to his day, upon the loss of a vessel, any cargo that was cast ashore belonged to the king; but Henry ordained that if any person escaped alive from a lost vessel, the ship should not be treated as a wreck, and property in her and her contents should not be held to have passed away from the original owner.

Maritime Adventure. It was in this reign that the peculiar genius of the English for maritime adventure first began to show itself. In 1102 Edgar, grandson of Edmund Ironside, undertook a crusading expedition to the Holy Land, and, five years later, one "Hardinge of England" appeared with the Christian fleet at Joppa during the siege of Jerusalem. This genius for adventure seems to have been aroused by the Continental Normans, who were already acquiring great influence in the Mediterranean and who soon found formidable rivals in their island kinsmen. It is an old maxim that trade follows the flag; and although, owing to the long continuance of the wars of the Crusades, the earliest adventures of the English in the Levant did not lead to the immediate opening of commercial relations with the East, they certainly paved the way for it, and enabled such relations to be entered into as soon as the establishment of peace permitted. English participation in distant adventure had another result equally important and more speedy. It brought about considerable improvements in naval architecture, a science which for several centuries had made very little progress. Men were not slow in discovering that the vessels which would serve well enough for a fine weather passage across the Channel were scarcely fit to brave the huge rollers of the Bay of Biscay, and to face the varying conditions of a long voyage. Whether many improvements had been made by the year 1120 is uncertain; but it is recorded that the *Blanche*—the "nef" commonly called the White Ship (p. 354)—had fifty oars, and that when she went to pieces there were lost with her about three hundred souls. Even if we admit that the number of passengers may have been exaggerated, we cannot easily avoid the conclusion that the *Blanche* was a much larger craft than any which belonged to William the Conqueror's fleet of 1066. William, Henry I.'s son, left the sinking ship in a boat, and might have saved himself had he refrained from attempting to rescue his half-sister, Mary; and we find no evidence that any of the Conqueror's ships had boats belonging to or accompanying them.

Another noteworthy circumstance connected with this period is the rise of Portsmouth as a place of naval importance. Robert, Duke of Normandy, when intending to invade England, landed at Portsmouth in 1101. Henry I. more than once made Portsmouth his point of departure for Normandy, and in 1141, when the Empress Maud came to England to assert her son's right to the crown, she disembarked at Portsmouth.

Henry II. is praised by Bromton, William of Newburgh, and Gervase of Canterbury for having commanded that shipwrecked persons should be treated with kindness, and for having forbidden, under heavy penalties, anyone to take their merchandise or goods from them. He protected the rising commerce of his kingdom more directly by

WRECK OF THE WHITE SHIP (MS. Claud. D. ii.).

enacting some of the earliest Navigation Laws. In 1181 he ordered the justices to declare in each county that no one should buy or sell any ship to be carried away from England, and that no one should induce any seamen to take service out of the country.

In his reign London and Bristol became conspicuously the chief commercial ports of the kingdom, the former trading with Germany and the central parts of the Continent, and the latter with the Scandinavian countries and with Ireland.

Maritime Commerce under Henry II.

During the early part of Henry's sovereignty, Ireland was still unconquered ; but first by the efforts of private adventurers, who were little better than pirates, and finally by the exertions of the king himself, who invaded Ireland with four hundred large ships in 1171, the sister island was brought under some kind of subjection. This had the effect of greatly increasing the trade of Bristol, the merchants of which soon acquired the reputation of being even richer than those of the capital.

Once more we find evidence of the increasing size of English vessels. The foundering of a single ship in the Channel in 1170 is said to have involved the loss of four hundred persons. Many commentators, who pin great faith to the contemporary representations of ships upon coins and in MSS., affect to believe that the statements of the chroniclers concerning the complements of the vessels of the period are exaggerated, but there seems to be little reason for this incredulity. The evidence of the coins especially has little or no value. Indeed, if we accepted all of it, we should be driven to the absurd conclusion that as late as the thirteenth century masted ships were often less than six feet long, and were so built that only by miraculous intervention could they be kept upright in the water. It is much more probable that all the representations of ships that have come down to us from the eleventh and twelfth centuries are purely and frankly conventional. It is tolerably clear, however, that ships still had never more than one mast, and they were still, for the most part, very small and indifferently seaworthy.

Maritime Affairs under Richard I.

The reign of Richard I. is, from a naval point of view, memorable in many ways. It witnessed the first distant maritime expedition that was ever undertaken by the forces of the realm, and the promulgation of the first laws for the government of the English fleet and merchant navy.

It was at Chinon, in 1190, that Richard issued the ordinances which have been very fairly described as the basis of our modern Articles of War. These ordinances directed that if any man slew another on board a ship, he was to be fastened to the dead body and thrown with it into the sea. If the murder was committed on shore, the murderer was to be bound to the corpse and buried with it. If anyone were convicted by legal testimony of drawing his knife upon another, or of drawing blood in any manner, he was to lose his hand. For giving a blow with the hand, without producing blood, the offender was to be plunged three times into the sea. If anyone reviled or insulted another, he was on every occasion to pay to the offended party an ounce of

TYPICAL MS. SHIP (Harley Roll Y, 6).
(St. Guthlac's Voyage to Croyland.)

silver. A thief was to have his head shaven, to have boiling pitch poured upon it, and feathers shaken over him, as a mark by which he might be known, and to be turned ashore at the first land at which the ship might touch. Another ordinance strictly required every person to be obedient to the commanders or justices of the fleet; and, as they regarded themselves and their return to their own country, they were enjoined faithfully to observe these regulations.

Allied to these ordinances was the code known as The Laws of Oleron. It is generally ascribed to Richard, or to his mother, Queen Eleanor, but the greater part of it is probably of older date, and was merely confirmed by Cœur

The Law of the Sea.

29

de Lion. The code did for the merchant service of the day what the ordinances above quoted did for the navy; but it went much farther. It consists of forty-seven articles, and its most interesting provisions are as follow :—If a vessel were wind or weather-bound, the master, when a change occurred, was to consult his crew, saying to them, "Gentlemen, what think you of this wind?" and to be guided as to whether he should put to sea by the opinion of the majority. If he did not do this, and any misfortune happened, he was to make good the damage. If a seaman sustained any hurt through drunkenness or quarrelling, the master was not bound to provide for his cure, and might turn him out of his ship; but if the injury occurred in the service of the ship, the man was to be cured at the vessel's cost. A sick sailor was to be sent on shore, and a lodging, candles, and one of the ship's boys, or a nurse, provided to attend him, with the same allowance of food as he would have received on board. In case of danger in a storm, the master might, with the consent of the merchants on board, lighten the vessel by throwing part of the cargo overboard; and if they objected to his doing so, he was to act as he thought proper; but, on arrival in port, he and a third of his crew were to make oath that what had been done had been for the preservation of the ship; and the loss was then to be borne equally by the merchants. Before goods were shipped, the master was to satisfy the merchants as to the strength of his ropes and slings; but if he did not do so, or if he had been requested to make repairs, and damage resulted, the master was to make it good. In cases of difference between a master and one of his crew, the latter was to be thrice deprived of his mess allowance before he could be lawfully discharged; and if the man, in presence of the crew, offered reasonable satisfaction, and the master still persisted in discharging him, the sailor might follow the vessel to her destination, and there claim wages as if he had not been sent ashore. In case of collision by a ship under sail running on board one at anchor owing to bad steering, if the former were damaged, the cost was to be equally divided, the master and crew of the latter making oath that the collision was accidental. This law was aimed at dishonest owners who put old and decayed craft in the way of better ones. All anchors were to be indicated by buoys or anchor-marks. If a pilot, from ignorance or otherwise, failed to conduct a ship in safety, and if the merchants sustained damage, he was, if he had the means, to make full satisfaction, and if not, to lose his head; and if the master or any one of the mariners cut off his head, the executioner was not to be held answerable; but before recourse were had to this fatal measure, it must be ascertained that the pilot had not wherewith to make satisfaction. This rule was aimed at a class of rascally pilots who purposely ran vessels ashore in places where by custom a third or a fourth part of wrecked ships belonged to the lord, with whom the pilots had, of course, an understanding. Nor were the wrecking lords themselves forgotten. A plunderer of wrecks was to be tied to a post in the middle of his own dwelling, and his house was then to be burnt over his head, its walls were to be demolished, its site was to be converted into a pig-market, and the man's goods were to be confiscated for the benefit of those whom he had robbed. People who, "more barbarous, cruel, and inhuman than mad dogs," murdered shipwrecked persons, were to be ducked in the sea and then stoned to death. Goods floating ashore were to be kept for a year or more, and, if not then claimed, to be sold by the lord, and the profits distributed as marriage portions to poor maids, and in other charitable ways.

The ships with which Richard carried on his distant **Warships** operations were of several types. The largest were galleys, **under** sometimes, if of great burden, called "dromonds," although **Richard I.** the name dromond was also applied loosely to any large vessel. The "buss" was a bluff-bowed capacious craft, chiefly used as a transport or store-ship. The "galion," or "galliass," was a swifter and smaller galley. The "visser," or "urser," was a flat horse-boat. The barge was probably a small vessel used for carrying goods. Snakes, or "esnecca," seem to have been light and swift passenger boats. And the "cog" was apparently a large ship, either naval or mercantile. The galleys were long and low, with seldom more than two banks of oars, and with a mast and an above-water spur. The largest of Richard's galleys in the Mediterranean in 1190 had thirty oars. The rudder had not yet been introduced, and steering was still effected by means of the paddle, worked on the ship's

starboard quarter. This paddle was, however, often attached
in some way to the hull, and was provided with a cross-head
or yoke, very similar to that of a modern boat's rudder.
The larger warships carried not only engines for the projection
of darts and stones, but
also Greek fire, and certain
squib-like explosives called
"serpents." They seem to
have fought under the
banner of St. George, which
from that time became the
flag of England, although it
was more than once tempo-
rarily supplanted.

SHIP, SHOWING METHOD OF STEERING.
(*Corpus Christi College, Cambridge.*)

In this reign there was
added to England the first
of her distant foreign possessions by the conquest of
Cyprus in 1191, but Richard
speedily sold his acquisition
to the Knights Templars
and, when they insisted
upon his taking it back
again, gave it to Guy de
Lusignan. After he left the
island for Palestine, the king
became the hero of a naval action, which, as it was the first
since the days of Alfred in which an English monarch bore
part, and as, moreover, it illustrates the naval methods of the
period, should be mentioned here. Nicolas has compiled the
following graphic account of it :—

"On the 7th of June, when near Beirut, an immense ship
was discovered ahead. This vessel, which was the largest
the English had ever seen, excited their wonder and admiration. Some chroniclers call her a dromon, and others a buss;
while one of them exclaims, 'A marvellous ship! A ship than
which, except Noah's ship, none greater was ever read of;'
and which he afterwards calls the 'Queen of Ships.' This
vessel was, they say, very stoutly built, had three tall
tapering masts, and her sides were painted, in some places

green and in others yellow, so elegantly that nothing could exceed her beauty. She was full of men to the incredible number of fifteen hundred; among whom were seven emirs and eighty chosen Turks for the defence of Acre: and was laden with bows, arrows, and other weapons, an abundance of Greek fire in jars, and two hundred most deadly serpents prepared for the destruction of Christians. Richard directed a galley, commanded by Peter de Barris, to approach and examine the stranger; and was told that the vessel was going from Antioch to the siege of Acre, and belonged to the King of France, but that the crew could neither speak French now show a French or other Christian banner. Being further interrogated, they varied from their story, and pretended to be Genoese bound for Tyre. Meanwhile an English galleyman had recognised the ship as having been fitted out at Beirut while he was in that port; and in reply to the King's question, he said, 'I will give my head to be cut off, or myself to be hanged, if I do not prove that this is a Saarcen ship. Let a galley be sent after them, and give them no salutation: their intention and trustworthiness will then be discovered.' The suggestion was adopted; and, the moment the galley came alongside of the ship, the Saracens threw arrows and Greek fire into her. Richard instantly ordered the enemy to be attacked, saying, 'Follow and take them, for, if they escape, ye lose my love for ever; and if ye capture them, all their goods shall be yours.' Himself foremost in the fight, and summoning his galleys to the royal vessel, he animated all around by his characteristic valour. Showers of missiles flew on both sides, and the Turkish ship slackened her way; but, though the galleys rowed round and about her in all directions, her great height and the number of her crew, whose arrows fell with deadly effect from her decks, rendered it extremely difficult to board her. The English consequently became discouraged if not dismayed, when the king cried out, 'Will ye now suffer that ship to get off untouched and uninjured? Oh shame! after so many triumphs, do ye now give way to sloth and fear? Know that, if this ship escape, every one of you shall be hung on the cross or put to extreme torture.' The galleymen, 'making,' says the candid historian, 'a virtue of necessity,' jumped overboard, and, diving under the enemy's vessel, fastened ropes to her rudder, steering her as they pleased; and then, catching hold of ropes and climbing up her sides, they succeeded at last in boarding her." [The use of the word "rudder" here is surely a mistranslation.] "A desperate conflict ensued: the Turks were forced forward; but, being joined by those from below, they rallied and drove their assailants back to their galleys. Only one resource remained; and it instantly presented itself to the king's mind. He ordered his galleys to pierce the sides of the enemy with the iron spurs affixed to their prows. These directions were executed with great skill and success. The galleys, receding a little, formed a line; and then, giving full effect to their oars, struck the Turkish ship with such violence that her sides were stove in in many places, and, the sea immediately rushing in, she soon foundered. All her gallant crew, except fifty-five, who were spared from no worthier motive than that they would be useful in the construction of military engines, were either drowned, or slain by the inhuman victors. So much importance was attached to the destruction of this ship that it was said that, if she had arrived in safety, Acre would never have been taken."

King John and the Navy. King John has been called the Founder of the Royal Navy of England. He does not deserve the title, which could only be given with justice to a monarch who had created a navy where none had been before; and it is impossible to mention any year in which, or any document or act by which, the navy was established. But John merits the credit of having very greatly improved the service, and of having devoted very careful attention to it, throughout his reign. He seems, moreover, to have been the first English sovereign to retain seamen in permanent pay and to pension officers for wounds, and the first seriously to assert the dominion of the Narrow Seas. The pay of his galleymen was sixpence and of his mariners threepence a day; and he found the crews of his ships in provisions, including herrings and bacon, and in wine. Moreover, he introduced the practice of paying men a certain portion of their wages in advance, previous to sailing. He had a number of ships of his own, in addition to the vessels which were supplied,

according to the provisions of their tenures, by the Cinque
Ports and by other maritime towns; and some of them must
have been of considerable size, for crews of seventy men were
not uncommon, and there are records of vessels, described
as "small ships," which were, nevertheless, capable of carrying as many as fifteen horses. Upon occasion both ships
and men were impressed, but there was also a system of
hire of vessels and of voluntary enlistment of seamen, and

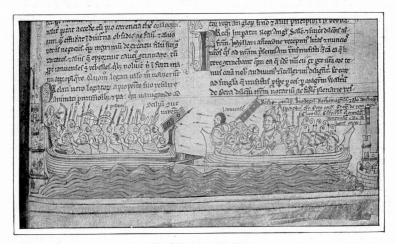

THE USE OF THE RAM.
(Corpus Christi College, Cambridge.)

a regular roll was kept of vessels which were permanently
liable to be called upon for service. The reserve of ships
thus constituted was administered by districts, each district
embracing four or five ports, and being under the superintend-
ence of an officer of rank. In 1205 the king's and the reserve
ships made up a force of over one hundred sail. The general
efficiency of the service was encouraged by a custom which
had the effect of giving to the seamen one moiety of all
prizes captured from the enemy. The prizes really became
the property of the king, and were either sold or added to
the navy; but the royal bounty always awarded prize-money,
and, dating from John's reign, there are many records of its
payment.

William de Wrotham, Archdeacon of Taunton, was, in

these matters, the king's right hand. He is variously designated as Keeper of the King's Galleys, Keeper of the King's
Ships, and Keeper of the Seaports; and he carried out many
of the functions of a modern First Lord of the Admiralty,
Controller of the Navy, and Admiral Superintendent, as well
as those of a Master of the Ordnance. He had something
to do with the original establishment of Portsmouth as a
dockyard and arsenal. In May, 1212, the Sheriff of
Southampton was ordered to cause the basins at Portsmouth
to be surrounded with a strong wall, as the Archdeacon of
Taunton would direct, for the preservation of the king's
ships and galleys: and he was also ordered to cause pent-
houses to be erected for the stores and tackle of the vessels.

**The Sove-
reignty of
the Seas.**
Selden is the authority for the statement that John
claimed the sovereignty of the seas. Selden quotes a folio
MS. "Commentary on Affairs Concerning the Admiral." But
Selden is not the only authority. Sir John Borough and
Prynne refer to it or to other MSS. to the same effect; and
although nothing is known of the originals, that fact is not,
in itself, suspicious; for many very important naval documents
of as late as the first half of the seventeenth century have
long since mysteriously disappeared, and nothing at all would
now be known of them had not their contents happened to
be promptly committed to print. The ordinance, which
Selden printed, was translated by him, as follows:—"If the
governor or commander of the king's navy, in his naval
expeditions, shall meet on the sea any ships whatsoever,
either laden or empty, that shall refuse to strike their sails
at the command of the king's governor or admiral, or his
lieutenant, but make resistance against them which belong
to his fleet, that they are to be reputed enemies if they may
be taken; yea, and their ships and goods be confiscated as
the goods of enemies; and that though the masters or owners
of the ships shall allege afterwards that the same ships and
goods do belong to the friends and allies of our lord the king;
but that the persons which shall be found in this kind of
ships are to be punished with imprisonment at discretion for
their rebellion." Whether the document may have been
genuine or not, it is intensely interesting as purporting to be
the earliest evidence of a claim which was afterwards proudly

and gloriously enforced by the English Navy during several centuries. There is no doubt that in the first half of John's reign the Narrow Seas were policed as they had never been before. To claim the dominion of them, therefore, would not have been unnatural on the part of the Power that spared no pains to keep them safe and open to the commerce of all nations.

In no department of life was the Norman's policy of "thorough" better carried out than in the matter of architecture. This was the work of William's spiritual mercenaries, who in intelligence, in discipline, in everything save numbers, were immensely superior to his lay soldiery. Nor were they numerically an insignificant body, for during the whole reign of the Conqueror (and under many of his successors) Norman and French and Italian priests were pouring into England. It was part of William's general scheme for the Normanisation of the country, everywhere to plant the foreign ecclesiastic by the side of the foreign soldier. Nor were the details beneath his personal supervision. As he had fixed on the larger towns as his principal places of arms, so he determined that these should also be the principal places of religion ; and it was for the more effectual carrying-out of the principle of the double garrison that he promoted the transfer of the bishops' seats from the small to the larger cities of their dioceses (p. 360).

R. HUGHES.
Art and
Architecture.

Wherever the imported ecclesiastic came from—whether he was an Italian, like Lanfranc ; a Piedmontese, like Anselm ; or a Norman, like Ralph the Torch—he had invariably a passion for building. The first thing, in fact, that we usually hear of the foreigners who supplanted Englishmen in English sees and abbacies is, that they set about rebuilding their cathedral or abbey churches. For this purpose the entire English fabric was usually pulled down ; sometimes, if the new church was built on the site of the old, the crypt was spared ; more often a Norman crypt was begun. It may have been effected later or earlier, but later or earlier every one of the English cathedrals disappeared. They were, of course, buildings of various merit ; a few, like Winchester, being considerable structures of stone, while more were only partly of stone, some wholly of wood.

Some dated from the time of Wilfrid and Benedict, others belonged to the revival under Dunstan, most were of the time of Canute or the Confessor. But the contempt for the rude and primitive Romanesque of the Saxon seems to have been universal, and whether the work was of the time of the recent Edward, or of the ancient Ethelfrith, it was equally English, and as such swept away. In country districts, of course, the architectural extermination was not so rapid: there was no such clean sweep of the English parish churches. This was due partly to the want of funds at the disposal of the local priesthood, partly to their want of architectural skill. In some few cases the Norman was even fain to rebuild in the Saxon manner, or only to add a Norman story, as at Deerhurst, or a Norman tower, as at Monkwearmouth. As a result, during the early days of William we have some buildings in the new style, some in the old, and some of a mixed character.

A very few new churches were also built at this time in the Saxon manner. At Lincoln, for instance—where William and Bishop Remi took, practically, the whole of the old town on the top of the hill, for the new castle and the new minster and monastery—the Saxon inhabitants were driven to the marshy land that lay in the valley. Here, while aloft the cathedral and castle were rising, they erected St. Peter's and St. Mary le Wigford—churches which resemble in general character, and indeed long passed as, typical Saxon. At Lincoln, therefore, we find genuine fragments of Saxon style built wholly in the time of the Norman, as at Westminster we have a genuine fragment of Norman style built wholly in the time of the Saxon. Both are Roman in origin, though the Norman style was, perhaps, the noblest form of Romanesque, as the English or Saxon was, perhaps, its meanest manifestation. Both, as we have said, are Roman, but the Norman shows its lineage most perfectly. The Norman round arch, supported on piers, is seen in the great aqueducts which the Romans built in France, in Spain, and in Italy. The round-headed apse is simply the ending of the Roman basilica. The Norman triforium (or first story) and the Norman clerestory (or second) are but developments of the architecture of the amphitheatre. In the matter of the central tower there is perhaps more originality, though here we have timidly applied hints taken from the architects of

The Norman Debt to Rome.

St. Sophia and San Vitale, and the Frankish Cæsar's copy of San Vitale at Aachen.

In plan the Norman church was invariably a Latin cross. **Norman** At the beginning the nave was supported by vast square or **Churches.** oblong piers, sometimes rounded into stumpy columns. Plain vaults without ribs for the narrower spaces, wooden roofs for the wider ones, were universal. The arch was either not

NORMAN PIERS, ST. ALBANS CATHEDRAL.

recessed at all, or only once recessed, or with the plainest round mouldings along the edge. The decoration did not get beyond simple arcades, with a sparse decoration of shallow zigzag or lozenge fretwork; and all this worked with the axe the use of the chisel being unknown. The capitals are also very plain— the upper stone square, the lower stone a hemisphere with the top of the sides chopped straight (or, from the mason's point of view, a square with the bottom rounded), so as to produce the familiar cushion shape, and occasionally—as in the White Tower in London—with a feeble volute at the corners, or in the middle

a cross shaped like the Greek letter Tau (**T**). The windows
are round-headed, without shafts or mouldings, and rather
long and small in aperture, and the doors square-headed
under a round arch. The central towers are exceedingly
low and heavy, the buttresses quite plain, and the porches
shallow, the doorways being recessed in the thickness of the
wall.

**Norman
Masonry.**   Simple indeed in every feature this Early Norman work is,

NORMAN WORK IN THE WHITE TOWER, LONDON.

but the low round arches, the enormous thickness of the piers
or columns, the sternness and austerity of the decoration, are, it
must be confessed, extraordinarily impressive. They look, as
has been said of the work of Rome and Egypt, as if the builders
meant to build for eternity, as if they meant to stamp on every
stone the Norman pride in Norman strength. It is to be feared
that the builders' motive was really less poetical. It was simply
that, in imitating the wide-jointed Roman work, they were
unable to make the adamantine Roman mortar, and recognising
the untrustworthy character of their material, they gave to pier

and column and arch a bigness that looks disproportionate to the weight it has to carry. The most distinguishing note of all in Early Norman work is the bad, wide-jointed masonry. The first Norman architects were, indeed, quite right; and when they laid aside this modest mistrust and attempted anything

THE TOWER AND NORTH TRANSEPT, WINCHESTER CATHEDRAL.

ambitious they usually had reason to regret it. The fall of Early Norman structures was, in fact, exceptionally frequent. Thus the tower of Ely, the south arches at St. Albans, and the tower of Winchester, all fell. This last cathedral had been fourteen years building; and the tower, finished in 1093, fell in 1107, nearly seven years after the wicked Red King had been laid beneath it.   It is, of course, impossible to disprove the popular belief that the vicinity of the body of the impious Rufus accelerated the fall of the tower of Winchester; but William of Malmesbury himself suspected that it was due to human clumsiness, rather than to Divine anger.   Some years later, probably about 1115 (the exact date is uncertain), the tower was raised again.   It is very low, but the piers on which it rests are enormous, and if they are as strong as they look, are capable of supporting three times the weight.

Effect of the Crusades.

The Anglo-Norman tradition of the thick column, which we so much admire, was, in fact, a tradition of timidity, inherited from the time when the masonry was bad, and persisting when, to use the words of William of Malmesbury, " the courses of stone were so correctly laid that the joint baffles the eye, and makes it fancy that the whole wall is composed of a single block"; for the bad stone-laying does not extend beyond the half-century that followed the Conquest.   By the end of that time the Crusaders were home again, having seen many men and the architecture of many cities, and their return is marked by a striking change not only in the masonry, but in the character and feeling of Norman work.   We have seen how the chronicler is impressed by the improvement in the new masonry; still more striking is the change from plainness to profusion of ornament, from the most simple to the most elaborate forms of decoration.

The Pointed Arch

Our earliest pointed arch was probably formed by the inter-section of two round-headed arches, an intersection which gives the perfect lancet form.   It first appears as a decorative feature only, as in the ornamental arcade at Canterbury, built about 1110, when Ernulf was prior, and repeated by him a few years later at Rochester, when he had been elevated to that see.   But as an element of construction, even of the most simple kind, the pointed arch does not appear until the second period of the Norman architecture—that is, until the end of the first quarter of the twelfth century.   In this respect the Norman architects were a long way behind some of their Continental brethren. Pointed arches had been in use in the South of France—a country through which many Crusaders passed—for more than a century, and they are found in the Church of the Holy Sepulchre, built by them after the taking of Jerusalem in 1100.

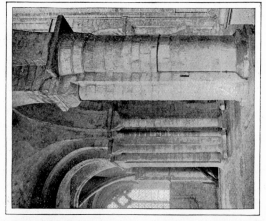

Wide-jointed Masonry, Winchester Cathedral.

Piers supporting Tower, Winchester Cathedral.

MASSIVE NORMAN MASONRY.

Photo.: Coe, Norwich.

Norman Pier, Norwich Cathedral.

It therefore becomes probable, though not strictly provable, that
the constructive pointed arch was also brought to England by
the warriors of the Cross. It was, apparently, first used here
about 1125 by Bishop Roger of Salisbury (p. 367), who rebuilt
the cathedral of Old Sarum. Not a stone of that edifice remains
in situ, but there are pointed arches of his in the Abbey of
Malmesbury, where they stand on massive Norman piers, and
where the work is in other respects of the plainest Norman
character. They appear a little later at St. Cross's Hospital,

Photo: A. F. Colborne, Canterbury.

THE ORNAMENTAL ARCADE, CANTERBURY CATHEDRAL.

built by Henry of Blois, the brother of King Stephen, where,
too, the intersecting round arcades form lancet windows in the
triforium. Henceforth, to the end of the century, the round
arch and the pointed arch are used indiscriminately, until, in
the last days of the transition from Norman to Early English,
the round arch is definitely abandoned for construction, and
when retained, retained only as decoration. The richest
Norman work coincides with this time of indiscriminate use,
though it must be borne in mind that the presence of the
pointed arch is not necessarily—nor, indeed, at all—associated
with any special richness.

Of this period, perhaps the most beautiful and most characteristic features which remain to us are the doorways and arches, both lay, as at Bristol, and ecclesiastical, as at Iffley. They are generally very deeply recessed through the whole thickness of

THE EAST END, SHOWING TRIFORIUM, ST. CROSS, WINCHESTER.

the wall, strand after strand of moulding running round the head, and being carried down on each side, and in many cases there is not a square inch of stonework which is not overlaid with ornament. The sculpture is also very deep and clean, and executed with the chisel, the use of the axe having been now

30

definitely abandoned.   The crane's-bill or beakhead, the cat's-head, the bead course, the medallions with figures, conventional foliage, or flowers, and the rosette—all are lavished in inexhaustible variety, and in combination with the old forms of the lozenge, the zigzag, the sunk star, and the round roll or billet.

Photo: Gillman & Co., Oxford.
IFFLEY CHURCH, NEAR OXFORD.

The piers now cease to be plain, and the columns grow taller, and twisted and banded shafts make their appearance.   The windows come in for a share of the decoration.   They are divided, and in some cases of the true lancet form, though the intersecting arches are still present.   Round lights also appear; at first, mere circular holes, but later the wheel-like beginnings which in time will develop into the perfect rose.   The plain

Photo: W. F. Kimberley, Kenilworth.

Chancel Arch, Stoneleigh Church.

Photo: W. F. Kimberley, Kenilworth.

Doorway, Kenilworth Church.

College Gateway, Bristol.

West Doorway, Lincoln Cathedral.

NORMAN MOULDINGS.

cushion of the capitals, which early took the scalloped form, become, with the advance in style, laden with ornament. The volutes are more openly copied, and a sort of feeble Etruscan

filigree pattern often runs over their square faces. Such are the main characteristics of the later Norman. It is not, of course, possible to date accurately the beginning or ending of any form of architecture; but dividing Norman into two periods of "early" and "late," we may approximately close the early period in 1120 (or fifty-four years after Hastings), allotting to the later period the next space of fifty-four years. This brings us to 1174, which is the date of the great fire at Canterbury, a disaster to which English architecture is immensely indebted.

BANDED PILLAR, CANTER-
BURY CRYPT.

The restoration of Canterbury, undertaken by William of Sens in 1175, undoubtedly marks the beginning of the transition, the mixed style

Transition to Early English. which belongs both to Norman and to Early English. It is not by the presence of the pointed arch alone that it is distinguished; that, we have seen, was common forty years before; but in the work at Canterbury we have not alone the free use of the pointed arch, but the budding of the pointed style, and we see that style in almost full bloom before the work is finished. By a fortunate accident the progress of the building has been recorded almost from year to year by a contemporary. The work of the first year is almost pure Norman in its detail, but it gradually changes, particularly after the death of the French architect, until at length every accessory, every moulding, every ornament seems Early English. The Romanesque column, however, remains, and a debased Corinthian or composite capital, borrowed probably from French examples. The builders of Canterbury were, in fact, pioneers, and the success which they achieved in the Metropolitan Church gave a great impetus to pointed work throughout England. Moreover, the superiority of the pointed to the

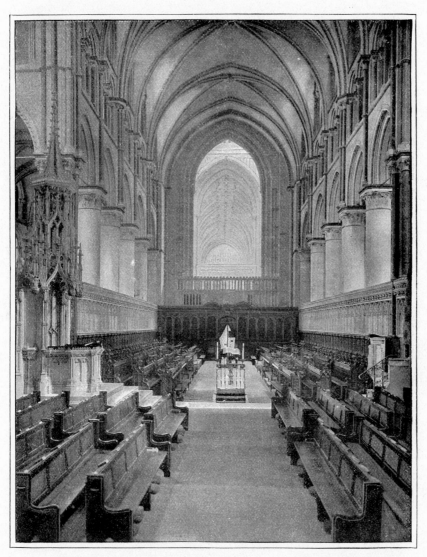

THE CHOIR, CANTERBURY CATHEDRAL, LOOKING WEST.

round arch, as a means of vaulting over large and unequal spaces, was undeniable, and helped to drive out the Norman style. Soon the pointed arches began to be preferred for their own sake, and we find them adopted in places where the round arch would have served as well or better. Another indication of the transition is to be found in the form of the windows, which now are frequently pointed without and round within, as at Oakham Castle, and with shafts at the sides, and with the violette, or dog-tooth, ornament, the typical decoration of Early English. So, too, we now find round arcades enclosing pointed lights, as at St. Hilda's above Whitby, and clustered pillars approaching the Early English form, as at Byland Abbey.

The Rival Arches. But besides examples such as these, in which the pointed method is generally triumphant, though the round arch holds out in decorative features, there are others where the exact converse occurs. Of these the Galilee, or west porch, at Durham is an instance, and, indeed, the most notable instance, where, so to speak, the body remains perfect Norman, while the soul of the building is perfect Early English. Bishop Hugh of Pusey, its builder, who was only appointed in 1180, died in 1197, and this very fine and expensive work must be attributed to the early days of King Richard, or the very last of King Henry. It was built in the interests of female worshippers, that they might have a place whence they should have the comfort of contemplating the holy places, which the stringency of the monastic rules did not permit them to enter. Certainly they are beautifully housed. The Norman round arch is used throughout, and the chevron ornamentation is also strictly Norman. Each of the arches springs, or sprang, from a tall and slender pier, though, perhaps, pier is hardly the right word to describe the two elegant shafts of Purbeck marble, of which alone each pier originally consisted. These have been altered for the worse; but the small forest of tapering stems, carrying the lightest of all stone arcades, remains, and is as graceful as any work of the later Gothic, and as far removed from the clumsy strength of the Early Norman. Mr. Freeman speaks of its Saracenic grace, and it is impossible not to feel the justness of the epithet. It was the very last word of the Norman style, and it must be owned that it was inimitably spoken.

The extraordinary architectural energy which had marked

the twelfth century showed, perhaps, some abatement at the very beginning of the thirteenth. This may well have been due to the phenomenal rapacity of Richard and John, which, falling heavily on all owners of property, seriously affected the religious houses, and made the Jews, who financed their building operations, unwilling to give evidence of wealth which might exasperate the royal extortioners. But the reign of John, which

THE GALILEE, DURHAM CATHEDRAL.

saw the birth of the chartered liberties of the nation, was also destined to see our first purely national architecture attain its majority. This, which we know as "the Early English style," actually came into being a little earlier, namely, in the reign of John's brother Richard, and is the one good thing that accrued to England under that most execrable of all our monarchs. Its birth was presided over by Hugh of Avalon (p. 395), Bishop of Lincoln, commonly called St. Hugh of Burgundy. He died in 1200, and was buried behind the high altar in his unfinished church. His work is remarkable in two ways: first, because it is the first example of pure pointed Gothic (of Gothic, that is, without the least tincture of Romanesque) to be found in

The Early English Style.

England, and not in England alone, but in all Europe; and
secondly, because though there is a youthful, we might say a
girlish, delicacy about it, it is neither tentative nor immature.
All the true characteristics are present.   We have the clustered
shafts, the elegant crockets (conventional out-curled leaves), the
pointed trefoil arch, the narrow lancet-shaped windows, the
stalked foliage of the capitals.   The history of the transition, of
course, makes it certain that it was, in fact, a case of evolution,
and not of a sudden separate creation; but the casual looker-on
would certainly be justified in thinking that the Early English
style, like Pallas from the head of Zeus, sprang full-grown and
full-armed from the brain of the architects at Lincoln and Ely.
This is true of St. Hugh's choir at Lincoln, built in the last ten
years of the twelfth century; it is emphatically true of the
Galilee at Ely, built in the first fifteen years of the thirteenth
century, than which no more perfect example is to be found
in the world.

The greatest and most important works in this noblest form
of Gothic, such as Salisbury, belong indeed to the next generation—to the reign, not of John, but of his son.   But the smaller
structures to which we have referred do not yield to them in
beauty, and show how completely the style of the Transition,
no less than the style of the Norman, had, at this early date,
become extinct.   In twenty years, or thereabouts, there has
been more than a change; there has been a complete and final
transfiguration.   Instead of heavy arches and solid piers, im-
posing chiefly by their mass, light clusters of delicate shafts
charm us by their airy grace.   Pointed arches carry, and pointed
arcades decorate, the walls, and possibly some of the high wide
roofs have exchanged their flat boarding for springing vaults of
stone.   Instead of the minute and laborious, almost missal-like,
ornament of the Norman carver, we have the free, almost
naturalistic, rendering of flower and foliage.   Instead of the
Norman beads, we have the violette.   The shallow square and
chamfer of the Norman mouldings is abandoned for boldly cut
rolls and fillets, and deep shadowy hollows in infinite variety.
The eye is no longer kept down to earth along the horizontal
Norman lines; on the contrary, everything points heavenward;
verticality is the law of the new order.   The round arch has
gone, not to reappear for centuries.

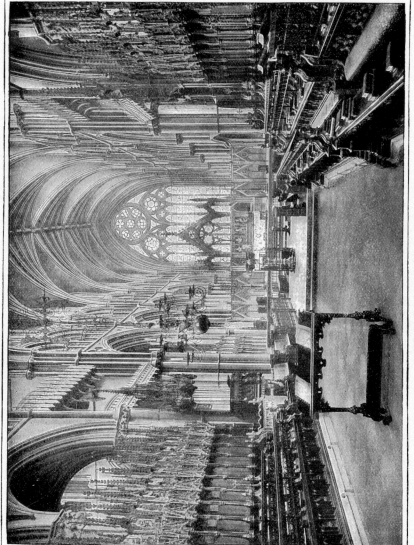

THE CHOIR, LINCOLN CATHEDRAL.

Norman Castles.

Great as was the change effected by the substitution of the Norman cathedral for the English church, it probably excited less wonder in English eyes than the substitution of the Norman castle for the English "burh." It does not appear that prior to the Conquest anything in the nature of a real stone fortress existed in England, and the famous French antiquary, M. de Caumont, by an exhaustive examination of the sites of the Norman castles whose owners fought at Senlac, ascertained that the same holds true of Normandy also. Like the English, they trusted to wooden walls and earthworks, fortified by stockades and defended by a deep ditch or moat. But these defences, however strong against assault, easily fell a prey to fire, and it was doubtless this consideration that induced the Conqueror not only to erect stone castles himself, but to encourage his great tenants to imitate his example. There is, indeed, evidence that some even of his earliest fortresses were of wood, for we read in Domesday of places like Stafford, where "the King has had a castle made which has lately been destroyed," and this could hardly have taken place by any other agency than fire, a means of destruction obviously inapplicable to such a building as the Tower of London. We hear, too, later, of immense numbers of unauthorised fortresses (*castella adulterina*) rising in troublous reigns like that of Stephen, and being destroyed, literally by the hundred, when law and order were restored. These also must have been of wood; but that William and his great barons generally built in stone is attested by the remains that are with us to this day. Some of these, like Winchester and Lincoln and London, were royal from the first; others were the work of tenants in chief, and also were held to be possessions of the Crown; while the few to which the royal claims were more doubtful were gradually, by escheat and otherwise, reduced into the king's possession.

The architecture of the Norman castle was simple. In form it was by preference a rectangular keep, the sides varying from twenty-five to a hundred feet in length, and varying equally in height. At the corners the walls come forward so as to form square towers, the faces being usually relieved by a flat pilaster-like buttress. The walls at the base are sometimes as much as thirty feet, and at the top as much as ten feet, thick. Below

was the store-room; higher up, to which access was given by
narrow staircases made in the thickness of the walls, were the
rooms for the garrison and for the owners, floors and roof being
of wood.   In every case a well was dug, some of these being of
prodigious depth.   Where practicable this keep was surrounded
by a moat filled with water; and though, of course, this was
not always practicable, a deep ditch of some sort was almost
invariably a defensive feature.   The doorway, which was small,

Photo: Chester Vaughan, Acton, W.

INTERIOR OF ROCHESTER CASTLE.

and gave access only to a small portion of the interior,
was defended by a drawbridge and portcullis, or some similar
mechanism.   But one peculiarity ever distinguishes these early
castles from the more elaborate constructions of later times.
They depend for their impregnability on the thickness of their
walls, not on any series of fortifications or ingeniously constructed *enceinte*.

The sites were selected with an eye solely to the subjection
of the country, though, of course, the old strong places (natural
and artificial) which had sheltered the Briton and the Saxon
were not neglected by the Norman.   The use of these older
sites led, however, to a modification of the type of fortress.   The

formation of the natural rock, or the weakness of the artificial mound, frequently obliged the Norman builder to abandon his favourite plan, and erect his keep as best he could, so as to form a shell round the highest and most defensible ground. This is the obvious origin of the kind known as the "shell," as distinguished from the "rectangular," keep. But that the Norman used the "shell" form unwillingly—from compulsion, not from choice—is proved by the fact that while the rectangular form is found sometimes on an old, and sometimes on a new, site, there is no single instance of the adoption of the "shell" where the castle was erected altogether on new ground. This is true even of the small pele[1] towers, the remains of which stud the northern Marches, and which are nothing but smaller editions of the great fortresses of Colchester and London. Of all specimens of military architecture, these rectangular stone castles are the grandest in outline. Most that survive are of the date of Henry I., a reign most prolific of castles; but very fine fragments remain of earlier masonry—such as the tower of Malling, built by Gundulf of Rochester, and considerable portions of London, Guildford, Bramber, Carlisle, Goderich, Walden, Wolvesey, and Colchester. There is but little difference between the earlier and later work, though at the end of the period under review the *enceinte* begins to play a more important part, and the round donjon, or juliette, occasionally takes the place of the square Norman keep. But it was always something of a foreign fashion, and we have no early work in this style by English masons that compares in grandeur with the impregnable towers of Coucy.

Other Norman Buildings
We know little of the other lay structures erected by the Norman architects of the twelfth century. Most that have survived formed part of the monastic buildings, and, indeed, amongst them it is not improper to class the chapter-houses of existing cathedrals. The Norman, and, indeed, the very early English, form of these was rectangular, and the few that remain show, as might be expected, that they conform to all the rules of the style in vogue. No doubt that wonder in its time, "the great Hall of Rufus," which has practically disappeared, was a characteristic round-arched basilican structure, with a boarded

[1 Or pele towers : small square towers of masonry with three floors, used as a dwelling and a refuge from raiders.]

Photo: Chester Vaughan.
Guildford Castle.

The White Tower.

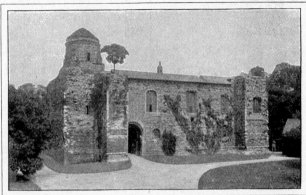

Photo: Graphotone Co.
Colchester Castle.

Photo: Chester Vaughan.
Rochester Castle.

St. Leonard's Castle, Malling.

NORMAN CASTLES.

roof and the cushion-capitalled cylindrical piers of the earliest days of the Norman style, just as Oakham Castle, with its

ILLUMINATED INITIAL.
(Trinity College, Cambridge.)

richly sculptured capitals which remain, was an equally characteristic example of its latest development. But great kings like Rufus, and great nobles like Ferrers, were exceptions, and it would seem probable that the architectural energy of the Churchmen was not, except in regard to castle-building, at all emulated by the laity. Portions of a few manor-houses and one or two buildings which tradition ascribes to Jews, like "Moyses Hall" at Bury (p. 671) and "the Jew's House" at Lincoln, survive, but they hardly exhibit any distinctive features. Probably the mass of well-to-do people continued to be content with wooden houses, and even the workers in stone seem to have been inclined to borrow wooden forms, as may be guessed from the exquisite external staircase at Canterbury, with its Norman balusters and arcades.

Illumination and Decoration. Of other arts there is not much to be said. The illuminators continue their delicate and laborious work, but though some of the specially English

Photo: A. F. Colborne.

FRESCO OF ST. PAUL AND THE VIPER.
(St. Anselm's Chapel, Canterbury Cathedral.)

MS. ILLUMINATION SHOWING THE VISION OF JACOB
(LAMBETH PALACE LIBRARY).

[To face p. 478

4

forms of decoration are abandoned, there is no real advance. Nor, indeed, could we expect any so long as the illuminations continued to be executed by monks, in the scriptorium of the monastery, instead of being, as at a later date they were, the work of the artist in his studio. We have already

ILLUMINATION TO PSALM I. IN THE CANTERBURY PSALTER.
(Trinity College, Cambridge.)

called attention to the missal-like character of the Norman sculpture. With the Transition greater freedom arrives, and in the Early English work we see flowers and foliage dealt with in a spirit that shows fine feeling, and the promise of still higher qualities. At the same time it remains the mere drudge of architecture, and almost the same is true of the decoration in polychrome and fresco, which were used—though exactly how, and to what extent, we do not know—from the tenth century onwards.

COIN OF WILLIAM I.

COIN OF RICHARD I., STRUCK IN POITOU.

Coins.   During the reigns of William and of his six successors the only English coins were silver pennies, and these were issued in the most casual fashion.   In some reigns no money at all was struck with the name of the sovereign upon it, Richard and John being satisfied to use, in England, the dies that bore the name and effigy of their father, although Irish coins of John, and Aquitanian coins of Richard, have been found.   They are all exceedingly rude, nor is there anything to choose in point of art between the earliest mintage that bears the head of the Conqueror and the latest that bears that of his great-grandson. The Conqueror's coins resemble in style those of Harold and of the Confessor, being, in fact, bad imitations of bad originals. On the pennies of the two Williams, evidence of their desire to pose as legitimate kings is supposed to be found in the presence of the Saxon Þ in place of W.   This letter in the hands of the Norman moneyer becomes transmuted into a P, so that both the Conqueror and Rufus appear as Pillem or Pilhelm. Throughout the whole period there is what seems meant for a portrait on the obverse, which, in the case of the two Williams, is usually of the most comical ferocity.   They have very strange headgear, but the smooth face and moustache are well enough shown.   There is usually, too, the sceptre and one or more stars, and on the back an ornamented cross with letters. The coins vary a good deal in shape, some of the earliest being

COIN OF WILLIAM II.

COIN, PROBABLY OF STEPHEN AND HIS QUEEN

perfectly round, while, later, some are so irregular as to appear to have been clipped with shears. The most interesting series belongs to Stephen's reign (pp. 369, 370), when they were coined, not only by the king, but by great lords like Robert of Gloucester, by great Churchmen like Henry of Winchester, by the king's sons William and Eustace, and by the Empress Matilda. The most interesting of these metal documents is one on which we read Stephen's name, and which shows two figures holding between them a lance topped by a fleur-de-lis. These personages were for a long time identified with Stephen and Henry Plantagenet, and the piece was supposed to have commemorated the Treaty of Wallingford. It is probably of slightly earlier date, and represents the king and his queen, Matilda, and may have been struck by that energetic lady while fighting for her imprisoned lord. Unfortunately, there is not a single coin of these princes which exhibits the least knowledge of the medallist's art, or possesses the limited element of beauty attained, four centuries earlier, under the Mercian Offa.

THE religious reformation of the eleventh century, which set the Latin Church once more on a career of victory, was accompanied by an intellectual movement not less penetrating in its results upon the history of education and the formation of human thought. The awakened interest in religious matters led at once to inquiry into the meaning of theological doctrines. It was from religious scruples that Berengar of Tours, towards the middle of the century, came to analyse the grounds on which the accepted doctrine of the Holy Communion was believed; and though in his attack upon the doctrine of Transubstantiation he left but few followers, still by virtue of the resistance he aroused, and the stimulus which was thus given to intellectual activity, he is rightly reckoned among the first of the pioneers of the scholastic philosophy. For the issue, on the one hand, broadened into a contest touching the claims of reason and authority, and on the other was diverted into a discussion as to the nature of the subject-matter of logic. In the controversy concerning the Holy Communion Berengar was opposed by Lanfranc, afterwards Archbishop of Canterbury. The logical dispute was brought into prominence some years

R. L. POOLE. Learning and Science; Theology and Philosophy.

31

later by Roscelin of Compiègne, who applied his conclusions to
the explanation of the doctrine of the Trinity, and was answered
by Anselm, likewise afterwards Archbishop of Canterbury.   In his
old age Roscelin was resisted by his own pupil, Peter Abelard,[1]
who sought to occupy a middle ground between the two schools
of logic. But Abelard, when he entered on the study of theology,
though he always accepted the traditional doctrine of the subordination of reason to authority, yet admitted explanations and
illustrations of the received dogma, which were taken to imply
that dogma needed the interpretation of reason; and thus
through his teaching and influence he roused the strenuous
opposition of St. Bernard. The whole controversy, logical and
theological, is included in the century that elapsed between
the first teaching of Berengar and the last condemnation of
Abelard by the Council of Sens in 1141. Whichever side had
the better of it in argument, the opinion of the time adjudged
the prize to the supporters of orthodox methods—to Lanfranc
and St. Anselm unhesitatingly, to St. Bernard with some waver-
ing. On the logical question of dispute, though St. Bernard did
not permanently succeed in resisting Abelard's new dialectical
method of treating theological discussion, still for the moment
the battle was won; and the conquerors were the Realist advo-
cates of authority, the beaten were the Nominalist or partly
Nominalist asserters of the place of reason in theological
inquiry. To understand these terms we must glance for a
moment at the method of teaching in practice at the time.

The Trivium and Quadrivium   The elements of education were embraced under two heads:
grammar, which dealt with words and their combination into
sentences; and logic, which was concerned with the combination
of sentences in discourse and reasoning, and thus fell into the
two branches of rhetoric and dialectic. The three Arts of
grammar, rhetoric, and dialectic were ranked side by side, and
formed the Trivium, or first course of training in the schools,
and the name logic was commonly appropriated by dialectic.
The second or more advanced course was the Quadrivium,
which comprehended arithmetic, geometry, astronomy, and
music; and the three and the four together made up the

[1 Strictly, the name is Abaielardus or Abaëlardus, the first syllable being
the Breton and Welsh Ab or Ap, "son." But the *aë*, mistaken for *æ* diphthong,
was corrupted into *e*, and the accent then shifted to the first syllable.]

FOUR LEADING MUSICAL AUTHORITIES: BOETHIUS, PYTHAGORAS, PLATO, NICOMACHUS.

(University Library, Cambridge.)

Seven Liberal Arts, so designated not because they were deemed to cover the whole field of human knowledge, but because they were regarded as the most proper studies for every educated man—in contradistinction to the professional faculties of divinity, law, and medicine.

Nominalism and Realism. Such a scheme of education gave no place for the study of philosophy, except so far as it could be embraced in logic, and consequently a branch of training requiring the most matured powers of the mind was thrust in among the rudimentary arts of the Trivium. For logic, it was clear, involved metaphysics, and it was on the metaphysical basis of logic that the whole scholastic problem turned. The main subject of controversy was the nature of universals. On the one side it was urged that logic was in fact concerned not with mere words but with things. The exponents of this, the accepted doctrine—the Realists— maintained that when we use terms denoting a class, *e.g.* white things, the whiteness which we attribute to all of them is a real thing or substance. The Nominalists held, on the contrary, that the particular thing only is real, and that the universal is a mere name, the creation of our own minds to express that which we have inferred from the comparison of observed facts. The one school proceeded from the highest and broadest conceptions of which the mind is capable—from the ideal, which to it was the only reality. The other held fast by experience, which declared only the individual. The difficulty of the Realist was to reach the individual. Could the individual be said really to exist? Was it not rather a bundle of attributes? This school had, however, the advantage in the readiness with which its principles could be brought into accord with the doctrines of the Christian Church—above all, with those of the Trinity, and of the change of substance in the Sacramental elements. The Nominalist, on the contrary, grounding himself on the dictates of reason, was inclined to arrogate for this a far higher rank than his opponents would allow; and logic, as the method which controlled the exercise of his faculties, became for him, not the mere " handmaid of theology," but itself " the science of sciences." Although by the middle of the twelfth century the Nominalists had been practically beaten out of the field, yet the Realism which remained supreme was profoundly modified in the course of the long debate; and through the fact that this debate had been necessarily conducted by means of logic, the importance which the Nominalists had claimed for the method was silently accepted by their opponents, and logic continued throughout the Middle Ages the dominant study of the schools.

It has already been said that logic from the first was applied to the examination of theological truths, and it was doubtless the result of the discrepancy of the conclusions at which Berengar, Roscelin, and Abelard arrived, with the accredited statement of those truths, that the school which opposed them won so unmistakably the upper hand. But as the Nominalist view of logic affected that of their rivals, so too did the logical treatment of theology acquire a currency which powerfully influenced its subsequent study. It was nothing new to compare and balance dogmatic passages from the Bible and the Fathers of the Church which at first sight might seem to contradict one another; but when Abelard in his "Sic et Non" ("Yes and No") arranged such passages side by side, classified under the proper heads, men felt at once that this was to expose the weak points of traditionary theology to the obvious attacks of the untrained or malicious. As a matter of fact, the systematic ordering of the discordant "sentences" was merely designed for the convenience of disputants; the logical method had become the method of theological discussion; and though Abelard's book was condemned, its plan was taken up, and became the model for the leading text-books of the schools. The "Sentences" of the Englishman Robert Pullan, and of Abelard's disciple Roland (afterwards Pope Alexander III.), are types of the appropriation of the dangerous method by the most orthodox divines. They contain theses or questions briefly stated, with arguments from the Bible and the Fathers, and conveniently arranged for use in a syllogistic form. But these and others of the same date were soon superseded by the "Sentences" of Peter Lombard, afterwards Bishop of Paris, which remained for more than three centuries the standard text-book of the European schools, the work upon which every candidate for a theological degree was obliged to lecture, and from whose classification the whole systematic theology of the later Middle Ages took both its form and its colour.

The earlier text-books of the medieval schools were almost

all the productions of the later Roman Empire.   Priscian and
Donatus supplied the grammar; logic was learned from Aristotle, mainly through the versions and paraphrases of Boëthius,
and, most of all, from a meagre compend attributed to St.
Augustine; and the whole circle of the liberal arts was studied
in the obscure rhetorical allegory " On the Marriage of Philology
and Mercury," by Martianus Capella, the treatise " On the Arts
and Disciplines of Liberal Learning," by Cassiodorus, and the
" Origins " of St. Isidore of Seville.   This last work provided
also a summary of historical knowledge, but the popular school
history was that of Orosius; and to some extent the other text-
books of the silver age had become superseded by the brazen
epitomes of Alcuin, the English counsellor of Charles the Great.
The minor works of the Venerable Bede, especially those on
rhetoric, metre, chronology, and cosmography, were widely used
by more advanced students.   Models of style were found in the
Church Fathers, above all in SS. Augustine, Jerome, and Gregory
the Great, and in the Vulgate or Latin Bible of St. Jerome.

Of any knowledge of the Greek language beyond the ninth
century, to which by a singular fortune it had survived in the
tradition of the Irish schools and of their descendants on the
Continent of Europe, there is in the West no certain trace; for
all supposed vestiges of it prove to be derived from glossaries
copied from older texts.   But the better classical literature of
Rome was by no means forgotten; or, if forgotten, was rapidly
recovered in the ages which followed the revival of the Roman
Empire by Otto the Great in the tenth century.   In the twelfth,
to judge by its most brilliant exemplar, there was not much of
that literature which lay altogether beyond the range of knowledge.   John of Salisbury, indeed, seems to have been ignorant
of Plautus, Lucretius, and perhaps Catullus; but he was familiar
with Terence, Virgil, Horace (not, however, his " Odes "), Ovid,
Lucan, Statius, Juvenal, Martial, Persius, and a number of later
poets.   If he had read little of Cicero's " Orations," he knew his
philosophical works intimately; and he was well acquainted
with Seneca, Quintilian, and the two Plinies.   With historians
he was more poorly supplied.   Cæsar and Tacitus were names to
him, and Livy he cites but once; but Sallust, Suetonius, Justin,
and, more than all, Valerius Maximus were constantly at his
hand.   No doubt his resources made him dependent to a great

extent upon the later classical writers—Gellius, Macrobius, Apuleius, etc.—but the range of his reading was certainly superior to that of most professed Latinists of the present day. Such learning was, without question, unique in the twelfth century; but the fact that it was possible is proof that the

PAGE SHOWING LATIN AND HEBREW.
(*Trinity College, Cambridge.*)

mass of Latin literature in attainable manuscripts was far greater than is commonly supposed. It need hardly be added that for educational purposes a very small selection of it was asked for.

Yet the variety, the elasticity, of educational methods was probably greater in the twelfth century than it became when

The Genesis of University Teaching. teaching was more highly systematised in Universities. It was often enough the teacher who made the school, not the school the teacher. A single man might, by his own personal attraction, create, as it were in a moment, a new centre of teaching. The material wants of the medieval student were few; he could move easily from place to place, with little baggage; and he asked only for house-room. We read of multitudes being drawn together by the lessons of Abelard, and building for themselves wattled huts round the place where the master taught. Sometimes a band of scholars, excited by some grievance, or moved merely by the spirit of novelty, would quit their school in a body, and from such a migration might spring a permanent new school, or even a University. But in order to understand the distinctive meaning of the word " University" we must glance for a moment at the educational arrangements which preceded the more complete organisation known by this name.

The cathedral churches and monasteries commonly had schools attached to them, and these supplied to the children of the neighbourhood at least the rudiments of education, though in practice probably only those intended for the clerical profession were sent to them. Where no school existed, the parish priest might undertake the duty, just as John of Salisbury, in Henry I.'s time, was handed over to a clergyman's charge " to learn his Psalms "; but in regularly established schools the teaching was entrusted to a particular member of the cathedral or collegiate body, who was called the *scholasticus*. In England commonly the place of the *scholasticus* was taken by the cathedral chancellor or the archdeacon; and this officer came in time to regard himself as too important a dignitary to devote himself personally to the work of giving daily instruction. He therefore employed a deputy, and it is in his official authorisation of teachers to do his work that we find the origin of the academical degree; for as the schools grew in popularity and in the numbers of students attending them, the need arose for several or many masters, all of whom required the recognition of their official chief. He gave them the " licence to teach," and this *licentia docendi* continues to the present day the essential element in the degrees in Arts conferred in the English Universities.

At the first the grant of this licence was a matter of favour, but the Lateran Council of 1179 made it obligatory to confer it upon all properly qualified scholars. Everyone now who desired to rank as a man of learning found himself compelled by usage to seek the licence, and the ambitious rivalry of the eager students of the twelfth century made its possession not merely a privilege but a necessity; for the licences of the most famous schools gradually acquired a European prestige, and became a passport to the master who wished to support himself by teaching. The stages by which the acceptance of the qualification became universal are obscure; but so soon as a licence held good everywhere, we have reached a condition of things in substance exactly identical with that in which the evidence of an academical degree is considered a sufficient warrant of a liberal education; and the degrees conferred at the present day by others than Universities —by the Pope, for instance, or by the Archbishop of Canterbury—are practically a continuation of the ancient licence modified by the analogy of academical graduation.

After the licence was granted, the new master at once proceeded to enter upon office. This he did—first, by the delivery of a lecture, and secondly by taking his seat (*cathedra*) among the established teachers of the place. A feast, given to them at his expense, concluded the ceremony. We have here the second main element in the formation of a University —namely, the existence of a society of masters who claim to have their say on the admission of a new member to their body. At first, no doubt, the society was of an informal character, but gradually it acquired an organisation. It became necessary for the masters to protect themselves against the possible competition of unqualified teachers, who might by some means have obtained the licence, and to secure the observance of an accredited system of study against wanton innovation. In this way there arose at Paris, not long after the middle of the twelfth century, a brotherhood or guild, or *universitas,* of masters, who by degrees succeeded in securing to themselves control over the method of teaching in the city, and over the reception into their body of other licensed masters.

A University, so far as the name is concerned, connotes no pretension, as has been supposed, of universal, encyclopædic

"Uni-
versity" a
Corpor-
ation.

study; it might busy itself with arts and theology (as at Paris) or with law (as at Bologna). The word means simply a corporation or organisation of any sort. The phrase *Noverit universitas vestra* in a medieval deed is nothing but the forerunner of the modern "Know all of you"; it might be addressed equally to the chapter of a cathedral church or to a body of merchants in a town. The special meaning only came with time. At Paris it was the teachers, at Bologna the students, who organised themselves for their own protection; and they were spoken of in the aggregate as the *universitas magistrorum* or *scholarium*. By an easy transition the *universitas* was used by itself to designate the organisation, but the proper name for the University, considered as a seat of study, was not *universitas*, but *studium*.

The Uni-
versity of
Oxford.

The migratory habits of medieval students have already been referred to. They were hardly checked by the formation of more and more permanent places of education. It was possible for students to leave their country, or to quit their school and remove to another land, for the universal use of the Latin language made any famous school of the Middle Ages international in a sense in which no modern school or university can be; and it is likely that the University of Oxford itself took its rise from a migration of a large body of English scholars at Paris about 1167. There is no evidence to connect the University of Oxford with any conventual school, or the students of that University with the disciples of any of the previous teachers whose work is recorded in that place. Theologians like Theobald of Étampes and Robert Pullan, and the lawyer Vacarius left, so far as is known, no tradition either of teachers or learners. It is of a sudden, about 1170, that we find at Oxford the beginnings of a population of students, and tradesmen whose dealings imply such a population; and from these students grew up the University. About 1186 Gerald of Wales asserted that he read his "Topography of Ireland" "before a vast concourse at Oxford, where the clergy in England chiefly flourished and excelled in clerkly lore." Still, until past the end of the twelfth century, Paris remained the school to which Englishmen preferred to go for the higher ranges of their education.

Among the earlier English scholars on the Continent after

PAGE OF MS. PROBABLY WRITTEN BY ADELARD.
(Eton College Library.)

English Scholars Abroad: Adelard.

the Conquest, Adelard of Bath claims the first place (p. 500). He belongs to the beginning of the twelfth century, before the Paris schools had attained their undisputed supremacy, and his studies in France are said to have been carried on at Tours and Laon. He is one of the earliest English travellers, and made acquaintance not merely with Spain, Sicily, and Greece, but also with the remoter regions of the Mohammedan world. That he learned the Greek language is doubtful, but it is certain that he drew from Arab sources a knowledge of physical science, to which the scholars of his time were strangers. In this Arabic learning he stands almost alone, but his studies in philosophy and dialectic do not seem to have profited by it, though in his day the works of Aristotle in their entirety were accessible only in Arabic translations. It was not until a later generation that they passed from the Arabic into common currency among Latin scholars.

John of Salisbury.

John of Salisbury was, perhaps, fifty years Adelard's junior. Like him, he went to France, to gain admittance to a tradition of learning which had no counterpart in England. His first master, on the hill of Sainte Geneviève, in the southern suburb of Paris, was Peter Abelard. From him, in 1136, he took his first lessons in dialectics. Later he removed to Chartres, where he entered into a field of humanistic scholarship which had been planted there by Bernard Silvester, and had grown up under his successors at the cathedral school, Gilbert de la Porrée and William of Conches. The philosophy of Chartres was Realist, but it was not in its philosophy that its chief distinction lay, but in its philology in the old and large sense of the word. " We are," said Bernard, " as dwarfs mounted on the shoulders of giants, so that we can see more and further than they ; yet not by virtue of the keenness of our eyesight, nor through the tallness of our stature, but because we are raised and borne aloft upon that giant mass." The study of classical antiquity was to him the indispensable basis of all true education. The Latin authors were to be read, not merely for their language, but for their sense. The style of different authors was compared in order that the pupil might find out for himself the qualities which make style. Nor was the value of the classics exhausted by their literary interest. Bernard was wont to use every art of illustration to bring out their hidden

meaning and make their study an ethical as well as an intellectual discipline.

The noble influence of the School of Chartres was soon
lost in the restless competition of the dialectical movement,
but it held its power through life over the mind of John of
Salisbury, who, after once more plunging into the dialectic
stream at Paris, decided that logic, helpful as it was as an
aid to other studies, by itself remained feeble and barren, and
incapable of yielding the fruit of true wisdom. On his return
to England he became secretary to Archbishop Theobald and
his successor St. Thomas, whose exile for six years he shared.
A theologian and ecclesiastic beyond reproach, John was also
by far the most learned man of his time, and his writings
reflect admirably the spirit he had caught from the humanists of Chartres, in which city as bishop he ended his years
in 1180. Through a career of unceasing activity he maintained the scholar's tastes and habits and quick curiosity.
The disciple of Abelard, he divined a middle course between
the accepted tenets of Realism and the theological perils
which underlay the qualified Nominalism of his master.
With his mature and all-embracing learning he was able to
assimilate the best elements of the philosophical discussions
of his day, and reject their eccentricities and excesses. He
has the virtues of the humanists of the fifteenth century,
but he is free from their vices. Imbued as he is with the
classical spirit, no man was ever less disposed to revive the
intellectual or moral code of paganism. He would choose to
be judged before all things as a divine, and his theology was
unquestionably based upon an extensive Patristic learning.
Sound as it was, its rigour was tempered not only by his
devotion to the Platonic tradition, which he took as he
received it, filtered through the teaching of many, but also
by that calm moderation of judgment which marked alike
his public life and the books into which he poured the
abundance of his thought. Nevertheless later generations
must be forgiven for judging him first as a scholar, for it is
his scholarship which distinguishes him from others to whom
his theology was common. His classical reading surpassed in
depth and range that of any writer of the Middle Ages. He
was always on the search for new manuscripts of his favourite

authors, having transcripts made, and even translations from the Greek. It is likely that to his energy we owe the first introduction to medieval students of the later books of Aristotle's "Organon." His correspondence is full of questions and points of classical interest. He was the literary adviser of all scholars, the central figure of the learning of his day.

Other Scholars of the Twelfth Century

Between John of Salisbury and even the most cultivated of his contemporaries there is a wide interval. Yet the record of English teachers and writers is a distinguished one, and their number daily increasing. Three of those whom John had known in his student years at Paris were of English birth—his masters, Robert of Melun and Robert Pullan (both authors of methodical compends of theology), and his friend, Adam of Petitpont. The second became a cardinal, the other two were rewarded by bishoprics at home. Later, among many more, Walter Map the satirist, afterwards Archdeacon of Oxford, and Gerald of Wales (p. 508), the cleverest and most unscrupulous critic of the life of his time, may be mentioned as English students at Paris. Those who proposed to study law, particularly archdeacons, thronged the schools of Bologna. King Henry II. himself was a pupil of the Chartres master, William of Conches, and all through his life was fond of reading and scholarly discussion; but it did not need his patronage

The Influence of Canterbury

to bring learning into favour. The Court of Canterbury, under Archbishop Theobald, formed a rallying-point for scholars as well as a nursery of prominent churchmen. It was Theobald who brought over the Italian Vacarius to give lectures in his house on Roman law, and these continued until they were forbidden by King Stephen. Here were trained the future Archbishops Thomas and Roger of Pont l'Evêque; John, Bishop of Poitiers and Archbishop of Lyons; Ralph of Sarr, Dean of Rheims. John of Salisbury himself was for many years an honoured member and guide of the society.

Nor did the Court of Canterbury stand alone. Every great man had his household and his chapel, and at least the houses of prelates were rarely without their circle of scholarly life and activity. Bishop Stubbs has sketched an imaginary tour of a foreigner on a visit to England in the latter years of King Henry II. He describes the learned men whom he might meet, and the historical, legal, philosophical works, the verses and satires, on which they were or had been engaged. The list is an astonishing one. " So far as books were concerned, there was such a supply of writers and readers as would be found nowhere else in Europe, except in the University of Paris itself." [1] The familiar names of John of Salisbury, Peter of Blois, Walter Map, Gerald of Wales, and the whole series of historians whose writings make the record of the second half of the twelfth century perhaps the best-known period of English history in the Middle Ages, are but samples of a type of culture that was universal in England; when in literary matters men talked and thought in Latin; when they read and studied widely and not without criticism, and wrote (unless they wished to be obscure) excellent Latin prose; and when their verses were only disappointing if they challenged comparison by the adoption of classical metres, their rhythmical poems having a vigour and fresh originality altogether their own.

Such, in outline, was the condition of learning in England at the time of the birth of the University of Oxford. In the next century it was profoundly modified by the growth of that University, by the extended knowledge of the works of Aristotle maturing the philosophy of the schools, and by the energy thrown into intellectual work by the newly founded and rival orders of friars.

IN the long chain of events which makes up the history of a people, no one link is, in strict truth, more essential to the final result than any other; and yet from time to time events do occur which seem to sum up in themselves the character and tendencies of much that has gone before, and which, because they easily attract popular attention, are convenient termini for the historian. Such links are spoken of as critical. A crisis of this nature is marked in our history by the 14th of October, 1066, when the battle of Senlac was fought, and the old heroic thegnhood of England—which had been celebrated by many a bard, from the singers of the deeds of Beowulf down to him who sang the death of Byrhtnoth—fell before the knightly chivalry of Normandy. Harold and his trusty men, falling one by one upon the hill above Hastings, slowly but inevitably

H. FRANK HEATH.
Literature.

---

[1] Stubbs : "Seventeen Lectures," pp. 145–154.

crushed by the better method and equipment of their Norman foe, are as clearly typical of the inevitable fall of Germanic civilisation before the Romance in the eleventh and twelfth centuries as the victories of Crécy and Poitiers mark its rally in the fourteenth.   The Norman Conquest was no cataclasm in our history, for it was a sure outcome of the weakened national life under Edward the Confessor and his immediate forerunners; yet it introduced so much that was new into England, and so largely changed the direction of development in the old, that at first sight we seem confronted by a break in continuity.   This is, however, more apparent than real, and we shall find the old methods in literature living on, though modified in form and no longer on the surface of the stream, but almost submerged by the flow of the new current. We must remember, too, that the substitution of a Norman for an English nobility, and the expulsion of the English from the higher ranks of the priesthood—the chief patrons, connoisseurs, and producers of the national literature—resulted in a very marked reduction in the amount of work produced and in a growing carelessness about the preservation of the old MSS., which the new abbots and bishops could not read and therefore despised.

At the same time the English priests and monks who were left in office after the change of dynasty remained the chief defenders of the English element against the Crown; and as their secular patrons had disappeared, we find that the bulk of the vernacular literature in this period consists of religious works on Latin models.   It is not till after the middle of the thirteenth century that the English made any attempt to rival the Normans in manner of life, for up to that time their whole energies were absorbed in the struggle for national existence, and in consequence it is not till after that date that we find any serious attempt to follow them in such a detail as literary excellence.   Leaving, then, for the present any nearer view of works written during this time in the mother tongue, we shall first consider what the new elements were which the Normans introduced.

It is to be remembered that these people were Germanic in origin, Danes or Scandinavians, like those who had harried and settled in England since the eighth century.   They had settled

Norman French Poetry.

in the North of France, had rapidly won recognition for themselves from the French king, and with more startling rapidity had adopted the language and culture of their new country.[1] They were a people of extraordinary earnestness and intensity, with a power seldom equalled of assimilating and making their own what was best in their surroundings. Withal, they were intensely practical; their motto was "Deeds not Words," and they had none of the emotional excitability which we have

A PASSAGE FROM THE CHANSON DE ROLAND (MS. Digby, 23).
(*Bodleian Library, Oxford.*)

learnt to associate with the modern French character. It is, then, only to be expected that the art and literature of such a people should reflect the national character. And so, in truth, it does. When the victory of Senlac came to be sung, it was not by an Englishman, in the long alliterative line which had told of the struggle against the Danes at Maldon, but by a man of Jersey named Wace, who, in syllabic measure, as was that of

[1] The grandchildren of the warriors who had conquered Rouen under Rollo in 912 had forgotten the language of their forbears.

32

the "Chanson de Roland,"[1] told how, as the Norman lines
moved up the hill to the attack—

> " Taillefer, qui mult bien chantout
>   Sor un cheval qui tost alout
>   Devant le duc alout chantant
>   De Karlemaigne e de Rollant[2]
>   E d'Oliver e des vassals
>   Qui morurent en Rencevals."
>   *Roman de Rou*, ll. 8035–40.

These few lines can teach us much about the changes which
that battle inaugurated. They show us that Norman-French,
the Court language, became, at least to some extent, a literary
language—the medium used by poets who appealed to the
barons and the princes of the Church as their public. They
show us that the French national epic verse was a measure of
short rhymed couplets—not based on a rhythmical system, like
the Old English, but with lines of eight syllables, four of which
were accented—a form of verse which was adopted in English
in the thirteenth century. And, still more significantly, they
show us how different was the Norman poet's method from that
of his Old English predecessor. In this poem of the " Roman
de Rou," and even more markedly in the earlier " Chanson de
Roland," we see all the severe simplicity characteristic of the
Norman race. The narrative is simple and straightforward,
leading the reader on from point to point, with none of that
tendency to shift the point of view and to repetition which
makes it difficult for the Old English poet to advance in his
story. The epithets may sometimes seem wanting in power and
originality, but at least they are never far-fetched, as those of
the Old English poet too often were. His simplicity and somewhat narrow horizon save the French poet from all " conceits,"
and restrict him to an even sparer use of metaphor and simile
than the English poet allowed himself. What the French epic
lost in variety of treatment, it gained in unity of composition
and firmness of outline, whilst passages like that describing the
death of Roland[3] are unsurpassed for power of conception and

---

[1] The oldest surviving MS. of this great French epic is one written by a
Norman settled in England, in a Norman dialect.

[2] This must refer to some old ballad of Roland, for the "Chanson de
Roland " was not written in a form adapted for singing.

[3] " Song of Roland," ll. 2375–96.

heroic passion, and scarcely excelled in the grim earnestness of the battle-scenes by anything in the whole range of Old English poetry. Of the Norman-French poets in England Wace is the typical representative. Without the depth of thought or heights of passion to be seen in the " Chanson de Roland," his laconic logical method, his smooth verses, and clear, temperate, and not ungraceful diction, reflect the practical, serious, and cultured nature of the Norman race. His work, however, is no longer national epic, which the " Chanson de Roland," in spite of romantic contaminations (such as Saracens, reliques, etc.), undoubtedly is. The " Roman de Rou " is Romance, which name implies less earnestness, less characterisation, more sentiment, and more room given to the trappings and mere machinery of the story. All this it will be necessary to remember when we come to deal with English work produced under Norman-French influences.

It was, however, the practical side of the Norman character which was naturally most prominent at first, and the bulk of the literature produced after the battle of Senlac dealt with either religious or scientific or historical subjects. These books, being intended for instruction, were written in the universal language of scholarship—Latin—and the large majority dealt with the third of the three branches of learning mentioned.

Among the religious works of this time were Archbishop Lanfranc's " Liber Scintillarum " [1] (*c.* 1080), dealing with the doctrine of Transubstantiation; Anselm's " De Incarnatione Verbi," " De Voluntate," and " De Concordia Præscientiæ et Prædestinationis," etc.—a work of great depth. [2] A large number of Lives of the Saints were also written, one of which, the " St. Malchus " (*c.* 1120) of Reginald of Canterbury, is interesting because it is written in leonine hexameters. [3] Laurence of

Religious Literature.

---

[1] " Book of Sparks."]

[2] " Of the Incarnation of the Word," " Of Will," and " Of the Harmony of (Divine) Foreknowledge with Predestination."]

[3] " Leonine" verses (hexameters or elegiacs) are those in which the last word rhymes with the word just preceding what is technically called the " cæsura," or division of a metrical foot between two words, at the middle of the line : *e.g.*:

" Hæc sunt in *fossa* | Bædæ venerabilis *ossa*."

The invention is attributed to one Leo, or Leonius, a canon of the Benedictine order in the 12th century.]

Durham wrote a Bible history called "Hypognosticon"[1] (c. 1150) in graceful Latin distichs; and the historian, Henry of Huntingdon, who also wrote lyric and didactic verse, produced eight books of Epigrams.[2] In this last kind of writing Godfrey of Winchester (died 1107) was the most skilled stylist at that time.

Science. The most famous man of science of the day was Adelard[3] (p. 492) of Bath, a keen and bold thinker, deeply read in the science of the Arabians. He translated Euclid, and wrote a number of treatises, among which were "Quæstiones Naturales," a book of physical science, and "De Eodem et Diverso,"[4] an allegorical argument for reason instead of authority as the final appeal.

History. When we turn to the historical works, it is not so easy to obtain a clear general view in any moderate space. We shall find, on the one hand, that under this head we must take into view productions both in Norman-French and in English, besides those in Latin, which, it is true, form the large majority. On the other hand, there are at least five different kinds of historical writing to be distinguished, and in dealing with the last of these we shall find ourselves in a domain where the books have far more interest and worth as literature than as science.

The various kinds of historical writing which should be distinguished are (1) biography, (2) history proper, (3) chronicles, (4) annals, and (5) pseudo-history. To which of these classes any particular work rightly belongs, the title used by the author is often little guide—and, indeed, the same work may be in one part little more than biographical, in another a chronicle, in a third no better than annals, and in a fourth mere pseudo-history. Under history proper must be understood a work of art which attempts to set forth events in their deeper relations of cause and effect. The only two writers who did work worthy of this name in the period were William of Malmesbury and his follower and disciple, William of Newburgh. Chronicles made

---

[1 He seems to have coined the word in the sense of "reminder," or "compendium;" it is a paraphrase of the Old and New Testament history.]

2 According to Leland, "De Scriptoribus Britannicis," p. 198.

3 The English form, which is seldom used, is Æthelward.

[4 "Of Identity and Difference."]

no attempt at selection or artistic arrangement, but gave a careful account of acts and an orderly arrangement of dates. " Imagines [1] Historiarum " they are called by Ralph de Diceto, quoting Cassiodorus. The English Chronicles and the " Gesta Regis Henrici II. et Ricardi I.," ascribed to Benedict of Peter-

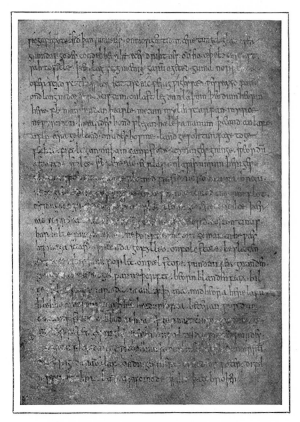

PAGE OF THE OLD ENGLISH CHRONICLE.
(Corpus Christi College, Cambridge.)

borough, are good examples. Another most important distinction between the chronicles or the annals, and history proper, lies in the fact that the author of the latter really used his authorities, throwing the whole work into his own literary form and diction,

[1] " Representations " : he adopts the title for the most important of his own works.]

THE ENGLISH CHRONICLE.

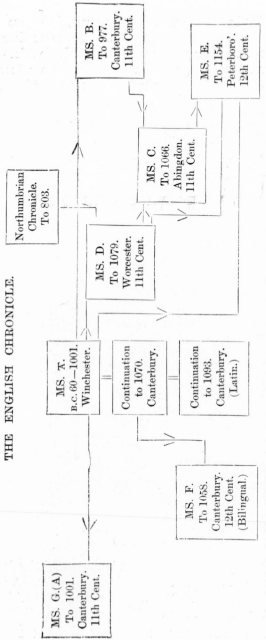

In this table double vertical lines show a continuation. The other lines show a continuation (through direct or indirect copies) for the younger one to which the lines are drawn. In each square stand the name of the MS. according to Prof. Earle's nomenclature, the date of the last entry, and the place and time at which it was written. If nothing is said about the language, it is in English. MS. E, the last to be discontinued, is important from 1066 to 1154, the date of the last entry. MS. 𝔸, now in CCC. Camb. (No. CLXXIII.), is the original of MS. G.(A), copied at Canterbury, and the basis of MSS. B, D, and E. MS. G.(A) is in the Cotton Library (Otho B. XI.), and was destroyed in the fire of 1731, except the entries for 837–71. *Cf.* Earle, "Two of the Anglo-Saxon Chronicles Parallel," 1865. His notation has been used for this table.

whilst the chroniclers and annalists were never original, except in describing contemporary events, copying for the earlier periods passages wholesale and word for word from the various books at their disposal. Sometimes they would compress, at other times enlarge, and often adopt as a whole, but with no claim to originality, except, as said, for contemporary events. It will be easily seen that the history, being an artistic work, produced in accordance with some theory of events, and dealing with them from this point of view, is not of such permanent value to the future historian as the chronicle, which only recorded facts in an orderly way. As literature, however, the history ranks higher than the chronicle, and its value is as permanent as that of any work of art. Annals are imperfect chronicles, mere jottings of events without any attempt at connecting them. Such are the two continuations written at Canterbury of the Winchester Chronicle. (*Cf.* Table on opposite page.)

By pseudo-history must be understood the skilful romancing under the guise of history introduced by Geoffrey of Monmouth, and continued by his translators and adapters down to Robert of Gloucester (in the earlier part of his chronicle) towards the end of the thirteenth century. There was, of course, a good deal of pseudo-history—in the form of legends, miracles, pure invention, etc.—incorporated into the historical works of writers before Monmouth. The pseudo-Nennius, his chief source, so far as he had any, is a good example. In the same way Monmouth's history of the Britons was afterwards accepted as historical material by uncritical writers like Henry of Huntingdon and the writer whose MS. Walter of Coventry used; but these are not, therefore, pseudo-historians. The proportion of truth can alone decide under which category any particular work falls. **Pseudo-History.**

It will be impossible here to do more than mention in detail the most important historical works of this time.

At the very outset we see in the continuations of the Old English Chronicle of Winchester [1]—which were made in the abbeys of Canterbury, Abingdon, Worcester, and Peterborough—an evidence of the continuity of prose-literature in the mother-tongue, at any rate down to 1154; [2] for, with the exception of **The Old English Chronicle.**

---

[1] Commonly called the Anglo-Saxon Chronicle.
[2] The Peterborough, the longest continuation, ends at this date. Each of

the bilingual version made at Canterbury (MS. F) and the second continuation of MS. A, they are all written in English alone.

Other Histories.   One of these continuations (that of Worcester), together with the " Chronicon Universale " [1] of Marianus Scotus, a monk of Fulda in Germany, Asser's " Life of Alfred," and Bede's " Ecclesiastical History" were the chief sources of information for Florence of Worcester's " Chronicon ex Chronicis," extending to the year 1117, which afterwards received two continuations of much less value, bringing it down to 1295. Of more value is Simeon of Durham's " Historia de Gestis Regum Anglorum " (to 1129). Eadmer of Canterbury, besides his " Historia Novorum " (1062–1122), wrote a valuable Life of Anselm in Latin; and ecclesiastical history found another exponent rather later in Ordericus Vitalis (1075–1143), author of the " Historia Ecclesiastica," in thirteen books, extending down to 1143.

Henry of Huntingdon (*c.* 1083–1155), poet, chronicler, and historian, was Archdeacon of Huntingdon, as his father, who was probably of Norman blood, had been before him. His " Historia Anglorum " [2] is not so valuable a work as that of his great contemporary, William of Malmesbury. The part of highest value is that dealing with the time in which he lived, and that immediately preceding it, of which he could learn through witnesses whom his position gave him many opportunities of questioning; but he cared more for attractive gossip than for accurate research, more for drawing a moral than for giving facts. He had ambition, literary taste, and intellectual quickness, but little perseverance, and less accuracy or judgment. If he wanders less from the subject than his contemporaries, it is because the material he used was scanty, and there was less temptation to stray. It used to be thought that he made use of many Old English popular songs; for in his description of battles in the fifth and sixth centuries he always adds picturesque details to the accounts in the English Chronicles, but

these abbeys had of course made direct or indirect copies of the old Winchester Chronicle, which they continued. For the relations of the various continuations to each other, and to the original source, with date of ending, time of writing, etc., *cf.* Table on p. 502.

[1] Not to be confused with the " Chronica Mariani Scoti," a later work.

[2] There were five editions of this work, the last of which brought the account down to the death of Stephen.

close investigation shows that he drew on his imagination for
these. He found Old English of even the tenth century hard
to translate, and makes astounding mistakes in rendering the

PAGE OF MS. PROBABLY WRITTEN BY WILLIAM OF MALMESBURY.
(*Lambeth Palace Library*, No. 224.)

" Battle of Brunanburh." He is important in the development of
historical writing as the last translator of the English Chronicles
and the first to accept Welsh tradition and romance without

question—a bad precedent.[1] The epigrams occurring in the history are probably from his hand, and the eleventh and twelfth books are wholly poetical.

William of Malmesbury (1095 to about 1143) was a south-country man, monk and librarian at Malmesbury, and, like William of Huntingdon, of mixed race. He was the first writer in England since Bede who made any attempt to digest the mass of material at hand, and to produce, by connecting cause and effect, a symmetrical work of wide view and ripe conclusions. The writers before him were mere chroniclers, with no conception of an articulated history. He was a man of sound judgment and cultured taste, and in consequence shows great love for delineation of character. He has considerable power of tracing the tendencies of important events and the development of political institutions. He is wonderfully broad-minded and free from party-feeling, in sympathy with Normans and English alike, while his work is made bright by humour and sharply pointed remarks. His " Gesta Regum Anglorum " in its third edition brings the history down to 1128 ; but the fifth book, as well as his " Historia Novella " (to 1142), commenced in 1140 as a sequel to the " Gesta Regum," are little more than rough drafts, intended, had life lasted, to be re-written and re-arranged. He also wrote a Life of Aldhelm, and seventeen other works.

William of Newburgh (1136–1208), who emulated the methods of Malmesbury, wrote an " Historia Rerum Anglic-arum " (from the Conquest to 1198), a trustworthy work. Except the first few pages, the whole is devoted to his own time, but it is not so completely original as was once thought. He clearly made use of Simeon of Durham, Henry of Hunting-don, the " Itinerarium Regis Ricardi " of Richard the Canon, and a lost work of Anselm the chaplain.

Giraldus Cambrensis or Gerald de Barri (1147–1223), sur-named Silvester (the Savage), a strong and passionate Welshman of Pembrokeshire, was many-sided, with great power of observa-tion and clear thought, but not free from vanity or superstition. He wrote on theology, politics, topography, history, and on himself in his " De Gestis Giraldi Laboriosis." His other works

---

[1] He copied at Bec in 1139 an extract from Geoffrey of Monmouth, which formed the subject of his epistle to Warine, the second of three incorporated in the eighth book of his history.

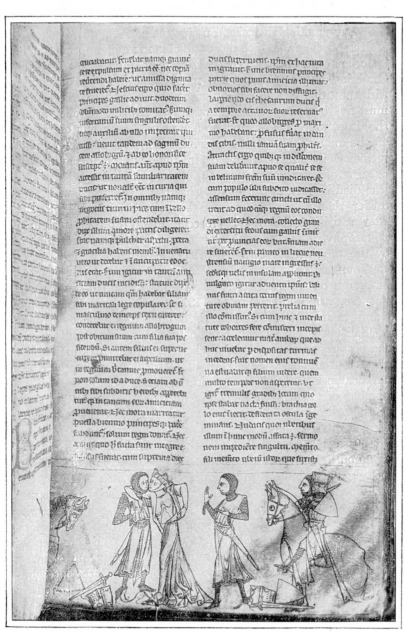

PAGE FROM GEOFFREY OF MONMOUTH'S "HISTORY OF BRITAIN."
(*Clare College, Cambridge.*)

are " Expugnatio Hiberniæ," an account of Henry II.'s conquest of Ireland, followed by a most valuable mine of information for historians called " Topographia Hiberniæ "; also a " Topographia Cambriæ," and a satire on the monks and the Papal authority with the title " Speculum Ecclesiæ."   Such satire on the Church must not be taken as indicating any active desire for reform— the times were not yet ripe for a Wycliffe—it is but one aspect of the melancholy and complaining tone so characteristic of medieval literature.   Similar in tone and tendency is the opening of the " Polycraticus " of John of Salisbury (b. c. 1120), who died in 1180 as Bishop of Chartres.   This work, which was earlier than Gerald's, appeared between 1156 and 1159, and, after satirising the Court, proceeds to lay down a system of philosophy, learnedly reviewing those of the classical thinkers by the way, in a lively, well-written style (p. 492).

Younger than John of Salisbury, less refined and learned, but more outspoken, witty, and worldly, though of high moral purpose, was Walter Map (c. 1137 to c. 1196), the friend and countryman of Gerald de Barri.   Under the influence of John of Salisbury, he gave a circumstantial account, full of the sharpest satire, of the Court and society in his day in his " De Nugis Curialium." [1]   Several Latin satirical poems, such as the " Apocalypsis Goliae," [2] " Praedicatio," and " Confessio," and a number of twelfth-century Latin and French romances,[3] some of them dealing with the Graal and Arthurian legends, have been ascribed to him.

These legends were first collected in England by Geoffrey of Monmouth, Bishop of St. Asaph (d. 1154), who, in his serious-looking " Historia Regum Britanniæ " (written 1132–1135), combined the Franco-Breton form of the Arthurian legend with the more historic Welsh version, connecting his hero, who was really of North British origin, with the Welsh saint Kentigern, the founder of Glastonbury.   Merlin, the prophet of Vortigern's Court, was, in the same way, a compound of many traditions.   To Geoffrey we owe the stories of Gorboduc, Cymbeline, King Lear, and Sabrina.   The Welsh were flattered by

[1 " Of the Trivialities of Courtiers." This was also the sub-title of the " Polycraticus."]

[2 i.e. the vision of an unworthy bishop, Golias (goliard=glutton).]

3 The " Lancelot du Lac " is generally supposed to be his.

the Chauvinist spirit of the book, and the Normans were not
displeased at a man who painted the English in no favourable
light, whilst he gave to the whole all the local colour of Henry
II.'s chivalric Court. So popular was it, in spite of the sneering
attacks of William of Newburgh and Giraldus Cambrensis, that
less than fifteen years after its issue Alfred of Beverley made an
abridgment of it with a continuation to 1129, and about the
same time Geoffrey Gaimar wrote an Anglo-Norman rimed
version, the " Estorie des Bretons," now lost, as sequel to which
came his " Estorie des Engleis " (to 1100). His version of Monmouth was soon cast into the shade by the more popular work
of Wace (b. 1124), the " Geste des Bretons "—or " Brut d'Engle-
terre," [1] as it is often called—written in 1155. The work, which
is in rimed octosyllabic couplets, with the exception of a long
section near the commencement, of later origin, in Alexandrines,
introduces the theme of the "Table Round," an element found
only in the Breton versions. Of Wace's other works the best
known is the " Gestes des Normans " or " Le Roman de Rou,"
spoken of already. Slowly the enchanting " lies " won their
way, and gained credence even with the English, until the
attractive but insulting story was rendered into English for the
first time by Layamon, the western priest, living by Sabrina's
stream. The " Brut " (*c* 1205) of the Areley priest is more than
twice as long as Wace's, on which it is based, with, however,
only ninety words of Norman-French origin in the whole poem.

This comparative purity of the mother-tongue leads us to **The Devel-**
notice that the influence of Norman-French upon it was rather **opment of**
of a negative than positive character. Some few sounds were **English.**
modified, such as the gutturals, which were palatalised, and one
or two new ones were introduced ; but otherwise the result was
only to hasten developments along lines which can be traced
before the Conquest, but which were allowed free scope directly
the old literary dialect of Wessex, with its controlling influence,
was destroyed. After the Conquest an increasing centrifugal
tendency is noticeable, which was not to be checked till Chaucer
came. The verse of the Brut is only another proof of the continuity of the old tradition, especially in the west country ; for
it is but a popularised form of the Old English alliterative line,

---

[1] It was Wace's book which served as basis for the greatest literary
creation of this cyclus, the " Parzifal " of Wolfram von Eschenbach.

with much greater freedom in the laws of alliteration, and, when alliteration is absent, a use of middle and end rime. This latter adornment, which had been sparely used even before the Conquest, caused the original long line to be thought of as a short rimed couplet of irregular form. The old verse in purer form is to be found in a group of Lives of the Saints written about the same time, of which the two best examples are "St. Margaret" and "St. Juliana." Like these, written in the south, but very different and much more important, was a sermon in verse called "A Moral Ode," which may date back in its earliest form

English Verse.

A PASSAGE FROM THE MORAL ODE.
(*Trinity College, Cambridge.*)

to the first half of the twelfth century. The poem is almost passionate in its depth of feeling, and is noble in tone, but the point of view is that of the Latin Church, not that of the old Germanic heroes. The simple, clear language shows Norman influence, and the verse is the iambic septenar (katalectic tetrameter) learnt from the Latin hymnology, and traceable to the measure of Terence and Aristophanes.[1] This metre, without

---

[1] A comparison of the following lines—respectively from Terence's "Andria," a famous mediæval drinking song, and the first line of the Moral Ode—will show the same *rhythm* in each :—

"Per omnes tibi adjuro deos nunquam eam me deserturum."
                                      Andria, IV. 2, ii.

the coupled rimes of the "Moral Ode," is found again in a Lincolnshire version of the Church homilies by an Austin friar named Orrm, who called his work the "Orrmulum" (*c.* 1205). The book is quite without literary value, but the careful distinction made in the autograph MS. between long and short vowels (by doubling the consonant after a short vowel) and between the various pronunciations of the letter " g,"[1] makes it of great value to the philologist. The septenar found its way after the middle of the thirteenth century into lyrical verse, and was a favourite form for "Robin Hood" and other popular

A PASSAGE FROM THE ORRMULUM.
(*Bodleian Library, Oxford.*)

ballads, influencing, together with the French Alexandrine, the old alliterative line in its popular developments.

The English prose-writing of this time is wholly religious, **English Prose.** and the most important and interesting example is the "Ancren Riwle" ("Rules for Nuns"), written (about 1210) for three sisters in a nunnery at Tarente in Dorsetshire. Besides the actual rules of conduct, the book contains much allegory and a

"Mihi est propositum · in taberna mori."
"Ich eom nu eldre thanne ich waes · a wintre and eac a lare."
Moral Ode, 4. **1.**
There are seven beats in each line, and hence the name.
[1] *Cf.* Professor Napier, *Academy*, March 15th, 1890.

remarkable description of the mystical love of Christ for the soul, and of the soul for Him, in the manner of the chivalric romance. This erotic note[1] in the religious literature we shall trace in the lyrics of a rather later time. Meantime in the secular domain the French epic was making itself more and more felt, despite the warnings of good men like Thomas de Hales, who saw in their stories the world and the flesh, if not the devil.

A. L. SMITH. Trade and Industry.

THE agricultural system is portrayed for us in outline at the beginning of this period by Domesday Book (p. 340, *seq.*), and in full detail by the Hundred Rolls. The latter display its completed form at the close of the thirteenth century, just before the changes which began the transformation to the

The Agricultural System.

system of modern times. The nature of the Domesday evidence is best indicated in the instructions to the Commissioners as recorded in the Ely Book. Their inquiries and the answers to them show that England was already divided up into manors; each manor contained both demesne (the lord's own land) and villein holdings. Villeins made up the great bulk of the population. Free tenants were scarce, save in the eastern counties and the eastern midlands; and it is more natural to suppose that they represented a survival of the ancient freedom in these districts, invigorated by Danish settlements, than that they had only lately arisen (*cf.* p. 302), and that serfdom had been the normal state of Saxon England. The number of slaves returned is small—some 25,000; and those chiefly in the south-west. The villeins proper, with a normal holding of a yardland (thirty acres) or half a yardland, are distinguished from the lower villein class of cottiers, *bordarii* and *cotarii*, holding sometimes only a cottage and garden, sometimes a cottage and a few acres, not often more than five, in the common arable fields. The normal villein would contribute a pair of oxen to the common plough; the cottier had no oxen of his own. The lord's plough of eight oxen, which tilled the demesne, was worked by the services of the villeins; these, moreover, had often to do service with their own ploughs and oxen. This all implies a great number of cattle, for whom there was ample rough pasture.

---

[1] *Cf.* also "The Wohunge [wooing] of ure Louerd," "The Wohunge of ure Leudi," "A god Oreisun of oure Louerd," etc.

Hay meadows were comparatively rare and valuable. Woodland was plentiful, and was measured by the number of swine it could feed. It has been estimated that as much as 5,000,000 acres were under cultivation, about five-twelfths of the present cultivated area. This would tally with the population, which may be fairly estimated at about 2,000,000. It would also agree

THE ELY BOOK: ETHELWOLD AND KING EDGAR.
(Trinity College, Cambridge.)

with the calculation that nearly one-half of the cultivated area was devoted to wheat, and that the production of wheat averaged about one-quarter to the acre. Besides leguminous crops, a good deal of barley and oats and some rye was grown; while the absence of root-crops or any systematic manuring implies a great extent of fallow, perhaps nearly one-third of the total arable area.

It is not easy to realise how essentially this whole arrangement of rural life differed from that of modern times. The

33

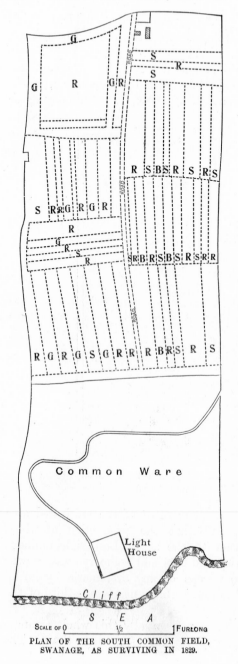

PLAN OF THE SOUTH COMMON FIELD,
SWANAGE, AS SURVIVING IN 1829.

great mass of the agricultural population are now landless; in the eleventh and twelfth, and, indeed, down to the seventeenth and eighteenth centuries, they were landholders. The class of farmers, whether on leases or yearly agreements, was then very uncommon, except on some Church estates. The relation between gentry and peasantry is now a mainly economic relation; in that age it was first and foremost a social and political relation. The villein must sit in his lord's court of justice, and follow him to war, as well as till his lands. They were bound together by mutual obligations; the lord could no more dispossess him, whatever unreal maxims the contemporary law-books chose to enounce, than he could shake off his lord and escape from the manor. But perhaps the most striking feature of all to a modern mind is the universal prevalence of community in cultivation, if not in ownership. A village was, indeed, one Communal Husban-dry. large common farm. To take the most typical case, each of the three arable fields was " open "; it was not enclosed or broken up into severalties, but only roughly marked off by turf baulks into acre strips, of which every fifth strip might be the lord's, every tenth the parson's, aud so on. The whole field would be ploughed, harrowed, sowed, and reaped, by the joint labour of all the holders. Each contributed, according to customary rules, his share of the labour, the oxen, the cost of the plough. A villein's holding of thirty acres might thus consist of thirty or forty detached strips scattered over a whole parish. Such a system was of course grossly wasteful; but it had grown up under needs with which economics have nothing to do. It was the natural outcome of a still ruder method of annual re-allotment of the arable strips; it was the expression of the old sense of kin-ship in the village community, and its cumbrousness was a determined effort to secure the absolute equality of each share. It must have had an immeasurable influence in silently moulding English character, drilling men into local self-government.

It is only within the last generation that Enclosure Acts Produc-tion: Prices Expenses have swept away almost the last of the " open " parishes. A few still remain. Fifty years ago they were still the majority. This singular tenacity perhaps implies that the system worked less badly than we should expect. No doubt, however, such a system helps to account for the low productivity of medieval agriculture. This and the imperfect means of communication and conveyance explain the great variations in prices which prevailed in neighbouring markets. There was evidently fre-quent local scarcity, even when there was no general bad season. But no fewer than nine years of dearth are recorded in the contemporary Anglo-Saxon Chronicle between 1070 and 1100. The only operation we hear much of for permanent improvement of the land was marling. On the other hand, orchards were common; a considerable quantity of native wine was made, and thirty-eight vineyards are mentioned in Domesday. Bee-keeping was universal, from the use of honey before sugar was known as a general mode of preserving food. Perhaps one of the greatest impediments to good husbandry was the great expense of iron. The cost of new irons to the plough is one of the chief items in bailiff's accounts in the thirteenth century; and to avoid this, wooden ploughs and harrows were often used, and the soil was in consequence scratched rather than ploughed up. In fact, there was little improvement in the art of agriculture till the Tudor period introduced a better rotation of crops, more thorough and varied use of manures, and the employment of horses instead of oxen. It must be remembered, however, that dairy produce and poultry were cheap and plentiful throughout the middle ages.

Changes between 1085 and 1250. The chief changes between Domesday Book and the middle of the thirteenth century can be best brought to view by selecting an instance from each of the chief documents which bridge over that interval.

In the Black Book of Peterborough 1125–8—to take the case of the first manor named in it—the normal holding of the villein was a virgate or "yardland" of thirty acres arable. Each villein has to plough in spring four acres for the lord. Each supplies two oxen to the plough-team, which was bound to be at the lord's call three days in winter, three in spring, one in summer. Moreover, each villein has to work for the lord three days a week, to pay a yearly toll of 2s. 1½d., a hen, and sixteen eggs. The cottagers, each holding five acres, render work of one day a week, besides twice a year making malt for the lord's use, and paying a 1d. for each goat using the pasture. On this manor there seem to have been 1,253 acres of arable held by forty-three villeins and eight cottagers; some 400 acres of arable farmed by the lord through a bailiff; a few dozen acres of valuable hay-meadow; a mill paying rent of 20s. a year; and an indeterminate but probably large area used for rough pasturage of the cattle, sheep, pigs, and goats, belonging both to the lord and to the villagers. The lord's demesne was tilled by the compulsory services of his men superintended by the bailiff. This one manor may be taken as typical of the twenty-five which are enumerated in the survey, and which constituted the estate of the abbey. In a few of the manors are found "socmen"—that is, freeholders, whose holdings might be no larger than those of the villeins, but who would generally, instead of heavy services, pay a fixed and not heavy rent.

THE PRIORY MILL, CHRISTCHURCH, HANTS (MENTIONED IN DOMESDAY BOOK).

In the Boldon Book, a survey made in 1183 of the manors of the Bishop of Durham, the chief differences from the above are that the services of carrying the crops, cutting wood, etc., are commuted for money payments, and that the cottagers' holdings are often as much as twelve acres each. Sometimes the whole mass of services was commuted for a fixed annual payment to the lord; *e.g.,* " The villeins of Southbydyke hold the township at a rent, paying £5 a year for it, and finding 160 men to reap in autumn and thirty-six carts to cart the corn."

The " Domesday of St. Paul's " (1222) shows that, besides the services, each villein paid in money and in kind a few shillings yearly to the lord, and that the number of free tenants had largely increased since the Norman Conquest.

The Register of St. Mary's Priory, Worcester, early in the thirteenth century, shows some further incidents of villein tenure. They could not, without the lord's leave, sell ox or horse, send their sons away or make them clerks, give out their daughters in marriage, or grind corn except at the lord's mill; and on a villein's death the lord could seize his best chattel, and impose upon the heir a " fine " at discretion. After this date there are innumerable similar documents—inquisitions, surveys, extents, cartularies,[1] and manor rolls.

The towns.   The period of Norman and Angevin rule initiated a great and almost sudden outburst of life and growth in the English towns. It is true that the immediate effect of the Norman Conquest was to bring disaster to the towns. The number of burgesses enumerated in 1086, as compared with that recorded for the reign of Edward, shows a falling-off of one half (8,000 as against 17,000). The advent of a new Norman lord and the building of a stone keep roused the desperate resistance of the townsmen. In the consequent struggles their poor dwellings were cleared away to make room for the castle outworks, or were fired and wasted by accident or for punishment; and the town pined under the labour and the dues exacted by the new lord. " In this town there are 478 houses so wasted and destroyed that they cannot pay any tax." This Oxford entry in Domesday Book might be paralleled

[1 " Extents " are valuation lists for the purpose of taxation ; "cartularies," collections of charters.]

from nearly every borough. But the Norman, almost from the first hour of his coming, gave more than he took. In his train came extension of trade-routes, intercourse with Norman and Breton, Poitevin, Gascon, and Spanish ports. Foreign merchants flocked to London and Winchester, to Ipswich and Boston and Lincoln. Foreign craftsmen settled everywhere, and all the trades of the mason, the carpenter, the glass-maker, the workers in metals, must have received an immense stimulus from the castles, cathedrals, and abbeys which began to arise everywhere in the new architecture. What we hear of Chester must have been true of many boroughs. It had suffered in the first years of the new rule, but by 1086 had recovered itself. "When Earl Hugh got it, there were 205 houses less than in King Edward's time; it had been grievously wasted. Now there are as many as he found when he came." At any rate, this was true of the towns as a whole long before the end of Henry I.'s reign. To the industrial classes, indeed, any exactions by their Norman sovereigns, if heavy in themselves, were but light compared with the relief from the insecurity and anarchy of Anglo-Saxon days, when even the stronger kings vainly bewailed "the manifold and unrighteous fightings that are daily amongst us" (p. 340). Nor was security of inland trade all that their new rulers could give. A charter from him who was Duke of Normandy and Maine as well as King of England; still more, a charter from Angevin kings, whose writs ran from Berwick to Bayonne, could lay open a range of free trade hitherto unexampled. To be "quit and free from all tolls, dues, and customs, at fairs or otherwise, in all harbours throughout all my dominions, both the hither side and the further side of the sea, by land and by strand," gave new life to the fettered and crippled commerce of the country. Commercial growth led to heightened constitutional claims; and constitutional progress itself stimulated commercial growth. The freedom of the English towns grew out of their prosperity, and the most critical phase of their history thus falls within the period whose beginning and end respectively are marked by William I.'s charter granted to London, and the Great Charter extorted from John. This stage of their history was critical, because it determined the form which the municipal self-government should take. Hitherto the English borough had hardly been

Royal Charters.

differentiated from the rural township. If it were too large to be treated as a single township, it ranked as a group of townships—that is, a " hundred." " This borough in payment of dues quits itself as a hundred" is the Domesday formula. All townships, and even some hundreds, had fallen into the hands of a lord. The same feudalising process had affected the borough. Boroughs in the later Anglo-Saxon period either belonged to one or more lords or to the king. By the side of the old moot, perhaps often supplanting it, had arisen the lord's court, in which the chief burgesses sat as the lord's **The Guild** vassals. This feudal character was for a time accentuated by **System.** the new Norman lords, with their clear-cut theories of tenure, and their classification of townsmen with villein tenants. But the feudal aspect was soon to give way to the commercial. The " hanse" or guild began to appear in every considerable borough. These guilds were unions of the traders, for their own protection, for the regulation of trade, and, it must be added, for the exclusion of rivals. Without a royal charter they would be " adulterine" and liable to be broken up. But with a charter they could receive and enfranchise serfs, and impose their guild bye-laws on the whole borough. Thus Henry II. grants to the guild-merchant of Oxford that no one outside the guild shall do any trading in city or suburbs; to the Nottingham guild control of the cloth-dyeing trade is given for ten leagues around; to the Lincoln guild, general control of the whole body of traders in the county. Hitherto the boroughs had aimed at two privileges, and two only, beyond the general ratification of their old local customs. These two were: the right to try in their own borough courts all but a few excepted cases, and the right to arrive at a verdict by the ordeal instead of the foreign method of " wager of battle." But now, strong in the rapid growth of trade and the success of the guilds, the boroughs set to work to commute their taxes for a fixed sum, and to collect and pay this themselves into the Exchequer. This would oust the hated tyranny of the sheriff, and this was generally accomplished under Henry II., and still more under Richard I., " in whose eyes all things were saleable." This step was decisive at to the future town constitutions. It was necessarily the guild to whom the Crown sold this privilege, and not to the ancient borough-moot, nor

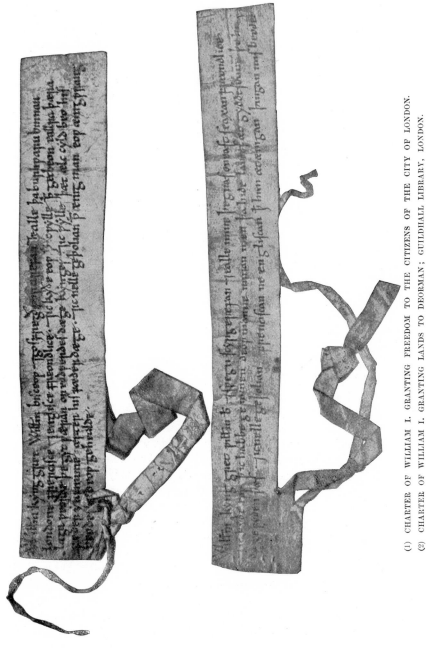

(1) CHARTER OF WILLIAM I. GRANTING FREEDOM TO THE CITIZENS OF THE CITY OF LONDON.

(2) CHARTER OF WILLIAM I. GRANTING LANDS TO DEORMAN; GUILDHALL LIBRARY, LONDON.

(By permission of the Library Committee to the Corporation of the City of London.)

to the court of vassals. These were now antiquated; the guild belonged to the new era. There is a curious illustration of the jealousy with which it was regarded in the language used by Richard of Devizes condemning the recognition in 1191 of the guild as the governing body of London: "What evils spring from these communes can be gathered from the saying about them, that they mean an upheaval of the rabble, a menace to the kingdom, and a lukewarmness in religion." The sign of this recognition was the allowing the borough to have its mayor. Thus the head officer of the guild became head of the town, the guild aldermen became his assistants, and the guildhall the headquarters of administration. This became common in John's reign; the other boroughs followed fast in the wake of London: *e.g.* Leicester got its "commune" in 1251. Fortunately, the boroughs still remained subject to the sheriff for certain purposes, such as "view of armour" and calling out of the militia, attendance before the royal judges on circuit, etc. Thus their position as part of the shire system was not lost — it was possible for them to sit in Parliament with the knights of the shire, instead of forming, as elsewhere in Europe, an estate apart; and to this was due the dual composition of our House of Commons and its unique indestructibility.

Craft-Guilds. While the merchant guild was becoming the governing body, the natural division of labour was at work to produce craft-guilds or associations of craftsmen, below the higher body and somewhat in rivalry with it. This rivalry was, it is true, far less marked than on the Continent. But still, a rule is often found in existence by the thirteenth century, that no artisan can belong to the merchant-guild. We know that as early as 1130 there were weavers' guilds in several of the larger towns, we find the merchants bribing John to revoke the weavers' charter, and the weavers buying it back again. After this date the craft-guilds succeeded in breaking down gradually the trade monopoly of the merchant-guild, and often in securing an independent jurisdiction for themselves.

The guild system, with all its restrictions, must not be judged by too narrow an application of modern economic canons. In an age when authority interfered everywhere, and when customers could do little to protect themselves, the guilds did much to inculcate a code of industrial morality; they came down severely upon short weights and measures, upon "shoddy" material and upon scamped workmanship. They also acted as benefit, insurance, and burial societies; and exercised social, educational, and even religious, functions, besides the regulation of hours of work, processes of manufacture, and wages and prices.

Much of the energy of English trading life was directed towards the exclusion of foreigners from the internal trade of the country. Till the thirteenth century the exports of England, still consisting almost wholly of raw materials, were in the hands largely of foreign traders. It was to the interest of the Crown to give, or rather to sell, wide privileges to these men. Early in Henry III.'s reign the Teutonic Hanse can be seen as a strong organisation resident in London within its own walled fortress—the Steelyard—on the Thames bank, with its common hall and refectory, its Masters, each with his suit of armour, and its gates closed at curfew. It had originated with the men of Cologne, but was amalgamated in the thirteenth century with the stronger Hanse identified chiefly with Lübeck and Bruges. A similar but rival organisation was the Hanse of the Netherlands. These bodies soon came to have branch establishments in the provincial centres. Even the less organised companies of merchants from Florence, Lucca, and Piacenza, when they appear in the twelfth century, making purchases of wool at Boston and Lynn, and doubtless bringing southern and eastern wares in exchange, have clearly some defined status and corporate rights.[1] A similar close connection with Genoa dates from the third Crusade. From Gascony, too, and from Lorraine came a large supply of wines. To meet the needs of this foreign trade, bills of exchange were introduced about 1200. But the great aim of English statesmanship was to secure a "balance of trade" for England in the form of silver. Henry of Huntingdon, in specifying the great cargoes of flesh and fish, wool, lead, and tin, that went to the Rhine, exults in the reflection that the Germans paid for these

Foreign Traders and Trade.

---

[1] A thirteenth-century list gives 177 monastic houses from which the Florentines drew their wool supplies.

in silver, and that in consequence the English currency was of pure silver. The same mistaken views led to prohibition of the export of corn. For contravening this, Richard I. burned some English ships caught at St. Valery, and the town itself, and hanged the shipmen.

Home Trade.

The internal trade of England depended chiefly on the great seasonal fairs. There were four such fairs a year at Cambridge. In 1189 it is mentioned that the Husting Court at London was suspended during the days that the annual fairs at Boston and Winchester were being held. During the seven days of St. Frideswide's fair at Oxford, the prior of that house had jurisdiction over the whole city. A court of " pie-powder " [1] dealt out summary " merchant's law " in such assemblages. All other trading in the town or district was generally suspended while the fair lasted. The wooden booths were assigned certain spaces, and arranged in streets according to their calling—goldsmiths' row, furriers' row, etc. The greatest of all these fairs was Stourbridge, near Cambridge (September 18th to October 9th). Here merchants from Hamburg, Bruges, and Strasburg, from Rouen and Bordeaux, and from Florence and Genoa, all met. The farm bailiffs came hither to buy their annual stores of pepper, of iron goods, and of tar ; and to dispose of wool and hides, cattle, corn, and hay. The manciples of Oxford colleges and distant abbeys came to buy the winter's provisions and stock of salt and spices, as well as Liège linen or Spanish wine, or furs from the Baltic, or Flemish cloth. A concourse like this, which covered a space half a mile square, shows that means of communication and routes of traffic were in very tolerable condition in the early Middle Ages. The dispersed character of the great lords' estates, and the flow of pilgrimage, helped to keep the roads good ; and that they were good is shown by diaries of journeys and expenses (*e.g.* from Oxford to Newcastle) ; by the moderate cost of carriage, even for heavy goods ; and, finally, by the frequency of inns. It was not unusual to have public or charitable funds set apart for maintenance of important bridges and roads ; besides that the common law laid this obligation on the parishes.

The Growth of London.

The rapidity with which trade and wealth were growing in this period may be measured by the case of London. In

[1 *Pieds poudrés,* "dusty feet," *i.e.* specially for visitors to the fair.]

Fitz-Stephen's contemporary description, written about 1174, its imports are gold and spices from Arabia, gems from Egypt, silks from India, furs from the northern lands, wines from France, and arms from Scythia. It had 139 churches. It had replaced Winchester as the capital: but its fighting force, given at 60,000 foot and 20,000 horse, must be reduced to perhaps one-tenth of those numbers. The citizens "ranked almost as nobles, for the greatness of their city." They elected their own sheriff and justices. They were, by royal charters, guaranteed their freedom of transit and of traffic, and their hunting rights in Chiltern, Middlesex, and Surrey. For the confirmation of these rights and the promise of the removal of weirs from the Thames and Medway they paid to King John £3,000 in 1199. It was the accession of London to the baronial side in May, 1215, that forced the king to sign the Great Charter. But London represented the high-water mark of municipal progress: few English towns of that age could have had a population above 10,000. The most prosperous were Exeter, Bristol, Winchester, **Other** and Southampton, in the south; Chester, in the north-west; **Towns.** Dunwich,[1] Norwich, and Lynn, in the eastern counties; Lincoln, Grimsby, York, Hull, and Newcastle, in the north. The coast towns were able to supply a fleet fairly numerous, though vessels of very small tonnage. Such a fleet was used by William I., in 1072 against Scotland, and by Henry I. in 1099 against his brother Robert. Henry II. had begun the creation of a royal navy, independent of forced levies of private shipping; so that though Richard I. was able to muster many galleys of his own, yet his large fleet was chiefly made of ships impressed or hired from his subjects. His reign supplies other evidence of the increasing wealth of the country; for his ransom was set at 150,000 marks, and Hoveden even declares that Hubert Walter informed the King that in two years there had been sent him from England 1,100,000 marks (about £750,000)—an incredible sum, being about twelve times the yearly revenue of Henry II. One thing is, however, clear—that England was already becoming, with the single exception of Italy, the wealthiest of European States, and without exception the best-ordered as well as the freest of all.

[1 Till 956 a cathedral town : since the fourteenth century gradually ruined by the encroachments of the sea.]

C. CREIGH-
TON.
Public
Health.

As an index of the miserable conditions of medieval life much has been made of the disease of leprosy. A good index of social misery it undoubtedly is, both for present and former times; but it is easy to overrate its importance. England in the Middle Ages was by no means the unhappy land of lepers which we might suppose from the attention given to those sufferers. Henry, Archdeacon of Huntingdon in the reign of Henry I., calls his country " Merry England " (*Anglia plena jocis*). The English, he says, were a free people, with a free spirit and a free tongue, and a still more liberal hand, having abundance of good things for themselves, and something to spare for their neighbours across the sea. Precisely those

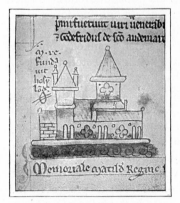

LEPER HOSPITAL, ST. GILES.
(*Corpus Christi College, Cambridge.*)

boisterous animal spirits, that very love of sports and jests, of good-fellowship and the pleasures of life, which marked the " average sensual man " and were the dominant national character, served to bring out in strong contrast the humility, the abasement, the penances mortifications, and morbid fancies of the religious few. As the history comes nearly all from ecclesiastics, we hear a good deal of the religious and morbid side of the national life ; and in that connection we hear much of lepers, who were the favourite objects of religious

A LEPER.
(*Trinity College, Cambridge.*)

care. The lepers were " Christ's poor," being named lazars, after Lazarus—indifferently the Lazarus whom Jesus loved, or the Lazarus who was laid at the rich man's gate full of sores.

David, King of Scots, the son of St. Margaret and of Malcolm
Canmore, was also Earl of Huntingdon, and founded a leper-
hospital there. Accordingly his biographer says of him
that he was received into Abraham's bosom beside Lazarus,
" whom he cherished." His sister Matilda, queen of Henry I.,
who founded the leper-hospital of St. Giles's, washed the feet of
lepers, believing that she was thereby washing the feet of Christ
Himself. The religious sentiment of the medieval world has
been contrasted with the joyous sentiment of paganism; but

A TWELFTH-CENTURY DISPENSARY
(Trinity College, Cambridge.)

it was in actual contrast with the boisterous workaday spirit
of its own time. It cared for those who were stricken, for
the helpless in the struggle; and it showered caresses upon
them, and treated them with morbid consideration or exaggerated devotion, just because these exercises of charity
afforded the relief and effusion that it needed in a hard and
cruel age.

The English leper-hospitals began to be founded after the
Conquest. Lanfranc, who held the see of Canterbury under
William of Normandy, built two hospitals—one for lepers, and
another for the sick poor in general. Several hospitals for
lepers date from the reign of Henry I., others were endowed by
Stephen, others under Henry II., and still others as late as the

reign of John, who, with all his odious qualities, was conspicuous among English monarchs as a patron of the lepers. The founders and benefactors were kings and queens, chivalrous nobles and pious ladies, bishops and abbots. The leper-houses were only a small fraction of all the charitable houses in England, perhaps a sixth or eighth part, and probably not more than fifty in all. One at Durham had accommodation for sixty lepers, men and women ; Matilda's hospital in St. Giles's Fields, outside London, had a chapel and hall for forty lepers, who must have slept elsewhere ; the hospital at Ripon, " for all the lepers of Richmondshire," had eighteen beds ; that of Lincoln had ten beds ; and the male leper-house of St. Albans Abbey had six beds. They were generally heavily staffed with ecclesiastics ; some were for leprous and non-leprous patients side by side, three or four of the former to six or eight of the latter ; others were for sick or " leprous " monks and priests, or for the same class when they " grew old, leprous, or diseased." As early as 1279 the leper-hospital of Stourbridge, near Cambridge, had been alienated from the leprous by the Bishop of Ely ; inquisitions in the reign of Edward III. showed that the leper-hospitals at Ripon, Oxford, and elsewhere, contained no lepers ; at St. Albans, for some years previous to 1349, only one, or two, or three of the six beds could find leprous occupants ; and in 1434 new statutes had to be made for the great Durham leper-hospital, by which it was provided that two beds should be reserved for lepers " if they can be found in these parts," in order to preserve the memory of the original foundation. In fact, even the few hospitals that were clearly designed, in whole or in part, for lepers were gradually diverted to other uses, and this, too, in some cases within living memory of their being founded ; and although that may have been owing in part to the avarice of the clergy, yet it must have been chiefly because there was no further use for them as leper-houses, or perhaps because there had been from the first something forced and unreal in the chivalrous movement which started them.

Not only did several of the leper-hospitals provide in their charters for a majority of non-leprous patients, but even those inmates that passed as leprous were a heterogeneous class of sufferers—from chronic or incurable sores, eruptions, tumours, and deformities. It is clear that the medical writers about the beginning of the fourteenth century knew true leprosy when they saw it, and that they had described it from actual observation; but it is also clear that "lepers" were immured on the word of persons who had no skill in diagnosis, and that the terms *lepra, leprosus,* and *lazar-house* came to have very elastic meanings. But even with all that comprehensiveness of diagnosis, the extent of "leprosy" in medieval Britain cannot be called great: there might have been a leper in a village here and there, one or two in a market town, a dozen or more in a city, a score or so in a whole diocese. Thus, in the records of the city of Gloucester, under date of 20th October, 1273, three persons are mentioned by name—a man and two women—as being leprous and as dwelling within the town, to the great hurt and prejudice of the inhabitants. The leper-hospital at Ripon, "for all the lepers in Richmondshire,"

PHYSICIAN AND PUPIL (MS. Harl. 1585).

made provision for eighteen. At no time in England was there leprosy to so great an extent as to make its ancient name of "Merry England" even a paradox. Leprosy is commonly supposed to come from bad food—semi-putrid fish or flesh; and in medieval times, when fresh food (except game for the lord or the poacher) was not to be had during many months of the year, and the salted food was often badly cured owing to the dearness of salt or the badness of it (the rock-salt of Cheshire was not mined until long afterwards), it is easy to understand that individuals here and there among the English may have fallen into leprosy, especially if they had acquired a taste for flesh or fish in a semi-putrid state, a taste which is widely spread among many savage or half-civilised and leprous

34

tribes at the present day. But the English have always had
a high standard in diet; they preferred to eat no bread

> " That beans in come,
> But of cocket or clerematyn, or else of clean whea
> Nor no piece of bacon, but if it be fresh flesh,
> Or fish fried or baked."[1]

More particularly they avoided rye-bread ("black bread"), which
was the staple food of the peasantry in France; and therewith
they avoided perhaps the greatest of all the dietetic maladies of
the Middle Ages—St. Anthony's fire or ergotism—from bread
made of mouldy rye, a more destructive and painful disease even
than leprosy, and one that figures even more than the latter, for
all its Biblical vogue, in the French legends of the Saints.

**Disease
and
Famine.**
If we assume that leprosy is rightly called a *morbus miseriæ*,[2]
and that it was due to corrupt food, one can readily believe that
there was a certain amount of true leprosy in England at the
time when the leper-houses were being founded; for the period
was a troubled one, and it stands out in the annals as one of
frequent famines and famine-pestilences. One great famine,
attended or followed by universal sharp fever (typhus), occurred
in the last year of the Conqueror's reign (1086–7); the chroniclers
yield to the temptation of epigram when they say that the fever
destroyed those whom the famine had spared, but they all speak
of the mortality as enormous, and even William of Malmesbury
for once descends from diplomacy and ecclesiastical history to
make mention of it. There was again sharp famine and mortality
under William Rufus, not, it would seem, from one or more bad
seasons, but because the peasants actually struck work, seeing
that the crops they raised were promptly confiscated as tribute
to the king. The same groaning under excessive taxes continued
under Henry I., whose reign is marked by numerous famine-
pestilences and murrains. The anarchy and civil wars of
Stephen's reign were attended by the same calamities; and
it is only on the accession of Henry II. in 1154 that these
entries in the annals cease for a time, and, with a single

[1 Piers Plowman, A. vii. 292. The language is modernised. Cocket was
the second best kind of white bread, only slightly inferior to "wastell," the
best. Clerematyn was also apparently one of the better sorts of bread. The
derivations of both names are unknown.]

[2 A disease generated by poverty and bad conditions of life.]

LEPER RELICS, HOSPITAL OF ST. NICHOLAS, HARBLEDOWN, KENT.

exception, for the whole of his long reign. Good government could not absolutely prevent famine and epidemic sickness, for two bad harvests in succession almost certainly produced them in any country of medieval Europe. One great famine-pestilence of that kind occurred all over England, in the reign of Richard I., during six months of the year 1196 ; it is the pestilence vaguely referred to in a few words in " Ivanhoe." The harvests had been bad for several years before, not in England only, but all over Europe ; the people had been dying of want, and at length a pestilential fever arose, " as if from 'the corpses of the famished," says the historian, which crept about everywhere, attacking those who had food as well as those who were in want. William of Newburgh saw it in Yorkshire, and Giraldus Cambrensis tells how the starving people besieged the doors and windows of the hospice in which he was then residing at Lincoln. The mortality must have been on the great scale, for ceremonial burials were omitted except in cases of the rich, and in populous places the dead were buried in trenches, as they were afterwards in the Black Death. Some part of that great mortality had not been due directly to famine. William of Newburgh, whose historical gifts inspire respect for his opinion, is explicit that those also who did not lack bread were infected, as if from the corpses of the famished; and he tells a strange story, related to him by an eye-witness, of how the village or small town of Annan, on the Solway, was desolated by a plague which was eventually traced to a particular corpse thrown naked into a shallow hole in the ground, and how certain wise men of the place stopped the epidemic by having the offensive body dug up and cremated.

D. J. MEDLEY. Social Life. POPULAR fallacies die hard. It is a familiar legend of our childhood that, at least well into the thirteenth century, Normans and Saxons dwelt side by side, but perfectly distinct. This view has been emphasised by Scott in " Ivanhoe " ; it forms the basis of M. Augustin Thierry's History of the Norman Conquest of England, and is graphically sketched by Macaulay in his review of the reign of Richard I. Any account, therefore, however brief, of the social life after the Norman Conquest must be prefaced by an assertion of the rapidity with which Normans and English became one people. Our great modern interpreters have conclusively shown, from the descriptions of contemporary writers and from the language of written documents that no such antagonism as that between Normans and Saxons ever held a prominent, much less a permanent, place in our history. In the first place, no one except a Scot or a Welshman ever described an Englishman as a Saxon. To himself, as well as to all other foreign nations, he was an Englishman and nothing else. In the second place, there *is* a contemporary contrast, but it is between French or Normans and English, not between Normans and Saxons. Under the term English very soon came to be included the Norman king's subjects of Norman birth and French speech, as well as those of English birth and speech. Thus when Anselm's biographer, the monk Eadmer, complains that Henry I. would give no high ecclesiastical office to Englishmen, he is alluding to the promotions of Normans and Frenchmen from over the sea, in preference to men, whether of Norman or of English birth, whose homes were on this side of the Channel. In fact, the lively Archdeacon Walter Map distinctly names the reign of Henry I. as the time when, largely through the action of the king himself, the division hitherto existing between the two peoples came to an end.

From the moment that the Conquest was completed influences are found at work which were bound to produce such amalgamation at no very distant date. William I. claimed to be, and tried to act as if he were, the lawful successor of Edward the Confessor. Hence he maintained the old English local courts, in which Norman and English alike came to mingle. And even though the circumstances of the Conquest caused the transference of great quantities of land, the Norman landowners were regarded by the king as stepping as nearly as possible into the position of their English predecessors; so that not infrequently their rights and duties were dependent on the testimony of native English. No doubt, the few innovations in the administrative system for which William was responsible were in effect out of all proportion to their number. But any breach which these might have made between the two peoples was merely temporary, and William and his successors did all they could to minimise the difference. The greatest, because the most fruitful, of these innovations—the method of

Fusion of Normans and English.

inquest or collection of information by a sworn committee of neighbours—was a strong appeal to the co-operation of the native English. The two institutions that might have dug an impassable ditch between Normans and English were the *duellum*—the trial by battle (p. 414)—and the exaction of the *murdrum*. But the *duellum* is only offered by William to the Englishman as an alternative : whether accuser or accused the Englishman may choose between battle and ordeal, while, on the other hand, as accuser he can compel his adversary to fight. As to the *murdrum*—the fine that protects the life of a Norman from the vengeance of the native English—from the first it is not held to apply to men of French race who had settled in England before the Norman conquest ; while at an early stage every man is treated as a Norman unless his Englishry can be presented—that is, his English birth can be definitely proved. But with the lapse of time such proof became exceedingly hard, if not impossible. Not that the pride of Norman descent grew less. But the original number of Norman settlers was probably not very great, while the separation of Normandy and England under William's immediate successors would cause those Normans settled in England to feel that their lot was definitely cast there and to intermarry with the native English. Hence the disappearance from England itself of the old triple division of Dane law and West Saxon and Mercian law. Hence, too, the explanation of Henry II.'s treasurer, Richard Fitzneal, that the English and Normans have so intermarried and the nations have become so intermingled that among the free classes it is impossible to distinguish between them. Indeed, even if it had ever been the case, there was no longer any slight attached to the name Englishman. Writing in the reign of Henry I., Ordericus Vitalis (p. 504), the son of a Norman and an Englishwoman, who spent all his life in a Norman monastery, nevertheless proclaims himself to the world as Orderic the Englishman. He and his contemporaries, whether in England or in Normandy, apply the terms Angli and Normanni almost indiscriminately to the troops of the English kings in their wars with France. The increase of Norman baptismal names would be due to the vulgar feeling of the superior social status they might imply : the surnames, so far as they yet exist and however they should be interpreted, are almost exclusively English.

The evidence of spoken language points in the same **Language.** direction. French was, and for a long time remained, the habitual speech of the palace and the manor house, while English was the language of the people. With the coming of Normans English ceased to be the language of laws and charters, but its place was taken not by French, but by Latin, which would be a common possession to the learned of both races. When in the middle of the thirteenth century French is becoming the medium of communication between government and people, the fusion of the races is complete, and the change is due to other influences than the predominance of a French-speaking people. For, meanwhile, the stream of vernacular literature, which was momentarily checked by the Norman Conquest, had begun to flow again (p. 509), and it is a striking as well as an interesting fact that the Provisions of Oxford in 1258 were issued in Latin, French, and English. But it is probable that by the thirteenth century all educated people in the country were as bilingual as the modern Welsh. At any rate, from the middle of the twelfth century the chronicles are full of stories that show a knowledge of, if not considerable familiarity with, English speech among the upper classes. Henry II. is noted as certainly understanding, even if he did not speak, it. Giraldus Cambrensis, of mixed Norman and Welsh descent, was so familiar with it that he could compare the dialects of different parts of the country. There is no reason to labour the point. A cursory glance at selected passages from contemporary writers might incline us to agree with Scott and Thierry; but a more careful examination leaves no manner of doubt that after the middle of the twelfth century at the latest the use of the term Norman to denote an inhabitant of England meant no more than a similar use of the term Huguenot at the present day.

The social history of any age cannot be exhaustively **Social** described in a few pages. But all societies, however complex **Con-** in structure, group themselves round a few common forms **ditions.** of social life. The more stationary the life the more will it ·tend to reproduce the same common forms. In the Middle Ages it will be seen that individuals were by no means so stationary as is ordinarily supposed. But in society generally there was a far larger stationary element than under modern

conditions; so that it is not altogether impossible to photograph the social circumstances of the twelfth and thirteenth
centuries. One broad division of life is common to all societies
that have emerged from the purely pastoral stage; life in the
town promotes needs and means of supplying them which
develop a totally different kind of character from that fostered
by the routine of the country; the quick-witted townsman
and the acquiescent peasant soon part company. But these
are types for all time and all places. There are, however, two
forms of social life which, though not entirely confined to the
Middle Ages, may justly be regarded as in a sense peculiar
to them. Life in the manor house and life in the monastery
are not unknown at the present day; but they are excres-
cences, or rather perhaps survivals; whereas the lord of the
manor and the monk are the two most typical characters of
medieval society. It will be convenient to confine ourselves
to them, and by a detailed study in turn of the buildings,
the organisation and the daily life of the manor house and
the monastery, to try to get as near as possible to the life
and thoughts of a remoter age.

Life in the Manor House. The baronial castle is generally depicted as the centre of
Norman life. But the Norman baron shut up with his family
and his men-at-arms in the gloomy walls of a comfortless
keep is a figure for romance. The earliest castles were mere
fortresses, and every sensible king took care that, by whom-
soever built, they should be garrisoned in the royal name.
When at a later period castles became residences of the great
nobility, the introduction of domestic comfort and ceremonial
splendour placed the life of their inhabitants on a level with
life in the largest manor houses. The noblemen of the
twelfth and thirteenth centuries, then, lived, like the knight or
more substantial free tenant of the same period, in a manor
house or, it might be, in several manor houses. For many landowners would possess more than one manor, and the different
manors might be at great distances from each other. The
time of a great number of lords will be largely spent in passing at intervals from one Hall to another, and in their journey
they would carry not only their families and servants, but all
their household conveniences and comforts. All conveyance
had to be done on horses and mules; and as the pace would

THE NORMAN HOUSE, CHRISTCHURCH.

be that of a led horse or mule, travelling was a tedious operation. Moreover, inns offered too poor an accommodation for a
large company; and although a monastery might open its
hospitable doors, one could not always be counted on; so that
it was necessary for any party of travellers to add to their
baggage the things necessary for spending a night in the
open air.

(1) Build-
ings.

It was almost a necessary part of such a life that the manor
house should be a simple structure. Whether it belonged to
the king or to a yeoman, it might differ in size, but for a
long period the details of its arrangement were substantially
the same. The central feature was a large hall on the ground
floor, flanked at one end by a vaulted cellar above which stood
the solar[1] or private room of the lord's family, and at the
other end perhaps by the stables. The building would probably stand between two courts. Of one of these, part would
be laid out as a garden for a lady, while the other would
form a poultry yard. The whole would be enclosed by a
quickset hedge, a palisade or a wall; while sometimes immediately round the house itself, cutting it off from the
pleasure grounds, but more often outside the wall which enclosed the courts, would run a moat to secure the buildings
from a too sudden hostile intrusion. The larger proportion
of early medieval houses were of timber. In many cases the
houses were "run up" with a celerity and a result emulative
of the work of the modern builder. True, the halls were
generally of stone, and all vaulted work such as the cellar
would necessarily be of the same material; but the solar or
even the kitchen, with all the attendant risks of fire, would
as often as not be merely timber structures. Some of the
timber work—often, for example, the kitchen—would be run
up for the occasion; but the greater portion of it would be
intended to remain until the owner could afford to build in
stone. Thus, as wants increased, a number of extra buildings
would gradually be dotted about the court—a bakery, a
brewery, a laundry, and such like; and the whole would ultimately be drawn together by a corridor of wood or stone.
This temporary nature of much medieval building shows
how largely life in the Middle Ages was a life in the open

[1 That is, the chamber where one can enjoy the sun.]

air. A study of medieval windows will make this clear. Even in the solar the windows were narrow, for they could only be protected by canvas or by wooden lattices or shutters. The expense of glass for a long time allowed only of the glazing of the upper lights in a window. The practical inconvenience of this is illustrated by an order of Henry III, which assigns as a reason for substituting glass for wood " that the chamber may not be so windy"; while the ineffectiveness of medieval carpentry comes out in a charge among the royal accounts of the same period, " for closing the windows better than usual."

THE SOLAR, CHARNEY BASSET, BERKS.

A medieval manor house, then, ordinarily consisted of at least a hall, a cellar, and a solar ; to these might be added a kitchen, a chapel, a lady's bower, a buttery, pantry, sewery, a brewery, bakery, laundry and, lastly, the stables and outhouses. The hall would be a square or oblong structure, generally of stone, covered in with a roof which was often supported on a double row of pillars so as to make the whole space into a nave and two side aisles. At the end opposite to the entrance would be a raised platform or daïs ; and the rest of the hall was sometimes known as the marsh—a name which, when it stood on the ground floor, in the absence of boarding it only too often deserved. Contrary to our ordinary idea, medieval stone walls were almost invariably plastered

over and whitewashed or painted on. Fire-places are seldom
found in medieval halls; a fire was lit on a hearth in the
centre and the smoke escaped through a louvre or lantern
in the roof. The hall served many purposes. It was the
scene of the lord's Court of Justice; it was the dining room
of the lord and his household, and it was the bedroom of the
household. The furniture was scanty and plain. Along the
daïs, across the width of the hall, would run a fixed or " dor-
mant" table for the lord, his family and honoured guests;
while at the side would stand a cupboard or dresser which
at meal-times would be furnished with a profusion of plate.
Down the sides or aisles would be placed movable tables
made of boards laid upon tressels. At night time these would
be removed and all round the walls would be spread mattresses
on the floor or on low wooden bedsteads, on which all the
household, male and female indiscriminately, would lie down
to sleep. Finally, the seats were mere benches, although the
lord and lady might be provided with a settee furnished with
arms and a back. Beyond the daïs-wall would be the solar.
Ordinarily the entrance to this room would be not far from the
hall, through which the lord could see and hear all that was
going on. It was the private sitting room and bedroom of
the family and of any distinguished strangers. Thus it would
be more comfortably furnished than the hall. The walls would
be wainscoted and tapestried all round; and whereas we hear
of no covering for the floor of the hall other than rushes and
boughs, in the thirteenth century carpets are mentioned in
connection with the solar. The room would also contain a
bed or beds somewhat luxuriously furnished and separated
from each other by tapestry or hangings. The fire place and
the chimney corner for the winter, the stone seat in the window
for the summer, are invariable concomitants of the only livable
room in a medieval house. Below the solar, if not below the
hall itself, would run the cellar—a large vaulted structure of
stone—which might be storehouse, brewery, and stables all in
one. Plenty of storage place was necessary, for the stores
could only be laid in at great annual fairs, and room must be
found not only for the supplies of winter food and for drink
in barrels, but also for all spare necessaries for the house and
farm. In the houses of the king or of the great nobles there

would be also special rooms known as wardrobes, which were both storerooms for the clothes of other seasons and work-rooms for the tailors. The supplies of drink and food when given out from the cellar would be placed respectively in the buttery (*i.e.* butlery) and in the pantry or sewery preparatory to their transference to the tables in the hall. The last, but not the least important, room in a medieval house which calls for notice, is the kitchen. Much of the cooking might be

Photo: Chester Vaughan, Acton, W.

THE HALL, OAKHAM CASTLE.

done in the open air; the kitchens, as we have seen, were often temporary structures, and the kitchen utensils would be among the most important furniture that the travelling house-hold carried in its train. Extant lists of such utensils show that the art of the cook was a much valued art. And yet to modern ideas the difficulties would be insuperable. In the ordinary kitchen built of timber the fire would of necessity be in the middle of the room. Roasting would be a laborious though not impossible process. But in any case the greater part of the meat was boiled; for the kitchen seems also to have been the slaughter-house, and the meat was either eaten in summer perfectly fresh from the knife of the butcher, or formed part of the store which had been salted down for winter use.

(2) In-habitants. The manor house would be inhabited by the lord, his lady and their younger children, by pages and squires and maidens— young men and women of good birth who were learning their respective duties—and by the attendants and menials, both male and female, of the household. It was a source of pride to the lord and lady that their household should be composed of as many noble youths and maidens as they could gather round them or support. A child would be sent from home at seven years of age to serve as page in some noble family. His education would be superintended by the priest; at fourteen, with certain ceremonies he would be inducted as a squire. His business was to learn gentlemanly accomplishments, to accompany the lord on his journeys and outdoor amusements or to attend him to the field of battle, while amongst the most important duties of his daily life would be his service at table and especially the knowledge of how to carve the joints. The maidens would be not merely the personal attendants of the lady, but her active helpers in the spinning, weaving and needle-work, both useful and ornamental, which under the conditions of life were supplied upon the spot. Social intercourse between them and the young squires was extraordinarily free and easy, and in a large measure accounts for the gross immorality which fills all the chronicles and romances of the time. The gallantry which we are accustomed to associate with the feudal age was only skin-deep, and the brutality of husbands to wives and of men to women quite disabuses us of our notions of medieval chivalry. For the rest, the household of a great lord would be composed of the heads of the various departments—the groom of the chamber to look after the hall, the butler, the steward, and many others, with their necessary attendants. When to these are added musicians and jesters it will be clear that even in a moderate-sized house the sum total of those who ministered to the needs and pleasures of the lord's family and friends must have reached no inconsiderable number.

(3) Daily Life. Late hours are the privilege of civilisation. The modern rhyme which associates early hours with health and long life, wisely does not attempt to define the hours. The medieval

equivalent is not so reluctant, and may be accepted as a statement of the times actually kept. It tells us that—

> Lever à cinq, diner à neuf,
> Souper à cinq, coucher à neuf,
> Fait vivre d'ans nonante et neuf. [1]

The day was begun by attendance at service at the private
chapel attached to the manor house or at the neighbouring
parish church; this
would be followed by
breakfast, which was not
a very formidable meal.
After this would doubt-
less come the business
of the day; arrangements
both within and without
the house had to be
made, the heads of the
various departments to
be interviewed, the
stables and kennels to
be visited. On days of
special obligation per-

MUSIC AND DANCING (MS. Royal 2 B. vii.).

haps a second service would summon those who could go to
church or chapel. At some hour between nine and eleven
the household assembled for dinner. Except in the halls of
the very great, the whole household seems to have sat down
together, the lord and his family and guests at the high
table on the daïs, the rest of the household at the tables in
the aisles. Meanwhile the household had washed their hands
at the lavatories, while to the high table was handed round
a basin and towel. To each person would be supplied only
a spoon, and between every two persons a silver or pewter
cup, for glass in this connection was scarcely known. On
great occasions the meat was brought in from the kitchen
with much ceremony and even with an accompaniment of
music. The large joints would be carved by one of the squires
upon the table, but the smaller roast meats were apparently

[1 To rise at five, to dine at nine,
  To sup at five, to bed at nine,
  Makes a man live to ninety and nine.]

handed round on the spits, often of silver, on which they had
been roasted, and every gentleman of the company cut off
enough for himself and his lady partner.   Silver and metal
plates were sometimes used, but ordinarily the meat would be
placed on slices of bread called trenchers and, like the cup,
shared between two neighbours ; each man would produce his
own knife, and though forks were not unknown, fingers were
invariably used.   The trenchers were eaten after the meat or
were thrown into the alms-basket.   Sweets and dessert would
sometimes follow.   When all was finished, the cloth and the

IN THE GARDEN (MS. Royal 2 B. vii.).

table itself were removed, a final draught of wine and spices was
served round, and after a second washing of hands the members
of the high table withdrew to the solar.   But during the dinner
the hall was filled with many occupants besides the diners.
First came the cats and dogs which lay upon the ground
devouring the bones and fragments thrown to them, and the
hawks which ladies and men alike seem to have kept upon their
wrists or upon the perches in the hall.   In the case of a great
nobleman the minstrels would be his own paid servants.   But
ordinarily there would be little to separate them from the
chance tumblers, dancers, and wandering jongleurs of all kinds,
or even from the beggars who could often only be kept out of
the hall at meal-times by the use of actual force.   After dinner
the amusements of the day would begin.   Out of doors there
was a quiet though ceremonious walk in the garden ; or there
were the more exciting and exhausting pleasures of hunting and

hawking. If the weather was unpropitious, there was much with which both ladies and men could occupy themselves indoors—chess for the sober, or some of the many gambling games with dice; cards were the invention of a later age. More violent exercise would be afforded by dancing or by romping games, of which blindman's-buff, called hoodman blind, was a type; while those who were inclined to sit still, would hear or play music, or even sit and talk, or read to the ladies as they sat over their embroidery. So the time would pass away pleasantly enough until five o'clock, when the whole household would

HOODMAN BLIND (MS. 264 Misc.).
(*Bodleian Library, Oxford.*)

again meet for supper. This was an almost equally formal meal with dinner, though perhaps not so elaborate. The hall was ordinarily lighted with candles, which were stuck upon a spike whether on a candlestick or elsewhere. On great occasions torches were carried about by the attendants or placed in receivers on the wall. The means of artificial light were too precious to be needlessly dissipated. Consequently, although sometimes supper was followed by carousals, dancing or games, very often after supper the household retired to bed. Even with the publicity inseparable from the absence of special bedrooms, medieval modesty did not provide a night-dress. An amusing set of instructions for the management of a household tells the lady of the house to teach her servants " prudently to extinguish their candles, before they go into their bed, with the

35

mouth or with the hand and not with their shirt "—that is, they were not to get into bed half-undressed and then put out the candle by throwing their shirts upon it.

Humble Life. The inevitable lack of material makes it almost impossible to describe the life of the poorer classes in an early stage of social development. We have seen that even the houses of manorial lords were of the simplest construction. The socage tenants,[1] and the better class of burgesses—in fact, the free tenants — may have dwelt in comparative cleanliness and comfort ; but judged from our standard, the arrangements of even a royal palace were sufficiently primitive, and were perhaps endurable only by reason of the size of the rooms and the plentiful draughts which swept unhindered through door and windows. The life of all classes alike was passed mainly in the open air ; the houses were merely places of shelter in which to sleep and to feed. The larger part of even the most substantial manor houses was built of wood ; carpenter and builder were synonymous terms. By the same standard, perhaps by any standard, the dwellings of the poorer classes must have been mere hovels, like the worst Irish cabins at the present day—four outside walls composed of wattles banked up with mud, and covered over with a roof of boughs or a thatch of straw. On the bare ground of the floor would stand a tressel-table and a bench or two ; the bed would be a mere litter of straw, on which the inmates would lie in the same clothes that they wore by day ; and the single room would possibly be divided by a rough partition into a sleeping space for the human inhabitants, and a shelter against inclement weather for the poultry and the pigs. The cooking would, no doubt, be done, when possible, out of doors ; but when it was necessary to light a fire inside, the absence of a chimney enables us to understand Chaucer's description of the poor widow's cottage :

"Full sooty was her bower and eke her hall."

All this would not necessarily denote an unhappy life, though it would certainly preclude an easy one. Attached to the cottage would be a plot of ground at least two or three

[1 The lower class of free tenants who did not hold their land on condition of military service.]

CHESSMEN AND DRAUGHTSMEN.
(British Museum and Ashmolean Museum, Oxford.)

acres in extent.   On this a stock of vegetables would be grown. Fowls would be a necessary adjunct to every cottage —the poorer tenants frequently paid part of their rent by the gift of a hen or a specified number of eggs.   Bees would supply the honey which filled the place of sugar in the diet of the time.   The only scavenger was the pig, for which even the humblest peasant found a place.   Ewe's milk was mixed with cow's milk to make the cheese which formed one of the staple articles of the peasant's food.   Thus upon the table of the poorest cottager might be found meat of pig's flesh and of domestic fowls of various kinds, vegetables and fruit, eggs and cheese.   The scantiest item of all seems to have been that one which we regard as the most necessary. A successful corn harvest would enable the cottager, who had no share in the common fields of the manor, to add a plentiful supply of bread and beer to his ordinary diet.   But harvests were precarious, and free trade in corn was practically unknown.   Hence meat seems to have been more plentiful than grain; and it is to the disproportionate consumption of meat, as much as to the filthy dwellings, that we must attribute the presence of those loathsome skin diseases which are somewhat gratuitously classed together as leprosy (p. 529). Thus in favourable years there must have been a rough plenty for all classes; but the constant liability to famine and its successor, pestilence, induced a recklessness of feeling and a cheapening of the value of human life which are the necessary counterparts of a precarious existence.   The labours of the peasant on working days must have been as un-remitting as those of the peasants to-day in many parts of continental Europe.   What time he could spare from the lawful demands of his lord's bailiff, or his share, if he had any, in the cultivation of the common fields, would be given to his own little plot of garden ground.   But the Church prescribed numerous holidays—more than were necessary to recreate the exhausted physical energies.   Attendance at mass would consume a small part of the time of enforced idleness; most of the remainder seems to have been spent at the neighbouring ale-house.   The English were notoriously hard drinkers.   Men and women alike would sit for long hours drinking, gossiping, gambling, singing, or listening to the

coarse performances of the wandering musicians and mounte-
banks, who frequented as much the taverns of the poor as
the manorial halls. Hence, when it was almost dark, would
they reel home to their hovels, and creep candleless to their
pallets of straw, there to lie until the morrow's sunrise
summoned them to the monotonous round of their daily
work. More wholesome recreation would be afforded by the

GLEANING : THE STORY OF RUTH AND BOAZ.
(*Lambeth Palace Library.*)

May-day, harvest, and Christmas festivities, which with much
feasting, combined dancing, singing and rough games of
various kinds. But these were only at long intervals.

It is difficult to imagine a life less well equipped with the
means of living. In summer, if the weather was propitious,
existence must have been tolerable, even pleasant. But in
winter, though the peasant might clothe himself more warmly
in a coarse garment of rabbit skins, the materials for a fire
might be hard to come by, and the choking smoke which
arose from the peat or the damp wood and leaves inside the
cottage was a doubtful alternative for the piercing cold against
which the fire was kindled and maintained. And even where
there were the means, there was little encouragement to thrift.

The boors must have escaped the royal tax-gatherer and the royal purveyors simply because there was nothing that could be taken from them ; but the more substantial villeins and the free tenants were fair game; and the household goods, as well as the live stock on their holdings, were forced to contribute now to the general needs of the State, now to the personal wants of the King's Court or the royal officials on their wanderings through the country. That men did rise from lower, even the lowest, social grades to higher ranks, we know; but for the most part the life of the mere peasant was a life, not of despair which is born of a desire for better things, but of reckless living for the moment, which scarcely separated them from the birds and beasts sheltering with them in the hovels which we miscall their homes.

Life in the Monastery. Our remaining time may be spent in a short examination of the buildings, the establishment, and the daily life of a monastic community. In common speech we distinguish between a monastery—a community of men, and a convent—a community of women. But no such distinction is admissible. The one is a Greek word describing the home of a solitary individual and applied by a misnomer to that of a separate community ; the community, whether male or female, habitually describes itself in Latin as a convent. Now, there were communities of various kinds and degrees—canons secular, consisting of priests who lived in separate houses within a cathedral close, but owed obedience to some kind of common rule,[1] and were dependent on the bishop ; canons regular, also priests living a collegiate life in obedience to some kind of common rule, but not bound by special vows ; monks, strictly so called, living apart from the world like the canons regular, not necessarily in holy orders, but bound by special vows. To these should perhaps be added the friars, in their origin not living in communities at all, but before long by a kind of irresistible necessity gathered into common dwelling-places, which gave them all the advantages without any of the restraints of a common life.

Buildings. Whatever the order, and whether composed of monks or canons regular, the buildings of the community would be modelled on a similar plan. They naturally centred round the church for whose sake it may be said that they existed. Hence

[1 Greek κανών, whence the name.]

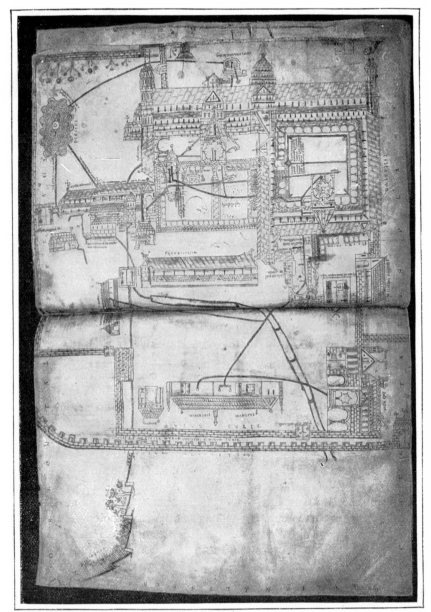

PLAN OF A CHURCH AND ITS MONASTIC COMMUNITY (CHRIST CHURCH, CANTERBURY).

(*Trinity College, Cambridge.*)

the care and wealth which were lavished on the church ; for its fame as a place of rare beauty, or, more important, as the shrine of some specially sacred relic, reflected credit upon and so brought wealth to them.   The church would be divided into two distinct parts by a screen, and the upper part or choir would be appropriated to the monks, while the dependents and visitors might occupy the nave.   There are some remarkable exceptions, but to the south of the church, as an ordinary rule, would lie the cloisters—a covered arcade in the form of a quadrangle running round an open grass plot called the garth, which might be laid out as a garden with a fountain in the middle. The cloister was not merely the means of communication between different parts of the monastic buildings, it was the chief scene of the monks' daily life.   In later times the open trellis work of the cloister was shut in by beautiful painted windows. But in the twelfth and thirteenth centuries there was no such shelter from the rays of the summer sun or the piercing winter blasts and the draughts which are peculiar to no season of the year.   No less than in the case of the inhabitants of the manor house, the life of the monk, although largely confined to the cloister, was essentially a life in the open air.   In one of the sides, alleys, or walks of the cloister would be held the monastic school.   Another walk would be fitted up with carols—that is, screened enclosures for study ; while a third would form an ambulatory where the monks might walk in meditation.   The cloisters would be bounded by the monastic buildings, and the usual arrangement, dictated largely by convenience, placed the church upon the north with the refectory opposite, while to the right or eastern side lay the chapterhouse, and to the west the dormitory.   The chapterhouse occupied the centre of the eastern side of the quadrangle, into which it opened by a long vestibule often furnished with benches as a waiting room.   For here all the business of the monastery was transacted—novices were admitted, offenders were sentenced, all internal arrangements for the church services and the monastery were made. The building obtained its name from the fact that in conventual houses a chapter of the rule of the Order was daily read in it.   For here the whole convent of monks or chapter of canons met in daily council after mass.   The refectory lay invariably to the south, so that the smell and noise which accompanied

the meals should be as far as possible from the church.
Usually, on the south-west side would stand the kitchen—a
more substantial structure for the stationary monks than was
needed by the migratory medieval lord. Sometimes the
dormitory would lie on the same side as the chapterhouse;
but in the larger
monasteries where
there was more than
one dormitory that
for novices or lay
brethren would lie
beyond the chapter-
house, while the fully
professed monks
would lodge on the
western side of the
quadrangle. In either
case the dormitory
would be upstairs, and
the ground floor
would consist some-
times of store-rooms,
sometimes of an
ambulatory or pro-
menade, to which
would be often added
a calefactory, a room
with a fire in it which
the monks were al-
lowed to frequent at

THE ABBOT'S KITCHEN, DURHAM.

certain times and on certain occasions. In either case also
the dormitory would communicate immediately with the
church, so that without leaving cover the monks could attend
the nightly services. It would be furnished at one end with
lavatories and would be divided, not into separate cells, which
was a peculiarity of the strict Carthusian order, but into cubicles
like the dormitory of a modern public school. Each cubicle
would be lit from a small window and would be furnished with
a wooden bedstead. In some monasteries the cubicles were
fitted with desks for study, and must have formed an acceptable

refuge from the heat of the sun in the cloister.   The mainten-
ance of discipline in the dormitory would rival that of a well-
conducted school.   The monks were shut in from the cloister
at a particular hour, lights were kept burning all night, and the
prior went round to see that each monk was in his cubicle.

The development of monastic buildings might be almost
limitless, but a few more deserve a passing notice as common
to a monastery of any size, and as playing an important part in
its daily life.   The Scriptorium or writing-room in a great
monastery would present a busy scene.   It would combine the
work of a modern land agent's office and a printing press.
Here would be drawn up the leases and other legal documents
incidental to the conduct of a great estate; the books and
music needful for school and church would be copied, and the
chronicle of the abbey would be compiled.   Equally characteristic of monastic work would be the Almonry lying often near
the church, whence the daily dole would be administered to the
poor.   Sick and dying monks were treated in an Infirmary
which often lay in a small cloister of its own with kitchen, bath-
house, hall and chapel attached, in one range of buildings and
so disposed that the sick monks in their beds could hear the
services.   Finally, the monasteries dispensed hospitality often on
a gigantic scale.   For this purpose they had guest houses, for
frequently there was more than one.   The guest house contained a hall, dormitory, and chapel of its own, and would be
somewhat apart from the rest of the monastic buildings.   The
accommodation for guests and for horses must have been
enormous, for we have seen that kings and barons travelled
with large companies.

**Organ-
isation**

The organisation of a monastery was most elaborate ; for the
minute subdivision of functions, and the multiplication of official
posts to which it led, must have been designed not only to give
as many monks as possible a feeling that the monastery was
their home, but with the even more important object of employing idle hands.   At the head of every monastery was an abbot
or prior.   Whether abbot or prior he lived apart from the
monks in a lodge which, with its hall, solar, and private chapel,
was on the scale of a large manor house.   He made all appointments, and the success of the house depended largely on his
administrative powers.   Abbot Hugh and Abbot Samson, whom

Carlyle has immortalised for us, were not, as types, peculiar to the great house of St. Edmundsbury. Where both existed, the relations between abbot and prior would be similar to those of the head of an Oxford college and its dean, to whom the prior has been aptly likened. For he was the executive officer of the monastery itself and would, if necessary, be assisted by one or more sub-priors. The heads of the various departments were

GUEST-HALL OF ST. AUGUSTINE'S MONASTERY, CANTERBURY.
(*Now the Hall of St. Augustine's Missionary College.*)

known as obedientiaries, and to each was assigned a definite and separate charge upon the abbey rents, out of which he could meet the expenses incurred in connection with his office. The chief of these were the Master of the Fabric, who looked after the monastic buildings; the Sacristan, who was responsible for everything connected with the services of the church; the Chamberlain, whose sphere of office was the dormitory; the Cellarer, who kept the stores; the Pitancier, who regulated all extra allowances; and the Almoner, who was the vehicle of the monastic charity.

The daily life of the monk was largely regulated by the **Daily Life.** number of services which he was bound to attend. Special

officials, such as the cook, and those whom the business of the
monastery carried to a distance from the church, might be
exempted; but the ordinary monk would be required to attend
the canonical " Hours " of the Breviary, which, indeed, had been
originally developed through the conditions and needs of monastic life.   Thus the monk rose and washed and was in his
place at church by six o'clock, where he said lauds and prime
and heard the matin mass.   This would be followed by the
holding of the Chapter.   On ordinary days he would then
break his fast with a light meal called the mixtum.   On days
of special obligation terce [1] at nine o'clock would be followed by
high mass, at which all within and without the monastery
would be bound to attend.   Until dinner the monks would be
occupied about their various duties—teaching, learning, copying, or looking after the concerns of the kitchen, the stables,
or the farm.   Those who were about the monastery assembled
again in the church at midday for sexts, to which on ordinary
days succeeded dinner.   But on fast-days—Wednesdays and
Fridays—there was no meal until after nones at three o'clock,
while during Lent there was even a more prolonged fast until
five or six.   Dinner would usually be eaten in silence while one
of the novices read passages from some edifying book.   Then
studies might be resumed in the cloister, or a few of the
lighter-minded monks would indulge in a quiet chat or even
play a game of chess.   Supper at five and vespers at sunset
would both claim the presence of all the inmates, and at six the
gates of the monastery were closed.   The day's round was ended
by compline [2] in the church, after which the monks passed in
procession to the dormitory.   Nor were the hours of the night
exempt from obligations.   The whole night was divided into
three nocturnes or watches, and a constant succession of Psalms
was chanted by relays of monks, the whole Psalter being accomplished at varying degrees of speed.

It is often supposed that the life of a medieval monk was
both hard and dull.   But such was by no means the case.   If
the inmates of a monastery did not live as luxuriously as is

[1 Terce, sexts, and nones are so called because they fall respectively at the
third, sixth, and ninth hour of the day according to Roman reckoning.]

[2 Compline, derived from the Latin *completus*, perhaps through an adjective
completinus, is the last service of the day, at 9 p.m.]

commonly supposed, at any rate they fed plentifully, though with due observance of the ordinances of the church. To us the greatest hardship of their life would probably be the winter's cold and the continual draughts; but in these respects they were no worse off than the inmates of the manor house or the palace. The monotony of their life, too, so far as it was monotonous, was no greater than that in other classes of contemporary society. True, the whole community did not move about like many lords of manors; but individual monks, especially the obedientiaries, would have not only opportunities, but even a necessity, for travelling far afield on the business of

MONK TRAVELLING (MS. Nero D. vii.).

the monastery. And for those who were not so fortunate, if they did not go into the world, the world came in no small quantity to them. Among their own number might be found persons who had played a great part in affairs before they exchanged the sword for the cowl; while in their wanderings, visitors of all ranks from the king downwards only too willingly accepted the hospitality of the monks. The monastic chronicles testify to the amount of news from the outside world which from one source and another reached the monastery. Day by day the items of news were noted on slips of parchment, which were inserted between the leaves of the Chronicle ready to be entered thereon. If to such breaks in the monotony of the daily round as have been already suggested we add those which come from the opportunities of sport afforded to a large land-owning corporation, from the lawsuits with the bishop of the diocese or with some powerful layman, and, finally, from the quarrels with their own tenants and the neighbouring townsmen, we shall perhaps be inclined to agree that the life of the quietest medieval monk in the most secluded monastery must have consisted of a succession of interesting episodes.

AUTHORITIES.—1066–1216.

Political History, 1066–1154.—The story of the Norman Conquest as it appeared immediately afterwards is told by William of Jumièges, by William of Poitiers (the Conqueror's chaplain) in the *Carmen de Bello Hastingensi*, and the Anglo-Saxon Chronicles, but best (for those who can read between the lines) in Domesday Book. For the reigns of William II. and Henry I. the Chronicle must be supplemented by Eadmer, and the monk Ordericus Vitalis. From this last writer, with the *Gesta Stephani*, William of Malmesbury (Rolls Series), the Hexham annalists, and the *Chronicle of Melrose*, we derive our account of Stephen's reign. The best modern account (to 1135) is Freeman's *Norman Conquest*, vols. iv. and v. (summed up in his *Short History of the Norman Conquest*). Stubbs's *Constitutional History*, from chap. ix., is invaluable. Dean Church's *Anselm* is an excellent biography. The facts and details are given fully in Franck Bright's *History of England;* Green's *Short History of the English People* supplies a brilliant sketch. The best summary is Stubbs' *Early Plantagenets.* In general, Round, *Feudal England;* Ramsay, *Foundations of England.*

1154–1216.—Of a crowd of contemporary writers on Henry II.'s reign, William of Newburgh, the so-called Benedict of Peterborough, and Roger Hoveden, give the best narratives. Ralph de Diceto may be added, while Giraldus Cambrensis, John of Salisbury, and the Rolls Series (collections of matters relating to Becket) are supplementary. For the reigns of Richard and John most of these writers are the primary authorities. These reigns are also illustrated by the memorials of Richard I. (Rolls Series), the various monastic annals, and the collection of Royal Rolls, and the selected documents in Stubbs' *Charters.* Modern writers as before.

Domesday Book.—The text of the *Survey* with that of the *Exon Domesday, Inquisitio Eliensis, Winton Domesday*, is in most public libraries. Facsimiles (obtainable separately for each county) are published by the Government. Sir H. Ellis's *Introduction to Domesday Book*, with indices (2 vols., 1833), is very useful; R. W. Eyton, *Domesday Studies* (analysis and digest of the Staffordshire survey), 1881; also *Dorset Survey* and *Key to Domesday.* Freeman, *Norman Conquest*, vol. v., is very useful and suggestive. [J. L. C. Mowat] *Notes on Oxfordshire Domesday*, 1892 (a good model for Domesday students). J. H. Round, *Domesday Studies* (in *Domesday Celebration* volumes), the best modern investigations on difficult points. The *Testa de Nevill* and *Hundred Rolls* and the *Domesday Book of St. Paul's* (published by the Dean and Chapter) are necessary for comparison of Domesday with later arrangements. Seebohm, *English Village Community*, excellent on open-field cultivation. See also Stubbs, *Const. Hist.*, i.; Maitland, *Domesday Book and Beyond.*

Religion.—The leading contemporary authorities besides those above cited are the works of Eadmer, Walter Map (Camden Society), Giraldus Cambrensis, Lanfranc, and Anselm (Migne, *Patrologia Latina*); the lives of St. Thomas of Canterbury, his letters, and those of Gilbert Foliot (Migne), and Walter of Coventry. When not otherwise specified, the above works are in the Rolls Series. A selection from the authorities as to Becket is given in English, in W. H. Hutton's *St. Thomas of Canterbury.*

Law.—Stubbs's *Select Charters* is indispensable, as also Bigelow's *Placita Anglo-Normannica*, and the various records published by the Record Commission and the Pipe Roll Society. The law books of the period are mostly printed in Schmidt, *Gesetze der Angelsachsen.* Dr. Liebermann is re-editing them, and has published the *Quadripartitus* and the *Conciliatio Cnuti.* Glanvill's text-book has often been published. The *Dialogus de Scaccario* is in Stubbs's *Select Charters.* Various scattered publications

tions of Dr. Heinrich Brunner (esp. *Die Enstehung der Schwurgerichte*) and of Dr. Liebermann are of great value. *See* also Pollock and Maitland, *History of English Law to Edward I.*

Warfare.—The evidence is scattered throughout the ancient chronicles, especially Froissart. Modern books—Hewitt, *Ancient Armour*, Oxford, 1860; G. T. Clarke, *Mediæval Military Architecture*, 1886; Oman, *Art of War in the Middle Ages.*

Naval Matters (1066-1399).—The *Black Book of the Admiralty*, the *Pipe Rolls. Close Rolls. Patent Rolls*, and *Rolls of Parliament*, the *Wardrobe Accounts*, the *Acta Regia*, the *Chronicle* of Melrose *Rolls Ser.es*, and the *Chronique de Normandie* may be mentioned, as also *elden s Mare Clausum*, and Prynne s *Animadversions*, and Bracton. Modern : Jal, *Archéologie Navale*; Laird Clowes, *History of the British Navy*. Most of the above texts have been published by the Record Commission.

Trade and Industry.—Allusions in William of Malmesbury, Domesday Book, and the lesser Domesdays (*e.g.*, St. Paul's), the *Boldon Book*, the *Chronicle of Jocelin of Brakeland*, and the town charters and other documents in Stubbs' *Select Charters.* The most useful modern books are : Freeman, *Norman Conquest*, vol. v. ; Green, *Short History of the English People;* Gross, *Gild Merchant;* Ashley, *Economic History;* Cunningham, *British Industry and Commerce;* Maitland, *Township and Borough.*

Architecture.—Freeman, *History of the Norman Conquest;* Fergusson, *History of Architecture;* Rickman, *Gothic Architecture;* Parker, *Glossary* and *Introduction to Gothic Architecture;* Murray's *Cathedral Handbooks;* Scott, *Mediæval Architecture;* Turner and Parker, *Domestic Architecture of the Middle Ages;* Clark, *Mediæval Military Architecture in England;* Winston, *Inquiry into the Difference of Style in Ancient Glass Paintings.* Coins, same as for chap. ii.

Learning and Science.—Hampden, *Scholastic Philosophy in its Relation to Christian Theology* (1833) ; Milman, *History of Latin Christianity;* Church, *Anselm;* Bass Mullinger, *The University of Cambridge;* R. L. Poole, *Illustrations of the History of Mediæval Thought*, 1884 ; H. C. Maxwell-Lyte, *History of the University of Oxford*, 1886 : Stubbs's *Literature and Learning at the Court of Henry II.* (in *Seventeen Lectures*, vi., vii.) ; Rashdall, *The Origins of the University of Paris* (*English Historical Review*, i., 1886) ; *Early History of Oxford* (*Church Quarterly*, xiii., 1887, and *Academy*, June, 1888); Prof. Holland, *Origin of the University of Oxford* (*English Historical Review*, vi., 1891) ; Poole, *John of Salisbury*, in *Dictionary of National Biography*, xxix.

Literature.—Freeman, *Norman Conquest;* H. Morley, *English Writers*, iii., etc. ; Earle's and Plummer's editions of the Anglo-Saxon Chronicles ; Gardiner and Mullinger, *Introduction to the Study of English History*, London, 1882 ; A. Chevalier, *Répertoire des Sources Historiques du Moyen Age* (Paris, 1877–1886) ; Nutt, *Studies on the Holy Grail* (Folk-lore Society, 1888) ; the publications in the Rolls Series, especially those edited by Dr. Stubbs. Of a specialist character are B. Ten Brink, *Geschichte der Englischen Litteratur*, i., Berlin, 1877 ; R. Wuelcker, *Grundriss zur Geschichte der Angelsächsischen Litteratur*, Leipzig, 1885 ; A. Ebert, *Allgemeine Geschichte der Litteratur des Mittelalters im Abendlande*, Leipzig, 1874–80 ; and A. Brandl, *Mittelenglische Litteratur* (in Paul's *Grundriss der Germanischen Philologie*, Strassburg, 1889, etc., ii. 1). The majority of the texts referred to in this and the following chapters have been edited by the Early English Text Society. A number have also been published by the Surtees and Camden Societies and the Roxburgh Club.

Social Life.—Costume :—Strutt, *Dresses and Habits of the English* (1842) ; Fairholt, *Costume in England* (1846; third edition, enlarged and revised, by the Hon. A. H. Dillon, in Bohn's Artists' Library, 1885) ; H. Shaw, *Dresses and Decorations of the Middle Ages*, 2 vols. (1843) ; Planché, *History of British Costume* (1847 ; third edition in Bohn's Illustrated Library, 1874); or, better still, the same author's *Cyclopædia of Costume*, 2 vols. (1876–9). Several of these contain a description of the military as well as the civil dress; for the former *see* Sir S. R. Meyrick's *A Critical Inquiry into Ancient Armour from the Norman Conquest to the Reign of Charles II.*, 3 vols. (1824) ; and Hewitt, *Ancient Armour*. On Furniture, etc., Viollet-le-Duc. *Dictionnairede Mobilier Français.*

CHAPTER IV.

FROM CHARTER TO PARLIAMENT. 1216–1273.

A. L.
SMITH.
The Reign
of Henry
III., 1216–
1273.

SIXTEEN years of troubled and factious, but eventually success-ful, government; seventeen tedious years of attempted absolutism and abortive efforts at resistance to it; seven critical years of civil war, baronial triumphs, quarrels, and failures; finally, eight uneventful years of peace and comparative good government: such is the varied story of the long confused reign of Henry III. (1216–1273). John's death left the kingdom in an alarming condition. Two foreign bands were quartered on the country— John's mercenaries and Louis's troops; and to Louis's cause nearly all the barons were bound by oaths. Langton was absent in disgrace, and a Papal Legate held the English Church in his grasp. The Justiciar was Peter des Roches, Bishop of Win-chester, a Poitevin, and thoroughly foreign in his views. There was a strong feudal party ready to seize any opportunity of disorder. But John's death had also removed the one exciting cause of all these troubles. A coalition was at once made between the English ministers and the foreign, the feudal party and the papal. Within three weeks the young king had been crowned (he was nine years old); the Charter had been reissued, and William the Marshall, Earl of Pembroke, made guardian and regent. In the spring of 1217 the barons were fast return-ing to their allegiance. On May 20th the battle called the Fair of Lincoln reduced Louis to take refuge in London; and the defeat of his fleet by Hubert de Burgh made him submit to the inevitable. By Michaelmas, 1217, England was at peace. But to restore order was a longer task. Barons like Ranulf of Chester had fought against a French prince chiefly to secure a monopoly of power to themselves. Foreign adventurers like Fawkes de Bréauté, the evil legacy of John, still held themselves entrenched in English offices; sheriff of six counties, captain of a band of ruffians, abductor of heiresses, and intimidator of justice, "he was more than a king in England," says the Dun-stable annalist. But before the Marshall died in 1219 much had been done. Much, too, was done after him by Hubert de **Hubert de Burgh.** Burgh, who as Justiciar was joined in power with Pandulf, the new Legate, and Peter des Roches, now guardian of the king's person, but to whose sole credit is due the work achieved between 1219 and 1227. This meant the extirpation of such pests as Fawkes de Bréauté, the vindication of royal authority over the feudal castles, and the restoration of Langton to the chief control of the English Church. In 1227 the king declared himself of age, but, fortunately for himself, not till 1232 was he strong enough to shake off Hubert, the great Justiciar, who

SEAL OF HENRY III.

stood between the king and the contempt and resentment of his subjects, and who checked the king's foolish schemes of Welsh, Scotch, and French wars. Hubert fell by a combination of hostile forces—the feudal party's vengeance, the intrigues of rivals, the papal influence, and Henry's own vanity and self-will. But the gratitude which the country owed him is typified in the story of the blacksmith who refused to forge irons for the man who had saved England. With Peter des Roches' return to office and Henry's marriage to Eleanor of Provence, Hubert's policy of England for the English was reversed, and "swarms of hungry bandits, horsed and armed" (in the vigorous words of Matthew Paris), trooped down upon the land and displaced the English ministers and officials. The barons met and threatened to depose the king if he did not dismiss Bishop Peter. The **Fall of Bishop Peter.** bishop fell in 1234, but not before he had betrayed the baronial leader, Richard the Marshal, to his death, and initiated the king

36

in a policy of personal government which caused the kingdom thirty-three years of misrule and strife, and nearly cost the king his throne.   This policy, following on the memories of

John's mercenaries, generated that hatred of foreign influences which is a keynote of English feeling from this time to the Tudors.

The outcry against "aliens" sometimes seems exaggerated. But it must be remembered that besides supplanting the English nobles and impoverishing the Crown, they encouraged the kings to aim at absolutism. Their hold on castles and seaports was a great danger; they menaced the new-created unity of England, and were a part of that oppressive system by which the wealth and welfare of the English Church were drained

HUBERT DE BURGH IN SANCTUARY
(MS. Roy. 14, C. vii.).

away to support foreign prelates. The Primacy itself was held by Boniface of Savoy, the queen's uncle; her two brothers were earls.   In 1252 Bishop Grosseteste of Lincoln, the foremost Churchman of his day, declared that papal nominees drew yearly from England moneys to thrice the amount of the royal revenues (p. 574).   Henry's weak and impressionable mind was overawed by the masterful character of a Gregory IX. and an Innocent IV. When the Popes demanded tithe from the English clergy, "the king became a reed to lean on"; and such exactions became almost annual. But baronial and ecclesiastical discontent could effect nothing without a leader. First Richard of Cornwall, the king's brother, next Richard the Marshal, then Edmund Rich the Primate, and the famous Grosseteste, successively headed movements against Henry's wanton wastefulness, and his perpetual violations of the Charters, the anarchy due to continued abeyance of the offices of Chancellor, Justiciar, and Treasurer, and the repeated gross breaches of faith on the king's part. He had once sworn "as a man, a Christian, a knight, a crowned and anointed king"; but this, too, he broke as lightly as he did the rest.

Matters had seemed to be coming to a climax many times— ir 1233, 1237, 1242, 1244. At this date Richard of Cornwall again stood forth to head the demands for reform, which became more urgent in 1248, 1253, and 1255. But it was a conjunction of peculiar incidents which produced at last the right man in Simon de Montfort. A foreigner by birth, but heir to the earldom of Leicester, he had won the king's favour and married his sister, and had served him well in the thankless lieutenancy of Gascony, only to experience Henry's ingratitude and suspicion. Simon had shown his sympathy with the reforming party as early as 1244, but not till 1254 was he much in England. The king had, in 1255, been lured into supporting the implacable papal war with the Hohenstaufen, though these princes were Henry's own kin by marriage. By conferring the title of " King of Sicily " on the vain king's second son Edmund, a mere child, the Pope gained the riches of England to draw upon, and had soon run up against Henry a bill of 140,000 marks. The king coolly asked the clergy for such a sum. " The ears of all tingled," says Matthew Paris, but they had to promise 52,000 marks. When next year the barons found that the king had pledged the country's honour for the whole debt, three times the annual revenue of England, they felt the cup was full. They had come armed to Oxford; the royalists called it the Mad Parliament.

The Barons' War.

The Provisions of Oxford.

But the Provisions of Oxford, though they banished the aliens, chose the ministers, and practically superseded the royal power by baronial committees, were temperate enough, if somewhat cumbrous, in their scheme of reform. The king could only govern through a council of fifteen, composed of royalists and barons alike; thrice a year this council was to meet twelve leading men elected from the whole baronage. This joint body was called a " Parliament "; and the twelve were said to " represent the whole community." Such an oligarchical scheme of reform was foredoomed

SEAL OF SIMON DE MONTFORT.

to failure. Perhaps Henry foresaw this when, to get his debt paid, he swore to the Provisions. If so, he was right; for, in a little more than a year, the excluded elements asserted themselves. Backed by Prince Edward, and probably encouraged by Simon de Montfort, "the body of the knighthood of England" attacked the baronial government for their self-seeking and exclusiveness, and extorted from them a further set of reforms. When the two great earls who had led the movement quarrelled, Simon represented the liberal, Gloucester the oligarchical party. The political advance of the former party, knights, freeholders, and burgesses, is what gives the chief meaning and interest to the turbulent, shifting, and seemingly futile story of these years of strife (1258–65). Twice over were the quarrelling barons frightened into reunion by their enemies' recovery of strength. For in 1261 Henry had got easy absolution by Papal Bull from all his oaths; and in November, 1262, Prince Edward, probably suspicious of Earl Simon's designs, had rejoined his father's side. On the other hand, in 1262, the old Earl of Gloucester died, and his son was a firm reformer. At last, after incessant wranglings and intrigues, sheer weariness forced both sides to submit the whole situation to the arbitrament of King Louis of France. His award naturally was adverse to the insurgent cause. But Simon fell back on the Provisions of Magna Charta, and the Londoners refused to accept an arbitration to which they had been no parties. The balance of military strength was now against him. He was driven into alliance with the rebel Welsh, and when at last it came to a pitched battle at Lewes, he was so overmatched by the king's forces that his less disciplined troops must have been defeated but for Prince Edward's making just the same mistake as Prince Rupert did in 1645 at Naseby. For Simon's

JUG SHOWING THE ARMS OF THE CLARES *(Guildhall Museum).*
(By permission of the Library Committee of the Corporation of the City of London.)

The Battle of Lewes.

party, the towns, the clergy, and the lower people, could not balance the fighting force of the barons, most of whom were now royalist. With vindictive fury Edward charged, broke, and scattered the Londoners, and pursued them for miles, to find on his return that all was over—his father, uncle, and cousin prisoners, and the Earl of Leicester the real ruler of England.

But victory gave Simon a position little less untenable. Under a thin veil of the king's name England was ruled for fourteen months by a council of nine, appointed by three men: and the three were Simon himself; his admirer, the young Clare, Earl of Gloucester; and his friend the Bishop of Chichester. But Simon's sons, with unpardonable folly, offended the Clares, allowed Prince Edward to escape by a very simple trick, were surprised by him, and so enabled him to outmanœuvre their father. "Sir Simon the righteous" fell at Evesham, and, with a ferocity rare in English warfare, his body was hideously mutilated. But his memory lived among the people; for generations he was worshipped as a saint; at

Photo: York & Son, Notting Hill, W.
TOMB OF HENRY III., WESTMINSTER ABBEY.

his tomb miraculous cures were effected. He was indeed a great man; and yet before he died the work which he could do was done, and that which was still to do remained for his greater successor, his pupil, ally, and enemy, Edward I. With the royalist victory, and the final submission of the residue of the malcontents to the Award of Kenilworth fifteen months later, the interest of the reign closes. When most of the Provisions of Westminster were, in 1267, drawn up as statutes in the Marlborough Parliament, much of what the barons had fought for was achieved. In 1270 Prince Edward started on a crusade; and while he lay wounded by the fanatic's dagger at Acre, Henry III. had died, proclamation of the peace had been made in the name of Edward I. and the oaths of fealty to his person had been taken.

A. L. SMITH. The Genesis of Parliament. THE origin of the English Parliament is to be traced back to the local institutions of the Germanic tribes. But the final stages of its growth are to be sought in the period between the accession of Henry II. and the close of Edward I.'s reign.

Up to the year 1213 its history is a history of the measures by which the royal power was drilling the local institutions to co-operate in carrying out locally the work of administration. From 1213 the scene changes, as it were, to Westminster; more and more definitely the localities are gathered together in one central assembly—a process completed by the formation of "the Model Parliament," 1295. But, meantime, important subsidiary processes were going on. Representation was assuming the elective form. Tenure as a constituent principle was weakening. The boroughs were gaining political weight. The clergy were constituting themselves into complete representative convocations. Taxation was changing in form; and juries of "recognition" were becoming the regular mode of assessing the new taxes on personalty.

The Elements of Representation. It would be impossible to trace all these growths concurrently. It is necessary to distinguish essential principles and trace each separately. These principles, four in number, can be distinguished in the writ of 1295, the year of the Model Parliament. The writ then issued to the sheriffs orders them to send to Westminster two elected knights from each shire, and two elected burgesses from each borough, to

have full and sufficient power for themselves and the community of each shire and borough to do what shall then be
by common counsel ordained. The essential points here
were :—

(A) The representation is of the shire. It was taken as
consisting of all freeholders, whether of country or town,
the former represented by knights and the latter by
burgesses.

(B) The representatives were elected ; that is, they were to
be real representatives.

(C) The purpose was taxation. They were not called
merely to discuss or to inform the Government, but to
do something, *i.e.* to make a definite grant.

(D) They meet the other estates (magnates and clergy).

The representatives are not merely the representatives of
localities, but also all together represent one estate, *i.e.* a class
with property and interests of its own ; just as the lords had
their separate standing, and the clergy, the spiritual estate,
had theirs.

(A) When the Anglo-Norman kings looked round for an **The Shire.**
ally against their feudal baronage, or the Plantagenets for an
ally against the aggressions of the Papal Church, they found
this ally in the old shire system of England.

The fact of this alliance is established by a series of
evidences, chief of which are :—

(1) The order of Henry I. distinctly announcing his intention that the shire court and its lesser division, the court
of the hundred, shall sit at the same time and place as in
King Edward's day, and that all in the shire shall attend
these courts.

(2) The use of shire and hundred courts by Henry II. as
instruments for royal needs ; *e.g.* to settle cases of fiefs[1] disputed between Crown and Church ; to co-operate in keeping
order and executing royal justice under the severe assizes of
Clarendon and Northampton ; to assess the personal property of individuals and their liability to taxation : and also
as an approved instrument for litigants to settle cases relating to lands, instead of using the brutal judicial combat.

(3) The status of the shire court in the reign of Richard I.

[1 Estates granted on condition of services to be rendered to the grantor.]

1194, when it had reached its fullest activity, and when its four leading knights would go round to arrange for a representative body of twelve knights or freeholders for each hundred, whose mere report could banish any notorious bad character from the realm, or put to the ordeal those suspected of crime; could decide what lands and feudal dues were the Crown's and what were not; could determine civil suits between subject and subject; and so on, down to the punishment of fraudulent weights and measures.

This was local "self-government" in the fullest and truest sense. To raise it to central self-government, there was only needed the calling of these local representatives to a central assembly, and the working out for that assembly the control of all government. To accomplish the former was the task of the thirteenth century (1194–1295), to accomplish the latter needed four more centuries and five revolutions.

As to the union of shires in a central assembly, the first step in this process was in 1213, the meeting at St. Albans of four men and the reeve from every township in the royal demesne, to assess the damage done to Church lands in the recent years of the Interdict. Later in the same year four knights from each shire were to meet at Oxford "to confer with the king on the affairs of the kingdom"; but this meeting never took place. In 1226, knights were called from eight shires to discuss some disputed articles in Magna Charta.

The early instances show that it was not till the struggle of the barons against the king's thirty years' misrule had forced men to reflect on the principles of government, that the calling of such a representative assembly came to be realised as important. The ministers had called the knights in 1254 as a last expedient to get a grant of money. In 1261 the barons having called knights to meet at St. Albans, the king was virtuously indignant at the idea of such an irregular meeting, and solemnly charged them to come "to Windsor and nowhere else"; and in the brief fifteen months of Simon de Montfort's actual power, he twice called a representative Parliament; one in June, 1264, and one more famous in January, 1265.

The fact was, that in the fierce political struggles of these years between the three groups of barons, who may be called

the Royalist, the Aristocratic, and the Nationalist, the great
question suddenly emerged: What was to be the constitution
of England? The form in which we should now put such
a question would be, How is the central assembly to be
organised? Is its constitutive principle to be baronage, or
military tenure, or representation? And if the last, What are
to be the constituencies, and who to be the representatives?

In the thirteenth century all this is summed up in the
question which meets us everywhere in the chroniclers, the
constitutional documents, and the political songs of the time,
What is the *communa*? **The Commons.**

Now this word in its various forms—*communa, communitas, commun*—was a term which sometimes was as wide as
our "nation," *communa totius terrae*, but often, practically,
was as narrow as baronial exclusiveness itself could wish;
e.g. the committee of barons, elected in 1258 *per communitatem*, are really elected by a knot of less than twenty
leading men. But in each and all of its meanings it has a
certain sense of organisation; and thus if men must take
tenure in chief to be the organising principle of the English
realm, then the *communa* must be the barons, and the
barons only. But it was too late for such a baronial
monopoly. Could military service then be taken as the
principle? If so, the assembly might be representative, but
would represent only the lesser chief-tenants and the rest
of the class of knights. But this would have been an
anachronism, now that the military aspect of feudalism
had become unreal, and the knights were no longer a
fighting class, but stay-at-home English gentry. Should
the *communa* then be taken to be all who dwelt on English
land? This would be too wide and vague a use. What
senses then remained? The sense in which it had been
consistently used, to denote the old shire-moot, the gathering
of all freeholders in the shire (*Communitas scirae*), whether
rural or urban. The assembly should be the house of assembled shiremoots (*Domus communitatum*). This is the
sense in which De Montfort's Parliament of 1265 was the first
House of Commons—the sense in which Edward I., in the
first Parliament after his landing in England, announced his
having got a grant from the "Commons of the realm." It

was the final triumph of the shire as the unit of the English system. The union of Anglo-Saxon local institutions with Norman centralisation had at last been effected.

The union of the two classes, burgesses and knights, distinguishes our early Parliamentary growth from that of any other country. Nothing, then, can be a more important fact, yet it is not, for all that, an isolated one, but a simple consequence of the composition of the shire itself. From our earliest history the boroughs had been counted as parts of the shire; they sent their leading men to attend at the shire court before the king's judges. The representation of the boroughs was a necessary corollary of the representation of the *communitas scirae.* The older writers therefore exaggerated when they spoke of De Montfort as the founder of Parliaments; they failed, too, to notice that he treated the boroughs not as a part of the shire, but almost as a separate estate —viewing them, in fact, as Continental *municipia,* not as English boroughs.

(B) The representatives were elected.

The Elective Principle. This was not so obvious and natural a thing as it now seems to us. Thus the feudal theory itself professed to supply a sort of representation; the lord grants an aid for himself and his vassals, even including the villeins.

In fact, the greater value of elected representatives over nominated was a financial discovery which was made during the latter part of the twelfth century, but was not distinctly applied to purposes of Parliament till 1254.

Again, it was quite possible that the expansion of the Great Council, which was seen to be inevitable, might be attempted by simply calling representatives of the lesser tenants-in-chief. This would have given an assembly of lesser nobles, whose class spirit would kill Parliament; and this was often in the fourteenth century declared, though erroneously, to be the proper theory of the Commons. Fortunately, tenure was already too effete by the middle of the thirteenth century to be relied on; and these lesser chief-tenants had sunk into the shire; the lesser nobles had become gentry.

(C) It was in this way that tenure was replaced by representation as the constituent principle of the legislative assembly. The one decisive influence throughout all this process was the influence of taxation.

Its importance in our English history has been immense; **Taxation as a Factor in English History,** the constitutional history might, in fact, be written, so to speak, in terms of taxation. The improvement of the judicial system in the twelfth century originated as a mode of gathering taxes; the royal administration was primarily a tax-collecting agency, and the growth of Parliament was necessitated by new forms of taxation. Thus the feudal aid, which was the earliest form of tax, being in theory a voluntary gift, established the principle that taxation requires the subject's assent. When the new taxes on personalty came in, this assent was made a greater reality by the tax-payers' help being required for assessment and collection; gradually the separate negotiations with each shire were simplified by calling the representatives of each shire to meet all at once and settle the grant. This is best seen by examining closely the action of Edward I. in the **and in the Formation of Parliament.** year 1290. He had in May called a feudal council to pass an important land statute; this council also granted him a feudal aid. Such an aid would be worth about £18,000; but in view of his great needs, it occurred to him that he might do better to get a wider national grant which would include personalty as well as land, and would be worth at least £40,000. He therefore called, in July, knights from each shire, who made the desired grant.

Thus it is clear that as late as 1290, so great a man as Edward I. still regarded the old feudal council as adequate for all purposes of government except the new form of taxation; for this, and this alone, he deemed a representative assembly necessary. The same feeling is clear in his treatment of the clergy; he laid down the maxim that they must at least pay, since the laity both pay and fight; the clergy possessed spiritualities, and spiritualities must bear their share of national burdens; and therefore the clergy must also be formed into a representative estate. In this policy, after a hard struggle, he succeeded; only his weaker successors yielded to a compromise which saved for the clergy their cherished independence, with results fatal in the end to themselves.

    (D) The last step to complete a Parliament was to bring the three estates together. The estate of the magnates had by long tradition been settled in the form of a small assembly of greater tenants-in-chief; what Edward I. did here was to intensify its tendency to restriction, practically reducing the number of peers to about one-half of what it had been, and exercising a considerable freedom of selection as to the individuals composing it. The clergy had been rapidly forming themselves for their own purposes into a representative body, or rather, two bodies—the Convocations of Canterbury and York. These Edward united into one Parliamentary estate of clergy; and at last, not till 1295, called all three estates at the same place and time to treat of the same business. It is curious to see that even after De Montfort's Parliament, containing magnates, though few in number, a great body of clergy, and a Commons of knights and burgesses, it still required thirty years to work out into permanent form the Parliament of three estates. There were probably seven Parliaments called in this interval, but in each there was some incompleteness and imperfection, such as absence of the burgesses or absence of the clergy; and 1295 was the first date in which each estate was properly constituted and all three met at once. An " Estate " means a class capable of a separate taxation; the three estates were thus—lands, spiritualities, chattels. By this means a double character was given to the Parliament; it was

a representation of the nation in its great classes, as well as a representation of the nation in its local communities. The former character it has now completely lost, there is no representation of classes as such; the latter is very much changed by the substitution of electoral districts for real *communitates*.

    A review of the early period of Parliamentary history brings clearly before us :—

(1) The slowness of its growth. It may be said that our jury-system and our Parliament, the two most characteristic and most imitated of English institutions, have the same root; and this root goes far back into the old Germanic life. The first use of elected representatives to act for their shires is at least as old as Henry I.; and even the calling them to a central body took eighty-two years (1213–95) to

work out. This means that the system was well tried and tested on the smaller scale first; representation was applied to petty local affairs long before it was raised to a greater sphere the Parliament stood firm because its foundations were laid deep in national habit; and English self-government has lasted for centuries, because it had been itself the slow product of centuries.

(2) The political system is a reflection of the social system. Nothing is more fundamental in the modern view of politics than the determination of the question, Who shall have the franchise—who shall have political right? This question, we should say, must be the very first point determined before any representative system can be set up. Yet this point, in the early days of our Parliamentary history, was never determined at all, was never even touched on; the first actual legislation upon the point was not till 1430—more than a century afterwards, when the right was declared to belong to freeholders of forty shillings a year and upwards. The point was, in fact, never explicitly determined in the early period, because it was never consciously raised. The political framework was merely the framework of society as it stood. That society, framed upon feudal ideas, regarded only the freeholder as an integral part of itself. The freeholders constituted the shire-moot. The House of Commons meant the House of assembled Shire-moots. So the Commons were simply the freeholders.

(3) The foundation of Parliament was no new departure; it was not a revolution. It altered none of the old landmarks; it made no new divisions. It was no electoral system, suspended in the air, invisible except when it descends to earth at polling times, with electoral divisions arithmetically marked out, and electors who have no tie or bond, except that once in seven years they all drop a paper into the ballot-box on the same day.

UNDER John the history of the Church is the history of the State. Under Henry III. the scene is changed. The Popes preserved the throne for the young king, and when he was firmly seated on it, and grown to man's estate, they demanded

W. H. HUTTON. The Church under Henry III.

the payment which their own designs made necessary. Demands for the Pope's wars multiplied, till the archbishop,
Edmund Rich, left England in despair. Protest after protest
was drawn up, the most famous being a letter of the rectors
of Berkshire in 1240, in which they exclaimed against the
scandal that had arisen throughout the world against the
Roman Church on account of its exactions, and declared that
the patrimony of other churches was in no wise liable to

Alien Ecclesiastics. assessment by or tribute to the Roman Pontiff. Again the
Church was flooded with foreign prelates. The king's half-
brothers and the kinsmen of his wife poured into the land to
fatten on the ecclesiastical revenues, and the Popes, by
"provision," gave the best benefices to men of their own
court (p. 562). The weakness of the king and the torpor
of the bishops allowed these abuses to be multiplied,
and the chronicles are full of cries of distress and appeals
to the tradition of national independence. Two gleams of
light alone relieve the darkness of the picture. One is
the life of Grosseteste, Bishop of Lincoln, the other the
coming of the Friars.

Grosseteste. Robert Grosseteste was for eighteen years, 1235 to 1253,
the foremost Churchman in the land; first in internal reform
of the Church, first in the support of barons against king,
first in resistance to papal aggression. He was the friend of
Simon de Montfort, and the tutor of his son, and the keen
supporter of all attempts at political reform. From him the
bishops, such as Walter de Cantilupe, learnt to stand together
for the freedom of the people. From him the clergy gained
courage to withstand the corruption of the times and the
exactions of the Popes. "Struck with amazement," says
Matthew Paris, "at the avarice of the Romans, he caused his
clerks carefully to reckon and estimate all the revenues of
foreigners in England, and it was discovered and found for
truth that the present Pope, Innocent IV., had pauperised
the whole Church more than all his predecessors from the
time of the primitive papacy. The revenue of the alien clerks,
whom he had planted in England, and whom the Church
had enriched, amounted to 70,000 marks, while the king's
revenue could not be reckoned at more than a third of
that sum."

When the Pope required him to institute to a prebend in his own cathedral his nephew, a mere boy, though ordained, and who had no intention of even visiting England, he replied in a letter which is the most striking instance of English feeling against Rome that is to be found in the history of the Middle Ages; and almost with his last breath he appealed " to the nobles of England and the citizens of London and the community of the whole realm" against the injury which the English Church was receiving from foreign intruders, " who not only strive to tear off the fleece, but do not even know the features of their flock."

Such protests as those of Grosseteste might seem to have borne little fruit. But the Church was being more surely regenerated from within (p. 615). In 1220 Dominicans first landed in England; in 1224 the Franciscans. Scholars and preachers, the former found a ready welcome at Oxford. The latter soon followed, and before long made the theological faculty their own. Both were not only leaders in learning, but expressed for the people from whom they were sprung the needs of the day, and the views of the villeins as to the great issues and the great men. The Oxford Franciscans had Grosseteste in 1224 for their rector, and twelve years later numbered Adam of Marsh among their brethren. The two were lifelong friends. Adam was one of the most eminent men of his day; he was a familiar guest at Court, as well as an assiduous lecturer at Oxford; a counsellor of Simon de Montfort, too, no less than of the king; and all the time he strictly followed the rule of St. Francis, " serving the wretched and the vile, and performing the prime and essential duties of a friar." For the early friars were not only the leaders of a great spiritual revival and the inaugurators of an intellectual movement; they were, above all, the apostles of a social mission.

The monastic orders had done their chief work in the country districts; the mendicants were the missionaries of the towns. During the twelfth and thirteenth centuries the cities had grown greatly, and outside the walls, in the crowded courts, or in the marshes by the river, there herded masses of men and women, neglected and outcast. Amid these multitudes the foul plagues confounded by the chroniclers

The Friars.

under the generic name leprosy (p. 528) found a ready prey; and there the friars from the first sought and found their work. All Franciscan novices were made to undergo a period of training in leper hospitals, and then the friars settled, where we may see the names of the friaries still remain, in

OPEN-AIR PREACHING (MS. Add. 10,292).
(*British Museum.*)

the most crowded parts of the towns. From their work came the first impulse of the Middle Ages towards the study of medicine, and the good that they did in the mitigation of some of the worst forms of human suffering is incalculable. The whole idea of the religious life was enlarged by their action; the gulf that had been fixed between it and the secular profession was bridged by their example. The enrolment among their numbers of men still engaged in their own callings and possessing their own property, but pledged to good works of charity and mercy under their guidance, must have enormously elevated the standard of social life. From the time when they abandoned the restrictions which St. Francis had placed on learning, they became the leaders of English culture; and before the end of Henry III's reign they were as supreme in the sphere of education as they were in missionary and philanthropic work.

Robert Kilwardby became Archbishop of Canterbury in 1273, and before this Bonaventura had refused the Archbishopric of York. Both were Franciscans. Alexander Hales, Duns Scotus, and Roger Bacon were the English leaders of a revolution in the world of thought. Thus, by the accession of Edward I., through the wisdom of individual prelates and the great work of the friars, the Church in England had more than recovered from the severe blows it had undergone at the hands of John. The corporate life of the Church was organised and consolidated : the clerical estate had organisation and did not lack leaders. It remained to be seen how to meet the difficulties that might arise between a strong church and a strong king.

The history of medieval England cannot be studied even cursorily without its being apparent that the Church exercised, politically and socially, as well as in religion, a profound influence on the national life. This influence was supreme in its own sphere, and unchallenged. During the period of which we have spoken there were practically no competing forces. There were no heretics and no dissenters. The foreign sect whose disciples reached England in Henry II.'s reign[1] made but one convert, and she was a wretched woman (*muliercula* says the chronicler) who recanted at the first sign of persecution. Within the church, theological warfare was at rest; outside, the Jews were the only non-Christian body of whom home-dwelling English folk had any knowledge. It is thus of great interest to know what was the attitude which the supreme religious society adopted towards the infidels within the area of its rule. The Church was not, as a body, harsh towards the Jews. There are many acts recorded of individual friendship and kindness. Jewish physicians were friendly and honoured by Christians; monastic societies held amicable relations with Jewish bodies; the

[1 A band of thirty Albigenses from Gascony, whose fate is described by William of Newburgh, II. c. 13.]

chroniclers, all of them monks or ecclesiastics, rarely, if ever, speak approvingly of outrages on Jews. Still, as time went on, and Jews in England grew rich upon the profits of the usury which they alone might exercise, more bitter feelings sprang up (p. 669 *seqq.*). From 1144, the date of the first recorded charge of murder of a Christian boy, the Jews

REMAINS OF THE SHRINE OF LITTLE ST. HUGH OF LINCOLN.

suffered from time to time from accusations most often false and judgments generally hasty. The prominent cases of this kind created quite a new cult in England. The boy martyr's shrine became not seldom the most popular in the cathedral. St. William of Norwich in 1144, Harold of Gloucester in 1168, Robert of Edmundsbury in 1181, a nameless boy in London in 1244, buried with great pomp at

St. Paul's, and St. Hugh of Lincoln in 1255, are the most prominent instances. It is difficult to refuse all credit to stories so circumstantial and so frequent; but on the other hand it may be said that the tales are too many for them all to be true, and most of them may be dismissed as wholly fictitious. It is at least clear that even here the clergy were not pledged to persecutions. We learn from Matthew Paris and from the Burton Annals that the mendicant orders successfully pleaded for the pardon of Jews charged with a crime of this kind. The general attitude of the clerical order then was tolerant, and the toleration may be ascribed to the undisputed power of the Church.

What this power was in greater towns, and in the nation at large, the general history of the time abundantly illustrates. More obscurely hidden are the facts which tell of its influence in the country districts. Here the work of the monasteries in the twelfth and of the friars in the thirteenth century was a direct work of evangelising and civilisation. Churches rose in the thinly populated shires which still bear witness to the practical nature of the popular devotion. Round the parish church the village life centred, and in the smaller towns the guild-association, starting quite in the heart of the country, as at Burford, in the eleventh century worked in close connection with a common faith and a common worship. The parish priests were generally simple, if ignorant, men. Their standard of life was at least as high as that of their superiors in office and much higher than that of the society in which they lived. Superstition, it is undoubted, was almost universal; but it was a kindly superstition, lit up by many gleams of intelligence. When we read that in East Anglia there appeared one harvest-time, no man knew whence, two children, a boy and a girl, "completely green in their persons, and clad in garments of a strange colour and unknown materials," we learn also that these strange visitors were most kindly welcomed, baptised into the fellowship of the Church, and cherished "till at length they changed their original colour through the natural effect of our food." William of Newburgh tells also a story of country religion which is not without a beauty, as well as a quaintness, of its own. One Ketell, a villein, in

The Church in the Rural Districts.

the service of a certain clerk named Ham, dwelling at Farneham in Yorkshire, had the strange gift of seeing the evil spirits who plagued mankind. Still he lived on simply as before, making no profession of superiority to his neighbours, only regarding not matrimony but embracing the single life, abstaining from the eating of flesh and the wearing of linen, and ever as his work allowed attending the daily offices in the village church, the first to enter and the last to depart. The spirit of devotion was kept alive by anchorites, living in caves and by unfrequented streams, to whom the people would make pilgrimage to learn from their simple faith, and wonder at their austere holiness. One of the most beautiful passages in the narrative of William, the prior of Newburgh, is his account of how he saw Godric, the hermit of Finchale on the Wear by Durham, a few days before his death—an old and ignorant man, but full of "a surprising dignity and grace." It is indeed a relief to turn from the wars and wranglings of the great barons and great ecclesiastics to watch the progress of humanity and gentle deeds as the Church spread her hands over the by-paths and the secluded nooks of country life.

F. W. MAIT-LAND. The Growth of Juris-prudence. 1154-1273.

DURING the period which divides the coronation of Henry II. (1154) from the coronation of Edward I. (1272) definite legislation was still an uncommon thing. Great as were the changes due to Henry's watchful and restless activity, they were changes that were effected without the pomp of solemn law-making. A few written or even spoken words communicated to his justices, those justices whom he was constantly sending to perambulate the country, might do great things, might institute new methods of procedure, might bring new classes of men and of things within the cognisance of the royal court. Some of his ordinances—or "assizes," as they were called—have come down to us; others we have lost. No one was at any great pains to preserve their text, because they were regarded, not as new laws, but as mere temporary instructions which might be easily altered. They soon sink into the mass of unenacted "common law." Even in the next, the thirteenth, century

EVIL SPIRITS DEFEATED BY ST. GUTHLAC (Harley Roll Y. 6).

some of Henry's rules were regarded as traditional rules which had come down from a remote time, and which might be ascribed to the Conqueror, the Confessor, or any other king around whom a mist of fable had gathered.

Thus it came about that the lawyers of Edward I.'s day—and that was the day in which a professional class of temporal lawyers first became prominent in England—thought of Magna Charta as the oldest statute of the realm, the first chapter in the written law of the land, the earliest of those texts the very words of which are law. And what they did their successors do at the present day. The Great Charter stands in the forefront of our statute book, though of late years a great deal of it has been repealed. And certainly it is worthy of its place. It is worthy of its place just because it is no philosophical or oratorical declaration of the rights of man, nor even of the rights of Englishmen, but an intensely practical document, the fit prologue for those intensely practical statutes which English Parliaments will publish in age after age. What is more, it is a grand compromise, and a fit prologue for all those thousands of compromises in which the practical wisdom of the English race will always be expressing itself. Its very form is a compromise—in part that of a free grant of liberties made by the king, in part that of a treaty between him and his subjects, which is to be enforced against him if he breaks it. And then in its detailed clauses it must do something for all those sorts and conditions of men who have united to resist John's tyranny —for the bishop, the clerk, the baron, the knight, the burgess, the merchant—and there must be some give and take between these classes, for not all their interests are harmonious. But even in the Great Charter there is not much new law; indeed, its own theory of itself (if we may use such a phrase) is that the old law, which a lawless king has set at naught, is to be restored, defined, covenanted, and written.

The Magna Charta of our statute book is not exactly the charter that John sealed at Runnymede; it is a charter granted by his son and successor, Henry III., the text of the original document having been modified on more than one occasion. Only two other acts of Henry's long reign attained

REMAINS
OF THE

GREAT CHARTER
(Cott. Ch. xiii. 31).

the rank of statute law. The Provisions of Merton, enacted
by a great assembly of prelates and nobles, introduced several
novelties, and contain those famous words, " We will not
have the laws of England changed," which were the reply of
the barons to a request made by the bishops, who were
desirous that our insular rule, " Once a bastard always a
bastard," might yield to the law of the universal Church, and
that marriage might have a retroactive effect. Among
Englishmen there was no wish to change the laws of
England. If only the king and his foreign favourites would
observe those laws, then—such was the common opinion—all
would be well. A change came; vague discontent crystallised
in the form of definite grievances. After the Barons' War
the king, though he had triumphed over his foes, and was
enjoying his own again, was compelled to redress many of
those grievances by the Provisions of Marlborough, or, as they
have been commonly called, the Statute of Marlbridge. When,
a few years afterwards, Henry died, the written, the enacted
law of England consisted in the main of but four documents,
which we can easily read through in half an hour—there was
the Great Charter, there was the sister-charter which defined
the forest law, there were the Statutes of Merton and of
Marlbridge. To these we might add a few minor ordinances;
but the old Anglo-Saxon dooms were by this time utterly
forgotten, the law-books of the Norman age were already unintelligible, and even the assizes of Henry II., though but a
century old, had become part and parcel of " the common
law," not to be distinguished from the unenacted rules which
had gathered round them. Englishmen might protest that
they would not change the law of England, but as a matter
of fact the law of England was being changed very rapidly
by the incessant decisions of the powerful central court.

W. LAIRD CLOWES. The Navy. So long as the navy of England was chiefly composed of
semi-irregular forces that were summoned to the king's
service only upon stated occasions, or when their help was
urgently required, there was always much lawlessness in the
narrow seas. This lawlessness was increased rather than
diminished by the growth of the influence and importance of

RUNNYMEDE.

the Cinque Ports, which, although they had possessed charters and privileges from an early period, did not become a considerable power in the realm until the reign of Henry III. That monarch, in 1229, issued an "ordinance touching the service of shipping" to be furnished by them, and, since the ordinance well explains their position and duties, and may fairly be regarded as the beginning of their greatness, it is worth quoting.

"These," it runs, "are the ports of the King of England, having liberties which other ports have not, that is to say, as more fully appeareth in the charters thereof made : Hastings, to which pertaineth as members one town on the seashore, in Seaford, Pevensey, Bulvarhithe, Hydney, Iham, Beaksborne, Grench, and Northye. The services thereof due to our lord the king, twenty-one ships, and in every ship twenty-one men with one boy, which is called a gromet. Winchelsea and Rye as members, that is to say, Winchelsea ten ships, and Rye five ships, with men and boys as above; Romney, to which pertaineth Promhill, Lyd, Oswardstone, Dengemarsh, and Old Romney, five ships, with men and boys as above; Hithe, to which pertaineth Westhithe, five ships, with men and boys as above; Dover, to which pertaineth Folkestone, Feversham, and Margate, not of soil but of chattels, twenty-one ships, as Hastings, with men and boys as above; Sandwich, to which pertaineth Fordwich, Reculver, Sarre, Storrey, and Deale, not of soil but of chattels, five ships, with men and boys as above; being fifty-seven ships, one thousand one hundred and forty men, and fifty-seven boys, in all one thousand one hundred and ninety-seven persons. The service which the Barons of the Cinque Ports acknowledge to do to the king at the summons of the service by forty days before the going out, viz. yearly, if it shall happen, for fifteen days at their own cost, so that the first day be reckoned from the day on which they shall hoist up the sails of the ships to sail to the parts to which they ought to go; and further, as long as the king will, to be kept by ordinance of the king." [1]

[1] Nicolas, "History of the Royal Navy," I. p. 261: quoting from Jeake, "Charters of the Cinque Ports" (pub. 1728), p. 25. In the total as above given, the contributions of Winchelsea and Rye are counted as part of that of Hastings, thus reducing the amount due from that town to six ships.

Besides the duty of furnishing ships and mariners, says Nicolas the barons of the Cinque Ports have, for many

SEAL OF FAVERSHAM.

centuries, performed an honorary service at the coronation of the kings and queens of England; the earliest instance of which was the coronation of Eleanor of Provence, consort of Henry III., in 1236.

Already, in 1226, the Cinque Ports had been very useful against Savery de Maloleone, a powerful French piratical baron, and others, and had, in the interests of their Sovereign, "slain and plundered like pirates." Forty years later,

under Henry de Montfort, they began to presume upon their power, and no longer attacked merely those who might be supposed to be the enemies of their country. To such an extent was their audacity carried, that when, in 1264, the Pope sent a cardinal legate to reconcile the king and the barons, they prevented his landing. Indeed, their piratical depredations at about that time were reported to have enhanced the price of all foreign goods

Piracy.

SEAL OF LYDD.

in England. The institution, therefore, though in war-time it was occasionally valuable, was by no means an unmixed boon. To put it plainly, the Cinque Ports, in their early years, were

"Gromet," a lad, is connected with the English word *groom* (A.-S. *guma*, man). "Not of land but of chattels," is interpreted to mean that the cost was borne by the latter only. Of the places mentioned, Bulvarhithe and Iham are in the neighbourhood of Hastings, and the latter was part of the Parliamentary borough till the Reform Act of 1885. Hydney (now non-existent) was near Eastbourne; Bekesbourne is three miles S.E. of Canterbury; Grench, Greneche, or Grange, is two miles from Chatham; Dengemarsh is one of the subdivisions of Romney Marsh; Oswardstone may be Orlestone; Fordwich is two miles N.E. of Canterbury; Storrey is presumably Sturry; Reculver (the Roman Regulbium, p. 103, note) is three miles E. of Herne Bay.]

little better than nests of chartered sea robbers.   More than once Henry III. made compensation to people who had been plundered by those freebooters.

They were, unfortunately, by no means the only pirates on the coasts at the time.   There was Sir William de Marish, a proscribed murderer, who seized Lundy, made of it a piratical stronghold, and even began to build a ship there. Lynn, Dartmouth and some of the small ports in Norfolk harboured pirates in plenty.   And there was the celebrated Eustace the Monk, who, though he fought sometimes for England and sometimes for France, was always a pirate in

SEAL OF WINCHELSEA.

his methods.   Akin to the pirates, and almost equally dangerous to peaceable persons, were the privateers, a class of irregulars which Henry III. was the first English king to license.   He granted, in fact, what later would have been called formal letters of marque.   " Know ye," declares one of these documents, dated 1243, " that we have granted and given licence to Adam Robernolt and William Le Sauvage and their companions whom they take with them, to annoy our enemies by sea or by land wheresoever they are able, so that they share with us the half of all their gain."

The increase in the dimensions of ships continued, and we read of vessels having decks and cabins, and more than one mast.   When Eustace the Monk was captured after the sea-fight in 1217, he was found concealed in the hold of one of the prizes ; and when, in 1228, a vessel was ordered to be sent to Gascony with the king's effects, a small sum of money was paid "for making a chamber in the said ship to place the king's things in." In 1242 the cabins for the king and queen were directed to be wainscoted. We do not know exactly what were the dimensions of the largest English ships of the period, but they may well have been similar, if not superior, to those of the largest of Continental vessels. The particulars of the finest of a number of ships furnished by Venice to France in 1268 have been preserved. She was

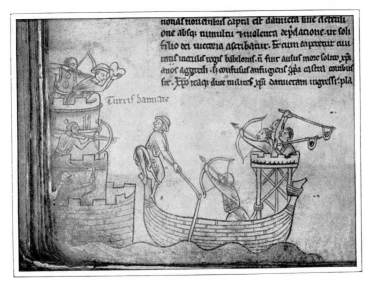

SHIP ATTACKING A FORT.
(Corpus Christi College, Cambridge)

110 ft. long, 40 ft. broad, and $11\frac{1}{2}$ ft. deep in the hold, and the height between decks on the main deck was $6\frac{1}{2}$ ft. Her complement was one hundred and ten officers and men. A vessel of these dimensions must have been of between four and five hundred tons burthen—about as large, that is, as a twenty-gun ship of Nelson's days. As for English seamanship, it was already celebrated. In 1270, during a storm in the Mediterranean, the English squadron was the only part of the allied fleet that escaped without loss. On the coasts lights and beacons began to be regularly maintained, quays

and piers to be built, and provision to be made to prevent the silting up of certain harbours and estuaries. There were dockyards of some kind not only at Portsmouth, but also at Rye, Winchelsea, Shoreham, and elsewhere; and vessels laid up in ordinary seem to have been usually protected by means of sheds. Naval pay did not increase. Masters were paid sixpence, and mariners threepence a day as in earlier times.

Tactics.   Of the naval tactics of the period we know something from the accounts that have been preserved of the great

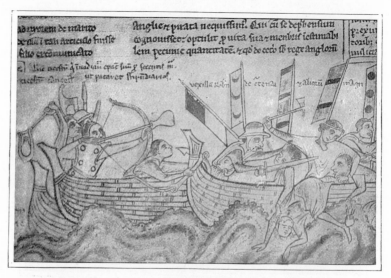

A SEA FIGHT.
(*Corpus Christi College, Cambridge.*)

English victory gained in the Strait of Dover in 1217. The English sought and secured the weather-gage, and then bore down, grappled the enemy, and maintained the closest possible action. Bows, cross-bows, slings, swords, axes, lances, and unslaked lime were employed; and the galleys, the over-hanging bows of which were shod with iron, were successfully used as rams. From the masthead of the commander's ship a banner was displayed by day, and a lantern by night; and directions were given by the officers of the Cinque Ports that in battle efforts should be made to cut adrift the hostile commander's banner, with the object of throwing his fleet into confusion.

THE DANGERS OF THE SEA. (*MS. Harl. 4751.*)

[*To face p.* 590.

[1273]

It is during the reign of Henry III. that the magnet seems to have been first commonly used for purposes of navigation by European seamen.[1] A Provençal versifier of the early part of the thirteenth century describes the rude compass of his day thus :—"This star" (the Pole Star) "moves not. They make a contrivance which, thanks to the virtue of the magnet, an ugly brownish stone to which iron readily joins itself, cannot lie. They observe the right point after they have caused the needle to touch it ; and they put the needle (placed in a rush) into water, without anything more, and the rush keeps it afloat. Then it turns at once its point with such certainty towards the star that no man may doubt it, nor will anything induce it to mislead. When the sea is dark and lowering, and they can see neither star nor moon, they place a light by the needle, and then they have no fear of going wrong." Another versifier speaks of a cork instead of a rush having been used as a float. But it is clear that even at this early period the properties of the loadstone had long been known.

Towards commerce the Government was well disposed. In his great Charter of liberties, Henry undertook that foreign merchants should have safe-conducts to enter and quit England, and, while in the country, might trade freely by land or water without injury, according to old and lawful customs, except in war-time. If any merchants belonging to a country that had declared war with England were in the king's territories at the outbreak of hostilities, they were to be attached, though without injury to their persons or goods, until the king knew in what manner the merchants of his dominions were being treated by the hostile State ; and "if our merchants be well treated there, theirs shall likewise be so treated with us." During several of the wars with France, trade between the two countries was actually interfered with only to a very slight extent ; and when it was interfered with, the interference was usually begun by France, and continued by England merely as a measure of retaliation.

[1 The earliest reference seems to be in the *De Utensilibus* of Alexander Neckam, a monk of St. Albans, who died in 1217. *Cf.* Mr. C. R. Beazley's Introduction to Vol. II. of Azurara's *Chronicle of the Discovery of Guinea* (Hakluyt Society), 1899.]

REGINALD HUGHES.
Architecture and Art.

WE have already seen how the Norman manner of building had slowly given way before the advance of the Early English style. The tide had begun to flow as far back as the reign of Henry; it had suddenly swelled to a great volume in the last years of Richard, until (under his brother John) the change was complete, and the last traces of Norman form, structure, feeling, and detail had been finally submerged. It was but natural, therefore, that the reign of John's son should not be a period of architectural change, for it represents the manhood and old age of the new style, just as the reigns of his father and uncle represent its boyhood and infancy. The elegant forms that had been carried from Canterbury to Rochester, and from Lincoln to Ely, are not changed—they are only developed and applied —in the chapter-house at Oxford, the choir of Worcester, the "nine altars" at Durham, and the south transept at York. The round termination to the east end has now practically disappeared, at least in thoroughly English churches, and the square end with its groups of lancets (Ely is perhaps, the most perfect specimen) has supplanted the apse.

By a piece of rare good fortune we have one great church which is built in this most perfect and national style, and which, owing to the fortuitous destruction of later additions, is an example almost throughout of pure Early English work. This is the Cathedral of Salisbury, commenced by Bishop Poore on a new site in 1220, and finished by Bishop Bridport in 1258. The spire is, it is true, "an afterthought" of the fourteenth century; but it was built by an architect who did not deem himself wiser than his forefathers, and is in admirable keeping with the rest of the church. Though by no means one of our largest cathedrals, it had the good fortune to be early recognised as the perfect national type, with the result that, when modifications of the old Norman cathedrals were undertaken, they were most frequently assimilated to the plan of Salisbury. No doubt it lacks the richness of the style that was to follow; no doubt it misses the sublime sense of strength that belonged to that which preceded it; but for excellence of workmanship, for magnificence depending on the ordered beauty of the composing

ENTRANCE AND INTERIOR OF THE GALILEE, ELY CATHEDRAL.

lines, for the elegance arising from the multiplicity of finely executed forms, it remains unrivalled. Elegance, indeed, appears to have spoken its last word in its clustered pillars with their light open shafts, in its tapering vaults, its light mouldings along the groins of the roof, its sparse enrichments of violette and the conventional folded leaf which we call the crocket. In Salisbury nothing seems done for effect, either in mass or ornament; the minimum of visible effort seems aimed at, and this difficult aim seems perfectly achieved. In one point only does Salisbury fail, and that is in the poor doorways and mean

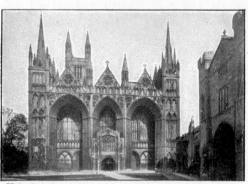

Photo: Poulton.
PETERBOROUGH CATHEDRAL, WEST FRONT.

and parcelled west front. It is just in the west fronts that almost all English cathedrals fail, and almost all French cathedrals succeed. The great exception belongs, it is true, to this style, and is found in the triple porch at Peterborough, which is probably slightly earlier than Salisbury; yet grandiose and magnificent as is this porch (the great arches are eighty-one feet high), it is a thing apart, having no reference to the cathedral behind it—an astounding *tour de force*, but constructively meaningless and insincere.

West-minster Abbey Trans-formed.
London, generally so poor in churches, is fortunate in possessing the great Abbey of St. Peter at Westminster; yet, strange to say, our national "abbey" is the most un-English of our great ecclesiastical buildings. It was in 1245, as Salisbury was approaching its completion, that Henry, mindful of the devotion he had towards St. Edward the Confessor, ordered the Norman church of St. Peter to be enlarged. To do the king justice, he had always been mindful of the Confessor, for in the fourth year of his reign he had laid the foundations of a lady chapel at the extremity of the old Norman choir. But now, twenty-five years later, he

THE CHOIR AND APSE, WESTMINSTER ABBEY.

proceeded to carry out a much more ambitious scheme. He
pulled down the whole of the east end of the church, the
Norman choir and transepts, and even part of the nave, and
then, with the aid of the "most subtle artificers, English and
foreign," he rebuilt them. The choir and apse, with the choir
chapels, seem to have been first built, then the transepts, and
one bay of the nave, while the work on the chapel-house
must have gone on with that on the choir. In the centre
he erected a stately tomb, and there he set the bones of the
Confessor. Nothing was spared by the king to make this
greatest of all our abbey churches sumptuous. He introduced
glass mosaic in the decorations, coloured glass in the
windows, and fresco painting on the flat spaces. The walls,
to the top of the triforium, he covered with diaper,[1] probably
gilt and painted as brightly as an illumination.

A special effect of richness, too, was given to the triforium
by a double arcading, by overlaying the mouldings with
sculptured foliage, the large arches being filled with two
smaller ones with pointed trefoil heads, and carrying above a
foliated circle with a triple ornament on the cusps. The
finest part of Henry's work is, however, in the transepts,
which are spacious and broad-spreading, and quite English
in character. This is, however, the only part of his work of
which this can be truly said, for the proportion of height to
the other dimensions of his choir and fragmentary nave are
quite unlike anything to be found elsewhere in England.
Beyond the transepts foreign influence is dominant, though
the east end of Westminster wears a less foreign air to-day
than in the century of its erection. Henry VII.'s chapel now
occupies a large part of the space where stood that dedicated
to our Lady by Henry III., and this, according to the
original design, formed the centre of a ring of apsidal

---

[1] The patterns known as "diaper" seem to have been originally taken from
Persian silks or other Eastern fabrics, and the word is probably Persian and
akin to jasper, the reference being to the various colours of that stone. The
word in its early use in France (whence it came to England) seems to have
meant rather an arrangement of variegated colours than a chequered design.
By a curious accident, the place in Europe which became famous for the
manufacture of textiles in which these designs were imitated was the Flemish
town of Ypres, and this has given rise to a false etymology (like that which
finds Mars' Hill in Areopagus) which explains diaper as a corrupt form of
d'Ypres.

chapels, an arrangement than which nothing could be more typically French. Westminster Abbey is, indeed, only one bit of evidence corroborating the fact that the King of England,

THE CHAPTER-HOUSE, WESTMINSTER.

who, by the loss of the Angevin and Norman provinces, was king of little else, was still half a Frenchman, and that the heart which after death was to belong to the Abbey of Fontevrault, had in life scant sympathy with the English genius.

It was the mere malice of Fate which made King Henry the builder of the chapter-house, where the Commons (that part of the hated institution of Parliament which he hated worst) was subsequently to find a home for two centuries. It is a typical specimen of the Early English chapter-house. In form it belongs to the rounded buildings, either hexagonal or octagonal, which entirely superseded the rectangular shape dear to the Normans. They had indeed erected at Worcester a monks' council-room of this pattern, supported by a central column, convenient for penitential purposes. This had been imitated at Lincoln, and reached its perfect development in the beautiful edifice at Westminster. It soon became the pattern of all future chapter-houses, until, in the time of Edward I. the central pillar was done away with, and a perfect Gothic dome was for the first time erected. To make this chapter-house of Westminster, the Abbey itself was, in Dean Stanley's phrase, "made to disgorge one-third of its southern transept" to form the eastern cloister by which it is reached from the chancel. Over its entrance from a mass of sculpture, gilding, and painting, the Virgin Mother looked down both within and without. The vast windows were filled with painted glass, and the walls covered with a series of frescoes. The existing frescoes from the Apocalypse, even the oldest of them, are not earlier than the fourteenth, and a portion are probably of the fifteenth century. But probably the original paintings were in part reproduced, and they may be regarded as giving some measure of the excellence attained in the art of design in Early English times. It is satisfactory to be able to note that this noble and most instructive example has been admirably restored, and the six windows, with their stonework replaced after the pattern of the seventh (a blank one), which fortunately survived, are being gradually refilled with painted glass. We may, therefore, soon be able to see "the incomparable" chapter-house, as Matthew of Westminster calls it, as it looked to the astonished eyes of the thirteenth-century Englishman. Nor was the art of painting limited to the decoration of churches, for in the account rolls of Henry's reign we find entries of heavy payments to artists. Thus in 1239 there is a payment to Odo and Edward his son

of 117 shillings and 10 pence for oil, varnish, and colours
bought, and for pictures executed for the queen's chamber;
and in 1259 a similar payment to Master William the

THE FRESCOES, WESTMINSTER CHAPTER-HOUSE.

painter, for a Jesse (*i.e.* a genealogical tree) for the mantel of
the king's chamber.

The sculptor's art seems to have found less favour at
Westminster. To see what Englishmen could do in that way
we must travel as far as Wells. That cathedral is another **Wells**
fine example of the pure architecture of this reign—at least, **Cathedral.**

so far as the nave and west front are concerned. In date
they are a little earlier than Westminster, as contemporary
authorities tell us that Bishop Jocelyn, having pulled down
all the west end, rebuilt it from the foundation, and
dedicated his work on October the 23rd, 1239. Of course,
such extensive operations occupied many years, and certainly
the nave looks a little older than the façade. But it is
possible that the slight differences observable may only
indicate that a different band of masons were at work on it,
and on the whole it is more reasonable to believe that the
west front is the earlier.

The Wells Sculptures.   It is not, however, for the architecture alone that Wells
Cathedral must be cited. It is because here—and here
alone in England—we have evidence of the sudden outburst of talent in those plastic arts in which, though some
Englishmen have attained high excellence in them, Englishmen as a rule have not excelled. Although isolated groups
and figures occur earlier, and some of these date probably
from the eleventh century, this work at Wells is the first in
which the sculptor can be said to have played a great and
independent part. Indeed, it would almost seem as if the
west front had been made abnormally wide, for the purpose
of better displaying that which is its most striking feature.
The number of figures is prodigious, and nearly half—more
than 150, in fact—are life-size or larger. There are crowned
kings and queens, mitred churchmen, armed knights, and
princes and nobles in costume, disposed in tiers, diversified
with medallions. " In the first tier," says the late Mr.
Cockerell, who devoted half a lifetime to their examination,
" are the personages of the first and second Christian missions
to England; St. Paul; Joseph of Arimathea; St. Augustine
and his followers. In the second are the angels chanting the
' Gloria in Excelsis,' and holding crowns spiritual and
temporal, the rewards of their predication. In the third tier
to the south, are the subjects of the Old Testament, and to
the north of the New. In the fourth and fifth we have an
historical series of the lords spiritual and temporal, and of the
saints and martyrs under whom the Church has flourished in
this country; King Ine, founder of the conventual church of
Wells; Edward the Elder, founder of the episcopal church;

King Edward the Elder and King Edwy.

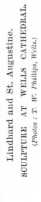

Lindhard and St. Augustine.

SCULPTURE AT WELLS CATHEDRAL.

(Photos : T. W. Phillips, Wells.)

Robert, Duke of Normandy, and
Fulk, Earl of Anjou.

the Saxon, the Danish, the Norman, and the Plantagenet dynasties. Together with these are the founders of dynasties; daughters and allies by marriage of the royal houses of England; the leading characters and lords of the Church—as Archbishop Brithelm, St. Dunstan, Bishop Asser, Grimbald the Earl of Mercia—surrounding Alfred. They form a complete illustration of William of Malmesbury and the early historians of our country—a calendar for the learned men as well as for unlearned artists."

This was indeed a sermon in stone, nay, an entire stone Bible, which all men with eyes could read, whereas previous efforts had not got beyond the plastic representation of a single text. Although it is impossible to accept all the conclusions of Mr. Cockerell — particularly as to the conscious illustration of chroniclers like Malmesbury—it is probable that a general idea such as he has endeavoured to outline runs through the work. There is less difficulty in making sure of the meaning of the medallions and some of the groups, such as The Creation of Eve and The Death of Jacob. It is not, however, the question of identity that is of the highest interest. The surprising thing is that we should find here figures which, besides being ingenious and expressive, exhibit genuine artistic feeling. The great Flaxman, indeed, whose passionate classicism made him a hostile critic of Gothic art, declared that, deficient in principle though they may be, and in places "rude and severe, they frequently possess a beautiful simplicity, an irresistible sentiment, and sometimes a grace excelling more modern productions." But perhaps the most wonderful fact about this wonderful work is its date. We cannot put it later than about 1230 or 1235,

Photo: T. W. Phillips, Wells.
THE CREATION OF EVE.

The Ark.

Noah Building the Ark.

The Final Resurrection.

The Mission of the Apostles.

The Resurrection of Christ.

SCULPTURE AT WELLS CATHEDRAL.
(Photos: T. W. Phillips, Wells.)

and nothing fit to rank with it was then being done in
Northern Europe—for the monumental porches of France,
formerly supposed to be contemporary, are now recognised as
of a later date. We must cross the Alps to find work comparable with this at Wells, and the famous Nicolas of Pisa is,
perhaps, the only contemporary artist who can fairly stand
by the side of our nameless and forgotten countrymen.

**Painted
Glass.**
Unhappily, sculpture was not destined to be in England a
great instrument of popular teaching. A rival was at hand
by which it was in this respect to be supplanted. The
presentation in stone was to hide its head before the glories
of the painted window. It has been well said by a distinguished architect that the best synonym for Gothic would
be the Painted-Glass style; and it is certain that the
introduction of this beautiful window material was a most
potent agency in architectural development. Plain glass had
been—as we have mentioned (p. 280)—used in churches as
early as the eighth century; though in early times the
material was, no doubt, either imported, or, if occasionally
made in England, made by foreign artificers. For a long
time, however, its capabilities as a form of decoration seem
not to have been recognised; and, in fact, until well on in
the twelfth century glass seems to have been applied solely
to the utilitarian purpose of keeping out the wind and rain.
It may have been first used for decoration by William of
Sens, who came from Becket's city of refuge to superintend
the restoration of Canterbury after the great fire of 1174. He
was doubtless cognisant of this, as of the other improvements
introduced a generation earlier at St. Denis; so that it is
probable that we owe to France, not only the Pointed style,
but the painted window, which now seems its natural complement. The earliest works of the kind were, however, rather
transparent glass mosaic than painted-glass windows; for the
outlines were formed by the lead beading, into which the
small plaques of glass (which were cut with a hot wire, the
use of the diamond being unknown till the fifteenth century)
were carefully fitted. This kind of design was, of course,
independent of colour, though colour was no doubt the
feature the addition of which gave the new windows such an
extraordinary popularity. It is doubtful whether a reasonably

complete specimen of a stained-glass window dating as early as the reign of John exists in England, though there are, doubtless, fragments of earlier date.

This earlier glass is recognisable by its extraordinary thickness, and owing to the fact that the colour is in the whole substance, and not merely—as in later examples—upon the surface, it is still unrivalled in richness of tone. It .is believed to have been first systematically employed at Westminster during the rebuilding by Henry III. It is of great interest to compare these windows of Henry's with those of La Sainte Chapelle in Paris, which was commenced almost at the same date and finished earlier than the work at Westminster. The geometric form of tracery, which gives the greatest space for colour, can scarcely go beyond this French work, while the English is still in the tentative form. It is important to note in this connection that the manufacture of coloured glass does not seem to have been established in England until centuries later, and the cost of the material seems to have made the development of tracery slower here than in France; but the result has hardly been regrettable.

There was, as we have seen, little positive change in the main structure of the church fabric during this reign; nor did the character of the ornament alter much. On the other hand, the windows were positively transfigured, and tracery, with all its possibilities of luxuriant beauty, was born. With the introduction of painted glass, the fenestration, if we may be allowed the term, became of supreme importance. **Windows.**

At the beginning of the reign the tall, narrow, lancet form of window prevails, widely splayed within and plain without. The splay, originally adopted simply as a means of getting more light, lent itself, when the windows were grouped together, to new and striking effects. The inner partitions of the windows were, by means of the splay, reduced to a narrow edge, and when these edges were covered, as soon became common, by delicate shafts and mouldings, three or more windows, which on the outside were quite separate, within formed a triple or multiple window of admirable composition. A still more important **Tracery.**

development grew out of the analogous practice of including
the group under a single arch, for this left between the
tops of the grouped windows and the top of the arch a
space of wall bare of decoration and unpleasing to the eye.
It was in the effort to get rid of this that tracery was
invented. The Early English architects were not, indeed,
the first who had attempted the task. The Norman builders
of St. Maurice's at York, of the choir of Peterborough, and of
the tower of St. Giles's at Oxford, had tried to abate the
eyesore by piercing the blank space of wall; but their
efforts had not got beyond a puncture, which barely relieved
the monotony of the surface. The new development consisted in the introduction of a window, circular or of quatrefoil design, cut in the wall above the window heads. These
openings are, indeed, the first steps towards tracery. Such
windows belong to the humbler kind, which the late Professor
Willis admirably christened " plate-tracery," as distinguished
from the later and more graceful forms, to which he gave
the name of " bar-tracery." The distinction is just and
luminous, for the former is, in truth, the decorative piercing
of a wall-space, while the latter is a decorative network laid
into a window light.

   Plate-tracery continues in vogue through the first half
of Henry's reign, but the solid portions of the " plate " get
smaller and smaller, narrow mullions supersede the solid
divisions of the light, the use of cusps or pointed attach-
ments becomes common until (at least as early as 1260) we
come upon veritable bar-tracery. The number of grouped
lights increases at the same time, and the openings in the
head are multiplied. The great stride towards perfect tracery
effected by allowing the mullions to cross each other in the
window-head must have been taken about the same time ;
and such windows are, in truth, in the form which was to
obtain through all the " Decorated" period. You have,
indeed, only to take the plain mullions from such a three-
light window as that of St. Mary le Wigford, at Lincoln,
and substitute for them bars on which the cusps are
actually carved—not laid on as external ornament—and
you have a perfect Decorated window. The circular windows
of this time—the eyes of the Church, as the French call

them—are equally instructive as to the gradual evolution of
tracery. They were not unknown to the Norman builders,
who, when the scale was comparatively large, frequently used
a wheel pattern of six broad spokes to break the monotony
of the light. This form persisted, and gave rise to such
early examples as the famous window at Peterborough, which
but for the elegant foliage which runs along the outer edge,
and the violette which adorns the truncheon-like divisions,

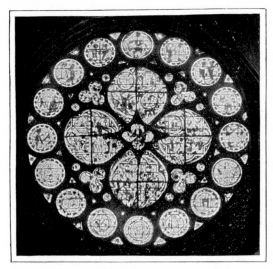

THE "DEAN'S EYE" WINDOW, LINCOLN CATHEDRAL.

might well be mistaken for a Norman work. So, too, of the
similar windows of Beverley Minster, where four round openings placed crosswise are pierced in the larger circular plate
and bordered with the half-violette, which in that form
better justifies its English designation of "dog-tooth." Perhaps, however, the highest point of Early English plate-
tracery is reached at Lincoln, where the window of the
north transept, formed by a ring of small circles, surrounds
four larger tennis-headed apertures, across the intersection
of which hangs a small equal-limbed cross, with a quatrefoil in the centre. The spandrel-like portions of the disc,
between the outer ring of circles and the tennis-heads, are
further pierced by trefoils and rounds, so that here the plate

form, though still distinguishable, has almost disappeared. Yet this window may safely be given to the first decade of the reign of Henry III., and none of them are later than the third. These are the natural forerunners of the great circular windows—rose, or marigold, or catherine wheel— which are among the principal glories of the Decorated style.

Secular Architecture: Castles.

Except in disturbed and frontier districts, like South Wales, the reign of Henry III. was not prolific as regards castles— at least, if we speak of castles built on new sites. The frontier castles, moreover, were rather places of arms, intended to keep at a distance a warlike but imperfectly armed population, than the impregnable strongholds of former and succeeding reigns. Their principal features are a strong curtain-wall, enclosing a considerable area fortified by round towers at irregular intervals, while the residential interior was constructed of wood. The round tower had come in as a French fashion in the reign of John, or possibly, in isolated cases, a little earlier; and these, as well as the older Norman keeps were, in this reign, generally strengthened by the addition of an *enceinte*. This was the case at London, and also at Dover, where the *enceinte* is double, the resulting stronghold fulfilling nearly all the conditions of the great concentric castles of the succeeding reign. An intervening form—a cylindrical keep with buttresses, such as is to be seen at Coningsburgh—is a little earlier, representing the transitional Norman form; while the round tower and the curtained tower defences, and the *enceinte* wall, represent the work of the Early English castle-builder. The round tower was not, perhaps, architecturally an improvement on the rectangular Norman keep; but it was far more economical of materials, and could be conveniently vaulted to carry on every story a stone floor, thus getting rid of the peril from fire involved in the old Norman planking. Wood, however, continued to provide the material for the most important part of the armament of these round keeps. This was the bretache, or covered wooden gallery, which ran round the top of the tower, from which every sort of missile was hurled on the besiegers. It was supported by wooden struts resting on stone corbels, and had a sloping roof. A portion of this crucial defence has actually been preserved at Coucy, in France, built about 1225 by the Sieur Enguerrand III. No such remains exist in England, though Norham preserves one of the doorways giving access to the bretache.

Much was done in this reign to render the castle habitable. Various conveniences were introduced or amended. The old Norman hearth—a mere recess connected with a smoke-vent—was supplanted by the regular fireplace. The wide ingles were adorned with elegant hoods of stone, and

COUCY CASTLE, NEAR LAON, FRANCE, SHOWING PLACE OF BRETACHE.
(*Photograph by permission of the French Government.*)

flues were built in the castle walls. The spread of luxury, of which the Court of Henry III. set the example, was, in fact, tending to revolutionise all English life. The nobles began to find residence in the rude fortalices of their fathers irksome, and, in the case of the smaller baronage, who were quite unable to garrison them, such residence was futile also. It was obviously absurd to inhabit, in circumstances of great discomfort, a fortress strong enough to keep an army at bay, when all that was required was a house which could resist the importunity of a robber or a neighbour. This feeling was all against the castle and in favour of the

39

manor-house; and we have positive proof, in the numerous permits to fortify granted by the king, that the fortified manor-house was all the fashion.

Nevertheless of lay, as distinguished from military and ecclesiastical, architecture, the specimens that have come down to us are comparatively few. Poor folk would still live in their wooden houses, and they of course have disappeared. But the new manor-houses seem to have been superior to those with which the Norman was content, and which have survived to fulfil the humble uses of a barn or a homestead. The new houses were comfortable enough to make it worth while for later owners to inhabit, and in time to alter them out of all recognition. Anyhow, Early English houses of this class are quite as rare as those in the Norman period. Among the most perfect specimens are the manor-houses of Cottesford and Cogges, which seem to belong to the earlier part of the reign; and Aydon Hall in Northumberland, Stokesay in Shropshire, Woodcroft and Longthorp in Northamptonshire, Little Wenham Hall in Suffolk, and Flore's House, Oakham, which are of somewhat later date.

Two most important buildings, which are neither churches nor fortresses nor ordinary residences, remain to be noticed. These are the King's Hall at Winchester and the Bishop's Palace at Wells; and they show very clearly that the lay architects followed, but followed slowly, the changes introduced by the free masons of the Early English cathedrals. The King's Hall has undergone many alterations and many restorations; but at the west end we come upon the early lancets of the original building, completely separate outwardly, but on the inside deeply splayed and grouped together by a moulding. These are not later than 1235, while the window inserted in the side wall, shortly before the accession of Edward, exhibits a simple form of plate-tracery. This is a genuine two-light window, so appearing both on the inside and outside of the building, each light being trefoil-headed, with a dividing transom and a quatrefoil above, the whole enclosed by a moulding. The episcopal palace at Wells looks later than the older part of the hall at Winchester; but probably it is not so in reality, for it was built by Bishop Joscelyn, who was promoted to the see in 1205, and the architects at Wells were a little in advance of those of the rest of England. Here we have the ground floor, used for domestic purposes, and storerooms lighted by single lancets, while the story above, where were the dwelling apartments of the bishop, has excellent double trefoiled lights, with a quatrefoil in the head and marble shafts at the sides. The lay architects, as a rule, showed little originality; and

AYDON HALL, NORTHUMBERLAND.

even in constructing prison chambers, like the vaulted rooms at Somerton, in the Tower of London, and Lincoln Castle, the imitation of the cathedral architecture is very striking, even to the use of the central pillar, universal in the round or hexagonal chapter-house of this reign.

This reign was remarkable for a strenuous effort to reform Coins. the coinage. More than one proclamation was issued against money which was not round, the royal anger being directed, not only against the obviously felonious practice of clipping, but against the humble habit of making change for a penny by chopping it into halfpence and farthings. The penny in silver continued, as in former reigns, to be the usual coin of commerce, though halfpence and farthings were issued; and there is some reason to believe that a groat was coined with a long cross reaching to the edge as a precaution against the malpractices of the Jews.   The old patterns were in use in

the early part of the reign, but in 1247, at any rate, a new coinage was undertaken.   From the point of view of art the coin-maker of the period was still behind his Saxon forerunners.   A rude attempt is made at a   portrait, but it looks rather like a feeble repetition of the no less rude

SILVER COIN OF HENRY III.

image of the king's grandfather.   Henry was, however, the first of the Norman or Angevin princes who ventured on adding a number to his title, and the appearance of the Roman numeral III., or sometimes the word *Terci*, suggests that he was inclined to consider the age of his dynasty worth mentioning.   The most remarkable numismatic event of the reign was, however, the abortive attempt to introduce a gold coinage.   Up to the middle of the thirteenth century Western Europe had found the Byzants of the Cæsars of Rome by the Bosphorus, helped out by an occasional dinar of a Saracen Prince, sufficient for all its needs in the way of a gold medium.[1]   In that year, however, a gold penny was issued in London by Henry III.   On

one side the king crowned is sitting on a chair of state, a sceptre in his right hand, and an orb in his left. The reverse shows a long double cross, and a rose with pellets in the angles.   The gold in these coins is the purest that has ever been

GOLD PENNY OF HENRY III.

employed in our national coinage, a circumstance which has, no doubt, largely contributed to its disappearance.   It was not a

[1 The golden byzant (so-called from Byzantium or Constantinople) varied at different periods in the amount of gold it contained.   Originally about a sovereign, it fell below half a sovereign.   Dinars (the name comes from the Latin *denarius*) may have been approximately equal to the Indian gold mohur, containing about as much as a sovereign and three-quarters.]

very beautiful coin, but more neatly executed than the contemporary silver. It was not, however, received with favour, probably because of its excessive value. The exchange was fixed at twenty silver pennies, and in purchasing value, according to our modern prices, it was probably worth several pounds. It was not long generally current, for the citizens of London petitioned against it, and it was accordingly redeemed by the king. It did not, however, pass entirely out of use, though no doubt mostly found in the royal exchequer, for in 1265, the famous year of Evesham, it was raised by proclamation to the value of twenty-four pennies. The coin is exceedingly rare, and the authentic specimens may probably be counted on the fingers of one hand.

THE University of Oxford may be said to have come into existence so soon as the brotherhood of Masters assumed something of a formal shape, and prescribed some sort of routine in study and ceremonial ; for instance, to take the example from Paris, in frequenting lectures and disputations, in wearing a scholar's cap, and in attending the funerals of other members of the body. But, unlike Paris, Oxford had no Cathedral Chancellor to give the licence to teach, which, we have seen, was an essential element in the scholar's recognition by his elders. It became necessary to invent an analogous officer, and, as a matter of course, he was connected with the see of Lincoln, in which diocese Oxford was then situated. The circumstances in which he was appointed are characteristic of the tumultuous life of the medieval students. In 1208 a murder committed by one of the Art students led to reprisals on the part of the townsmen. King John, it was understood, favoured the latter, and the scholars —we are told, three thousand in number—resolved to quit the place. At the beginning of 1209 Oxford was emptied. The town soon awoke to the loss it had suffered, and when a Papal Legate arrived in England in 1213 it was not sorry to purchase the hope of restoration by an ample penance. In the ordinance regulating this penance mention is made of "the Chancellor whom the Bishop of Lincoln shall set over the scholars " ; and when the office is actually established it

R. L. POOLE. Learning and Science: The Universities.

is that of the Bishop's representative, conferring the licence and exercising judicial authority over the Masters and scholars of the University. Yet it is probable that from the first the Chancellor was elected by the Masters and only confirmed by the Bishop : so that, instead of there arising, as at Paris, a constant struggle between the Chancellor and the University, at Oxford he was by a natural process absorbed into the academic body. He presided over the Congregation of the University, but his jurisdiction in substance passed to the Congregation itself.

The Proctors. Early in the second quarter of the thirteenth century Oxford borrowed another constitutional feature from Paris, where the Masters of Arts were divided into four nations, French, English, Norman, and Picard, each with its representative, or Proctor (Procurator), to act on behalf of the Masters when it was necessary to defend their rights. At Oxford there were but two nations, the Northern and the Southern, and hence there were, and are, but two Proctors. By this organisation, and in consequence of their numerical strength, the " Artists " succeeded in engrossing the real power in the University and leaving the higher Faculties of Theology, Law, and Medicine little besides the dignity of precedence. But it would be out of place here to examine at length the constitutional history of Oxford. It may be sufficient to notice that the first recorded Statute dates from 1252.

In spite, however, of the growing stability of the University, it was long before it could be said to be definitely fixed at Oxford. We have seen how a general migration took place in 1208. In 1240 a number of the Oxford clerks removed themselves to Cambridge, where the sister University had sprung up in the first years of the century. A little later Cambridge, too, suffered a dispersion, which went near to establishing a third university at Northampton. Here, in 1264, the young school was recruited by the mass of the Oxford scholars, who, after a great conflict with the townsmen, feared with reason that their privileges would be cut short. At Northampton, when, just afterwards, King Henry III. besieged the place, the Oxford scholars were foremost with their slings and bows, and were only reduced to a timid neutrality by the king's oath that he would hang every man of them. It was not until the victory of Simon of Montfort —for politics had a good deal to do with the Oxford riot— that the scholars were enjoined to return. Even so late as 1334 there was so considerable a secession to Stamford that fears were felt for the very existence of the University, and strong measures were taken to stamp out the schism. So long, indeed, as the students lived as they pleased in lodgings or grouped themselves round a Master in his private house, there was no certainty that the University would remain fixed in one place. The academical stability of Oxford and Cambridge was determined by the rise of the colleges; and the colleges, though the idea was borrowed from the University of Paris, arose under the stimulating example of the Mendicant Friars.

In order to understand the distinguishing characteristics of these new brotherhoods, we must bear in mind

BRASENOSE COLLEGE GATE, STAMFORD.

that at the time of their foundation there were in Latin Christendom two classes, and two only, of persons professing a religious rule: the Monks, who followed the Rule of St. Benet; and the Canons, who followed that bearing the name of St. Austin. Cluniacs, Carthusians, and Cistercians were alike in essence Benedictines; Regular Canons and Præmonstratensians were alike Augustinians. Now the Lateran Council of 1215 expressly prohibited the foundation of any new Order. St. Francis had, it is true, a few years earlier, in 1209, obtained Innocent III.'s approval of his missionary aims; but the scheme was too inchoate for formal confirmation. St. Dominic was in Rome at the time of the Council; and he, when he sought the Pope's authorisation of his preaching brotherhood, was bidden to choose the rules of one of the existing orders

The Friars at Oxford.

to conform it to. He chose, therefore, to remain what he was himself, an Augustinian canon; and from the Augustinian canons the Friars Preachers are lineally descended. The Franciscans, on the other hand, or Friars Minor, preserved their freedom, and only after many changes of government adopted a code of constitutions, in which the influence of the Dominican rule is strongly marked.

The two new orders are distinguished from their predecessors in several ways. The brethren were not bound to continue in the religious house where they were professed. They were not burthened with the duty of manual labour in the fields. Above all, they were to live on alms—they were Mendicants. And this leads to another point of distinction of the highest importance. If they were to depend for their bodily support on the gifts of others, their lives must be devoted to the service of others; and this, in fact, was the profession of both orders. They were in principle missionaries, but with a difference: the Dominicans applied themselves to the work of opposing heresy and error, and of bringing over the heathen to the true faith; while the Franciscans sought with a more directly personal aim to revive the life of Christ and His apostles. But the distinction of precept and example was not long maintained in practice. The Franciscans, it is true, were conspicuous in the mission they found of carrying the civilising influences of Christianity among the neglected populations of the towns; but they too, although their founder's example was firm against worldly studies, soon became teachers, and a long and mainly honourable rivalry arose between Friars Preachers and Friars Minor, which should hold the place of pre-eminence in learning and in the schools—a rivalry that lasted until the transition into modern times. The Franciscans extended their connection in a wide circle by the recognition of Tertiaries, or half-members of their Order, who lived in the world and only observed the rule with modifications. Two other societies were formed or reorganised about the same time; and both, the Carmelites and the Augustinian Hermits, adopted the Franciscan constitution before the middle of the thirteenth century. These were known as the White Friars and the Austin Friars.

The Friars Preachers were the first to come to England.

1273]

This was in 1220, and their first house was established at Oxford. The Franciscans followed them in 1224, and they at once found their way to Oxford; in the same year they settled at Cambridge. The choice was a natural one; for not only did a university town offer a large field, in its mixed population, for their missionary labours, but it also promised a goodly harvest of recruits to be gathered from among the students. Besides, as we have said, to the Dominicans learning was a matter of obligation. Their younger members were instructed in philosophy before they entered upon the theological training which was required of all those in the Oxford convent who had not already been admitted to degrees in the Faculty. But the rules alike of the Dominicans and Franciscans forbade a Friar, after his profession, to take a degree in Arts. Consequently, when the University made such a degree the necessary preliminary to a degree in Theology, the Friars were in danger of losing the chief academic privileges altogether; and it was only after a struggle which came to a head in the early years of the fourteenth century that a practical compromise was arranged, whereby, while the University upheld its rule, it was permitted by grace to dispense from it sufficiently trained candidates presented to the Chancellor by their respective Orders.

At the first the Friars, probably from necessity, appointed their teachers from outside. The first Lector of the Oxford Franciscans was Robert Grosseteste, afterwards Bishop of Lincoln, one of the most famous men of learning of the century, and his three successors likewise belonged to the secular clergy. But soon the school had teachers of its own, and Friars were lecturers also in the convents of Cambridge, Bristol, Hereford, and Leicester. They were, indeed, more than able to hold their own in the contests of the schools and in independent advancement of knowledge; though this, in the case of the Franciscans, was a defiance of their founder's injunctions. It was impossible for them to possess any books or scientific instruments, and Roger Bacon could only obtain ink and parchment by the special leave of the Pope. Nevertheless, their care for the poor led them constantly into connection with sickness and disease, and a knowledge of medicine became for them a necessity. Medical involved physical studies, and the great mass of Franciscan scholars, whatever their eminence in other branches of learning, were distinguished also by their acquirements in physical science. The original rule of the Order could not be maintained; some sort of possessions the Friars must have, and the "moderate use" of worldly goods which Pope Nicolas the Third, in 1279, allowed them was happily ambiguous in practice. The widened range of knowledge which they brought into play in turn reacted upon their secular brethren; and even when the force of the scholastic movement was spent, and academical studies were far on their decline, we may still observe that the influence of their example was not wholly forgotten, and a varied course of training in mathematics, natural philosophy, and natural science was still pursued by those who aimed at rank among scholars.

It would be unfair to judge the Friars alone by their learned work. If many of them were great scholars, more were also great preachers; indeed, their learning was designed to prepare them for their life of activity among the people. They were the most popular of preachers; and their sermons told with a direct force that sprang from the spiritual earnestness not less than from the theological completeness of the preacher's equipment, and was brought home by his plain language, his humorous touches, and his good stories. By a sharp and not unnatural contrast the severity of the Friar's profession was balanced by a light-hearted temper and a merry countenance. He had the repute everywhere of a pleasant fellow. To those who read the accounts of the early years of the Franciscans, the warmth of their reception and the rapidity of their conquests are easy to be understood. Nor was it otherwise with the Dominicans, although, great as is the part they play in the history of English learning, they never filled the same place in the minds of Englishmen at large as did their Franciscan rivals.

The Collegiate System.   The Friars' distinction in the schools of Oxford and Cambridge acted as a spur to their secular rivals, who could not but observe how their zeal and method in study were assisted by their manner of life. They dwelt in houses or convents of their own, and the convents formed each a

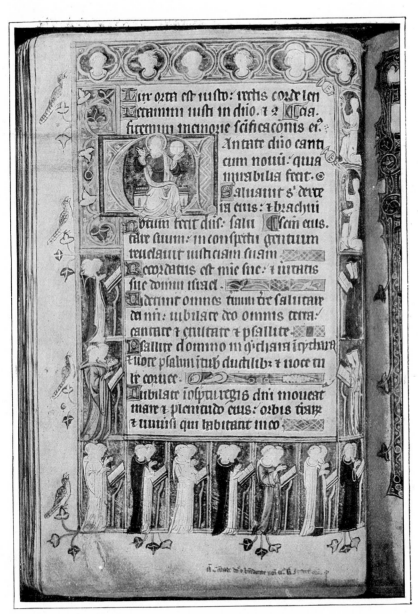

THE MONASTIC ORDERS, FROM A PSALTER.
(*Sidney Sussex College, Cambridge.*)

miniature *studium* in the midst of the greater academic body of the place. The advantages of this common and regulated life were manifest, and it was natural to seek to adapt the system to the requirements of those who had no mind to attach themselves to a lasting rule. The first speci-men of such an adaptation was perhaps that of John Balliol and Dervorguilla his wife, not long after 1260; but their **The House of Balliol.** endowment, modelled on the example of the earliest colleges at Paris, constituted at the outset a mere almshouse for a few poor students. The first real beginning of the Collegiate system, the archetype of the colleges both of Oxford and Cambridge, was made by the foundation of Walter of Merton, Chancellor and afterwards Bishop of Rochester, which he established in 1264, and planted definitely at Oxford ten years later.

Merton College. Merton College consisted of a Warden and a certain number of Scholars, who lived together in conventual buildings designed on a grand plan. The Scholars were to engage themselves in the study of Arts, and then proceed to Theology, a few being allowed the choice of Canon or Civil Law. If anyone received an ecclesiastical benefice or entered a religious Order, he at once lost his Scholarship. Otherwise he remained a Scholar or Fellow (the names are used interchangeably) so long as he resided in the College. The elder Scholars were largely employed in College busi-ness, in keeping the household accounts, and overseeing the estates. All dined and supped in the common refectory; they were bound to keep the canonical hours and hear Mass in the College Chapel. But, four Chaplains being provided, they were under no obligation to enter Holy Orders themselves. The foundation further supplied a number (up to thirteen) of "poor boys" with a mainten-ance and education until they were old enough to become Scholars.

Walter of Merton's scheme was taken as a model, though with variations in detail, by the founders of later Colleges; and through their establishment neither Oxford nor Cam-bridge was in serious danger of ceasing to be the home of a university. But it would be altogether a mistake to suppose that the colleges occupied anything like the dominant position which they acquired in later times. By far the majority of students throughout the Middle Ages lived either in lodgings by themselves or in halls or inns managed by graduates. The non-collegiate student of the present day represents not merely the earliest but the normal type of the English university student; and it was not until the fifteenth century that the lodging-house system was checked, and not until the reign of Charles the First that the Colleges succeeded in engrossing the entire government, and absorbing nearly the entire population, of the University. It is plain that when Oxford counted several, if not many, thousand scholars, but a very small proportion could find room in the four Colleges of the thirteenth century, or even the nine Colleges of the fourteenth, each with an average number of at most thirty or forty members. The life of the student was then less formal and less regulated; such uniformity as there was, was obtained rather by the system of study than by any strict rules of discipline.

The methods of study had, indeed, undergone a revolution since the time when John of Salisbury learned at Paris or Chartres; and this revolution was due first to the introduction of new dialectical appliances from the Byzantine school of logicians, and secondly to the opening out of the whole works of Aristotle to the Western world. We have seen that in John's own lifetime all the books of the "Organon"[1] were already known, but they passed but slowly into the educational system, and St. Edmund Rich, afterwards Archbishop of Canterbury, is claimed as the first to lecture on the last book—the "Sophistici Elenchi"[2]—at Oxford, in the third decade of the thirteenth century. The knowledge of Aristotle's complete logical exposition only excited the desire for further teaching as to the metaphysical questions arising about the basis of logic. The desired information was found in other works of Aristotle which were made accessible in Latin by the beginning of the thirteenth century. The translations were taken in some cases from the Greek

(margin) University Studies.

[1 "The Instrument" (*i.e.* of reasoning), the collective name for Aristotle's treatises on logic.]

[2 "The Refutations of the Sophists": a treatise on various fallacious arguments and logical puzzles to which prominence was given by the professional teachers and disputants of Aristotle's day.]

originals, in others from Arabic versions, themselves made indirectly from the Greek by the vehicle of Hebrew or Syriac translations. But in one way or the other the whole of Aristotle was now in the hands of Western scholars, and the effect upon the method and even the subject matter of their philosophical studies was prodigious. Instead of moving within the circumscribed field to which their previously existing materials confined them, they now found a new world of speculation ready for them to explore, the very crabbedness and ambiguity of the translations supplying ever fresh openings for nimble invention, for fine distinctions, for originality. For if, viewed absolutely, originality is not to be asserted of the productions of scholastic thought, nevertheless, in relation to the philosophers and their times, there is a fertility of original conceptions, and with it a subtlety of manipulation, which only suffered from the ease with which it might degenerate into legerdemain.

The Study of Aristotle.　With Aristotle Western scholars became acquainted also with the commentaries of the Arab doctors Avicenna (Ibn Sina, died 1037) and Averröes (Ibn Rushd, died 1198), and their teaching might seem inevitably tainted by its Mohammedan source. Moreover, some were led, by the study of the "Physics" of Aristotle, to conclusions the heretical character of which was so manifest that in 1209 the work itself was forbidden to be read at Paris. Six years later the proscription was extended to the "Metaphysics," and it was not until 1231 that the Greek philosopher received a qualified toleration in that university. The diversity of treatment applicable to the same material, as seen in the Arab commentators, could not but produce an uncertainty about positive truth; and while some wandered away into scepticism, most were glad to correct the indecision of human reason by enforcing the absolute and sole authority of an unerring revelation. The British philosopher, John Duns Scotus (died 1308), who represents the extreme of this tendency maintained that there was no true knowledge of anything knowable apart from revelation; we could not of ourselves prove the existence of a God. The Italian, St. Thomas Aquinas (1224–1274), on the other hand, while admitting that some truths were beyond the discernment of human reason, sought to effect a harmony of reason and faith by positing reason and revelation as two independent sources of knowledge, each sufficient in its own plan of action. Whether the final conclusions of the Arab philosophers were accepted or not in full, the influence of their method was long paramount. While the German, St. Albert the Great (1193–1280), held by Avicenna, and Aquinas followed Averröes, they decided alike that the Mohammedan superstructure was faulty, and that recourse must be had in the end, as in the beginning, to the Aristotelian foundation. It was hence that Aquinas promoted the execution of a new translation of Aristotle, which was made by William of Moerbecke shortly before the saint's death.

ARISTOTLE TEACHING (MS. Roy. 12 G. v.).

The renown of Albert and Thomas made the authority of Aristotle at once the guiding one for their Order, the Dominican. The Franciscans, on the other hand, held for a time fast by the Platonic tradition as it had passed to them from St. Austin. But it was impossible for them to remain long untouched by the influence which had won so powerful a currency through the teaching of their rivals, and even Alexander of Hales (died 1245), senior in years to Albert, was profoundly affected by it. The questions at issue involved the nicest problems of psychology, and it would be impossible here, without a technical discussion unsuited to the character of this book, even to sketch their purport. It must suffice to notice that the new studies raised difficulties about the immortality of the soul, which the hardy inquirer was apt to solve by a pantheistic or a materialistic theory; and Aquinas himself was charged with erroneous doctrine, which was condemned by the Bishop of Paris in 1277. At Oxford also a like controversy was dealt with in the same way by two successive Friar Archbishops of Canterbury—the Dominican Kilwardby and the Franciscan Peckham.

Grosseteste as Scholar. Among the leading masters in the English scholasticism of the thirteenth century Robert Grosseteste, Bishop of Lincoln, claims a foremost place. He was already a prominent man in the University of Oxford when, early in the second quarter of the century, he was called upon, though a secular, to preside over the Franciscan school there; and when he became bishop of the diocese within which Oxford lay, his moderating and enlightening influence was constantly felt in the University as in the nation at large during the many years which followed until his death in 1253. But his personal authority was less than that which he wielded as a writer, and this authority continued until beyond the end of the Middle Ages. He commented upon Aristotle, wrote philosophical treatises as well as works on physical science. Poems in French and set treatises on theology indicate the breadth of his intellectual training; and when it is added that he was skilled in medicine and in music, and credited with a knowledge of Greek and Hebrew, it will be seen that his acquirements might easily pass as unrivalled in his age.

Adam Marsh and Roger Bacon. His younger contemporary, Adam Marsh, lecturer also at the Franciscan school at Oxford, was more famous as a teacher and organiser of teaching than as himself an author, though his works (now lost, excepting his letters) are said to have borne out his character as a worthy successor to the all-accomplished Bishop of Lincoln. His record lies rather in the school which, more than any other, he brought to maturity—the school whence issued Roger Bacon, John Duns Scotus, and William of Ockham. Roger Bacon, it needs not be said, stands quite by himself—not by any means because he limited himself to the physical studies by which in modern times he is renowned, but because, having learned all that could be learned of the current philosophy, scholarship, science, and literature of his day, knowing Greek, Hebrew,

and Arabic, and having advanced in some directions far
beyond the limit of performance then deemed possible, he
was able to judge the existing state of knowledge, and appor-

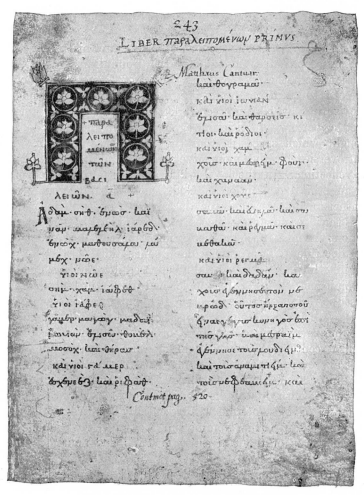

LEAF FROM GREEK MS. USED BY GROSSETESTE.
(*University Library, Cambridge.*)

tion its excellences and its defects from a point of view
immeasurably more independent than any other man. He is
not merely the original investigator and discoverer of physical

40

truths, but the wisest critic of the learning of his age. He seems to have felt that the scholastic method had already run its course by the years 1267–1271, in which he completed his principal works, and that it was time that new lines of inquiry should be pursued in the directions of physical science and philology.

Duns Scotus.

Duns Scotus, partly in order to liberate his Order from the philosophical ascendancy of the Dominicans, partly in a reaction from the overpowering weight of Aristotle's authority, reverted to an uncompromising Realism. But his chief service is that by his unmatched logical faculty he was able to erect a battery of criticism against the dominant school of thought which saved it from the perils of absolutism. The controversies for the moment cleared the air and gave room for reflection. In theology, while substituting an intellectual for an ethical conception of God, Duns ran dangerously near Pantheism, and asserted the doctrine of free-will in such a way that recourse was necessary to revelation for its correction; he also headed the Franciscans in their defence of the doctrine of the immaculate conception of the Blessed Virgin, which had been steadily opposed by Aquinas and the Dominicans. With Duns, logic had been the subtlest and most powerful of instruments ; his pupil (as is commonly said), William of Ockham, proposed for it higher claims still, and he revived in a maturer form the Nominalism of the twelfth century. Universal ideas were to him the mere arbitrary creations of the mind. But in theology and ethics the impress of Duns's teaching was lasting with him ; in matters of faith, indeed, he continued orthodox, but the whole character of his doctrine was essentially sceptical. It is not strange that the new Nominalism took firm root among the critical spirits of the University of Paris and flourished there for many generations.

If the British Islands had produced Alexander of Hales and Roger Bacon among the great names of the thirteenth century, and John Duns Scotus and William of Ockham, the greatest at the opening of the fourteenth—all Franciscans— the attractive forces of Paris were too strong for them not to seek there a more public and more ambitious field of study and teaching than they could find in England. Bacon alone returned to Oxford; the rest are numbered among the foremost doctors of Paris. Yet Duns's famous commentary on the "Sentences" bears by an old tradition the title of *Scriptum Oxoniense*, his Oxford treatise, so that he may be fairly claimed to have accomplished a weighty part of his work as teacher and writer before he left England. Far from dying, as is commonly said, at the age of thirty-four, he was fully that age when he departed for Paris in 1304, and he died as lecturer at Cologne four years later. Ockham is related to have been a pupil of Duns, in all probability at Paris, since he lived on at least until 1349: certainly it was at Paris that he made his reputation as a logician. His after history, as the champion of the Emperor Louis IV. in his contest with Pope John XXII., illustrates the application of the principles of a sceptical logic to the solution of political questions. To give power to the secular authority he holds better than to give it to the ecclesiastical; but this is mainly because the Church, in Ockham's view, should be kept pure from worldly affairs, not because he has any confidence in the abstract fitness of the civil state. The decision in matters of faith he would entrust, not to the Pope, but to general councils formed alike of clergy and lay folk; but these, too, he admits may err, and in despair of human infallibility he is obliged to revert to the old doctrine of the authority of the Holy Scriptures. Still, though Ockham's conclusions are hesitating, his great political treatise, the "Dialogue," marks an important stage in the history of political theory, even as his "Sum of Logic" marks a revolution in that of dialectic. From Ockham onwards, though in one or two points there is an advance in logical manipulation, and though there are still a few great names, such as those of Archbishop Bradwardine and Walter Burleigh, generally it is a period of steady decline; and the schools busied themselves with the weaving afresh of old stuffs until there was no fabric left, and thought became entangled in the mass of words until it was well-nigh hopeless to unravel it. The educational system was labouring under a congestion which needed the drastic remedies it received from the Humanists of the fifteenth and sixteenth centuries.

William of Ockham.

H. FRANK HEATH.
Language and Literature.

FOR a century and a half, the English race and language had been forced to yield up their supremacy before the Norman invasion, the English literature almost its very existence. But this was not destined to last. The conquerors were too weak in numbers, the conquered too sturdy in character and physique, to make extinction or even permanent servitude possible, and the inevitable result was a slow but certain fusing of the two elements. This process was greatly aided by the course of political events during Henry III.'s reign. The tyranny and administrative weakness of the Crown led to rebellion among the barons; but ultimate success was reserved to the side which could win the support of the English yeomen and labourers. This support the barons succeeded in obtaining, partly because constant and closer contact with their tenants gave them a personal influence which quite outweighed the theoretical authority of the Crown, partly because any opposition to the Court seemed to open out to the English a prospect of revenge upon the hated Norman conqueror. And so, after many preliminary squabbles and peacemakings, followed by open war, a decisive check was given to the royal prerogative by the barons and their English allies, all of which resulted in the beginnings of our present Parliamentary government and the disappearance of the old racial antipathies and opposing interests. Then it was that the national spirit became once more conscious of itself and its powers, and began again to find its expression in literature.

Norman-French, Latin, and English.

We find, therefore, that the relative position of the three languages which occupied the social field changes somewhat during the period now under consideration. For the previous hundred and fifty years Anglo-Norman had been the speech of all who made the slightest pretence to position or culture, and naturally of all the literature produced for them. Latin was the universal language of the learned, of the law, and of the Church, and English was only spoken by the yeomen and lower orders, and written in the very small body of literature which sufficed for their needs. In 1154 the last of the English annals, those compiled at Peterborough, were closed; and from then till the second quarter of the thirteenth century English found its almost exclusive use in the religious literature produced for the edification of the masses.

Soon after the accession of Henry III., however, things began to change. In consequence of the loss of Normandy, just eleven years before this date, the barons were forced to look upon England as their only home, and to seek their pleasures and interests here; so the Anglo-Norman dialect naturally began to die out as the language of home-life, though it kept its place at Court and in the law. But even at Court it gradually gave place to Central French, from which it was so different that English soldiers found it difficult during the French wars to understand their foes, and the sons of nobles were often sent to France to learn what was considered the more aristocratic way of speech.[1] French remained the language of the Court till the end of the next century, and Anglo-Norman was the language of government and law until within fifty years of that time, for it was not till 1362 that cases began to be tried, or the proceedings of Parliament held, in English (p. 404). It is noticeable, however, that during the whole of Henry III.'s reign, and for some little time longer, all reports of law cases were written in Latin, and it is not till the next century that French was used side by side with it for this purpose. In the administrative departments also Latin was used almost exclusively till the middle of the thirteenth century, and English was not used as a rule till the third decade of the fifteenth century. There are instances of the use of both French and English earlier than these dates, such as a French document of Stephen Langton's, issued 1215, and Henry III.'s famous proclamation of 1258, which made use of English and French side by side; or again, in a royal proclamation at Worcester in 1299,[2] or in a document granting privileges to the City of London, dated 1327, both in English; but these are only isolated

---

[1] *Cf.* Gervase of Tilbury, *Otia Imperialia*, c. xx. l. 13, *seq.*, in Leibnitz's *Scriptores Rerum Brunsvicensium*, I., p. 945, where he is speaking of his own time. The chief peculiarities of Anglo-Norman were :—The dropping of inflections and unaccented vowels in all parts of the word; the pronunciation of *ä* as *n* and *ü* as *u*; the introduction of English words, etc., as we see from such comic pieces as the "Fabliau de deux Angloys et de l'anel," "La pais aus Englois" (*cf.* Wright, Political Songs), and others.

[2] "Annales Monastici" (Rolls Series), IV. 541.

cases, and at most point to a growing interest of the Government in the English-born section of the people—or, rather, to their growing wealth and influence.

About private documents in this century we have unfortunately no evidence; but that they were probably always written in Latin we may infer from the fact that the Countess of Stafford, making her will in 1438, thought it necessary to explain why she made it in English (Halliwell, Dic. I., p. x., note). On the other hand, Anglo-Norman was naturally the language in which the education of the upper classes was conducted. They were educated either at home or in the house of some abbot or bishop, or sometimes, as we have seen, in France. It can hardly be doubted, however, that English was used at least as much as Anglo-Norman in the cathedral-abbey-, and grammar-schools, for the sons of the commoners were most unlikely to have learnt anything but English at home. At the universities, of course, Latin reigned supreme. To sum up, then, we see that Latin and Anglo-Norman hold their own in university, public, and Court life to the end of our present period and beyond it, though there is a tendency noticeable for the latter to infringe upon the former in legal and other documents. In private life, however, and in literature, as we shall see, English is beginning to regain lost ground at the expense of Anglo-Norman.

Changes in English. At the same time it was inevitable that this English should be much modified in form by constant contact with the French dialect spoken on all sides, and we find in consequence that the language of such a writer as Robert of Gloucester, who flourished at the end of the thirteenth century, is something very different from that written just before the Conquest or even from that of Layamon, who though living at the beginning of the century, was distinctly archaic in tendency. As has been remarked, the first effect of the Norman Conquest was a negative one, leading to a fresh splitting up of English into a number of dialects, of which the main divisions are Northern, East and West Midland, and Southern. The last was spoken south of a line coinciding with the Thames as far west as Oxford and thence over Evesham and Worcester to the Severn. The first includes Yorkshire, Northumberland, Durham, and the Scottish lowlands. All who lived between these two districts spoke Midland. It was not till the beginning of the fourteenth century that any very large number of Romance

Linguistic Divisions
—— of the ——
BRITISH ISLES.
About 1250.

words was adopted into English, but from 1200 onwards Anglo-Norman words were slowly being absorbed, especially in connection with ecclesiastical ideas and those of general culture. Later came words connected with the State, knighthood, dress, hunting, the castle and the kitchen, for which there had either been no English words or they had fallen out of use during the period of degradation following the Conquest. In some cases doublets were the result, such as *work* and *labour*.

It must be remembered, of course, that these borrowed words did not retain their native form, but in most cases suffered more or less modification, especially in the position of the accent, which was in time thrown back upon the first syllable, in accordance with the English principle. This, combined with the fact that the English accent was a much stronger one than the French, led in time to the weakening of the unaccented syllable, thus :—Anglo-Norman *resoùn* becomes Middle English *resoùn*, and then later *réson*; this passed into Modern English, *réason* (pronounced reezn). It was not, however, till the sixteenth century that there was any uniformity in this matter, the borrowed words being capable of bearing either Romance or English accent during the M.E. period. Meanwhile native words were undergoing important modifications. There was a tendency before 1250 to lengthen the quantity of all monosyllables ending in a consonant and of all vowels standing before the combinations *mb*, *nd*, *ld*, and *ng*,[1] while long vowels before a lengthened consonant were shortened. After 1250 short vowels were lengthened if they stood at the end of an unaccented syllable—*e.g. brǫ-ken* passes into *brǭ-ken*. The changes in quality are no less marked. The Old English diphthongs (*e.g.*) became monophthongs—though much more slowly in the South than in the Midlands and the North—and a new set of what are called "secondary diphthongs" appeared, due to the combination of a primary vowel with a vowel developed from an original consonant; thus—Old English *dæg* becomes Middle English *dai* or *day*. This naturally leads us to notice that some of the consonants underwent a change. The O.E medial palatals *c*, ȝ, were affricated; *e.g., læccean* passes into Middle English *lacchen* = Mn. E. *latch*; and O.E. palatals often disappeared altogether, especially in weak syllables, or were vocalised and combined with other vowels to form fresh diphthongs, as described above. The initial sounds found in the

---

[1] This was known to the Anglian and late West Saxon dialects before the Conquest.

words "*chief*" and "*joy*" were borrowed from Anglo-Norman. Finally we must notice the gradual disappearance of inflections, due to weakening of the vowels in final unaccented syllables. This, in turn, affected the syntax of the language, making necessary a more logical arrangement of words in the sentence.

When we turn to the literature we find, as would be *Literature.* expected from what has been said, that most of the work produced during the first half of the reign is written in Latin ; and the most important books fall under the head of history. The long line of chronicle and history writers in the *The Devel-* twelfth century is continued into this, and culminates in *opment of Historical* Matthew Paris. A great advance is noticeable in this kind *Writing.* of writing in the thirteenth century. Chronicles give way to histories, chronological accounts of a string of events give place to a method of presentation which attempts to connect events with their causes, to estimate and to pass a judgment upon the characters of the chief actors, and to trace out the tendency of their actions. The famous northern school of chroniclers of the twelfth century came to an end with Roger Hoveden (died about 1201), the greatest of them all. The centre of this form of literary activity then moved southwards to St. Albans, a town most favourably situated for obtaining information, being on the great north road, and within an easy stage of the capital. Here lived during the thirteenth century a series of monks who produced most valuable historical work.

The first was the compiler of a chronicle afterwards made *The* much use of by his successors, Roger of Wendover and *St. Albans School.* Matthew Paris. Dr. Luard has shown with a fair amount of certainty that this compiler is to be identified with John de Cella, who was abbot 1189–1214. On this compilation, which has no historic value and accepts all sources of information as equally valuable, Roger of Wendover (d. 1236) founded the first part of his " Flores Historiarum." He re-wrote and enlarged his original up to 231, copied it verbatim to 1012, then introduced a few alterations to 1065, from which year he again copied closely with occasional additions to the year 1188, where his own work begins. Even here its historical value is of the slightest—at any rate in regard to the amount of discrimination shown in weighing evidence. Wendover is, however, anxious to be impartial and, except where the interests of his order are concerned, succeeds fairly well. He is laudably outspoken in his criticism of all orders of men, and chronicles their deeds in a plain, straightforward style, which lacks all distinctive character.

MATTHEW PARIS WRITING HIS
CHRONICLE (MS. Nero D. vii.).

His successor, Matthew Paris (b. *circa* 1200, d. 1259), who, in spite of his name, was of English origin, showed great advance in his work upon that of the Northern school and that done before him at St. Albans. He vas not only an historian, but a raveller, politician, and, most dif-

Matthew Paris. ficult of all, a courtier to boot. The first portion of his work, the "Historia Major," like that of Wendover, was transcribed with a few alterations from the compilation by John de Cella; and when this source of information ceased, he used the "Flores Historiarum" up to the year 1235, but with very considerable alterations from 1199 onwards. A condensed form of this earlier portion of the "Historia Major" afterwards formed the first part of a compilation going under the name of Matthew of Westminster. From 1235 to 1250, where the first edition ended, the work is original. Subsequently the work was revised and extended to 1253, and an abridgment made under the title "Historia Anglorum" or "Historia Minor." Finally, at the close of his life the author added a further continuation to 1259, which he never revised. Matthew Paris is among the very best of medieval historians. His style is vivid and picturesque, and his book gives us a series of brilliant criticisms on the men and events of his time. He is honest in purpose, a lover of truth, a keen observer, and, on the whole, just, though occasionally he gives vent to violent expressions when he feels ecclesiastical interests are at stake. He is practically the only authority for the years of Henry's reign between 1248 and 1253, and he shows much knowledge of contemporary affairs in the Empire, France, and Rome. He is, as a rule, quite trustworthy, far more so than the forerunners in his school. Where parallel authorities exist they bear out his truthfulness, and recent investigations have in every case confirmed it. He is even more fearless than Wendover in his outspoken blame of those who deserve it, no matter what their position in society. Even St. Louis is remonstrated with because he extorted money for his crusade from the Church of France. The picture he draws of the English king is very vivid; he paints him as a man weak in purpose but brave in battle, passionate and untrustworthy, avaricious; he calls him "regulus mendicans" (a beggar princelet), and at the same time a spendthrift, devoted to foreign favourites. Towards the end of his life, when he had learnt to know him better personally,[1] he began to think he had possibly been rather extravagant in some of his criticisms, and he revised his work, cutting out many a hard word about Henry and modifying others. He was a fearless critic, and therefore not afraid to retract.

MATTHEW PARIS, DRAWN BY HIMSELF (MS. Roy. 14 C. vii.)

William Rishanger, whose "Cronica" extended from 1259 to 1306, was also a monk of St. Albans. He evidently made use of the same sources as Nicholas Trivet in his "Annales

William Rishanger.

---

[1] Henry III. was on a visit to St. Albans in 1257.

sex Regum Angliæ," etc., from which Chaucer drew his "Man of Lawe's Tale." Finally the monastic annals of Burton, Winchester, Waverley, Dunstable, and Worcester must not be forgotten. Those of Winchester give a very full contemporary account of the decade following the battle of Evesham, whilst those of Waverley afford a valuable supplement to Matthew Paris between 1219 and 1266.

Literature in English. When we turn to the English literature of this time we find that the productions of the first half of the reign are confined to religious and moral subjects. It is not till after the battle of Lewes that the rising national life finds its expression in literature as in politics. One of the first English works produced in this reign is a metrical version of a Latin "Physiologus" by Tebaldus, and called a Bestiary (between 1220 and 1230), in which the various animals with their mystical properties and symbolisms are described. The verse is very irregular; at one time short rimed couplets, at another short-lined stanzas with cross-rime, at another lines with alliteration and no rime. These latter seem used generally in the descriptive, the two former in the moralising passages. The metre, too, shows a curious mixture of the national and romance principles of structure. In the poetical version of "Genesis" produced not much later, and, like the "Orrmulum" and "Bestiary," in the East Midlands, romance influence is much more evident. The verse consists of short rimed couplets of regular construction, according to the French or syllabic principle. This invasion of even religious literature by foreign influences is only another sign of the advancing tide already noticed. The author's chief source is not the Bible but Petrus Comestor's "Historia Ecclesiastica" (written 1169–1175). In the same way another poet, perhaps of the same monastery, produced not long afterwards a metrical "Exodus" in the same style and based on the same source. Among the lyric poems of this time—several of which show the influence of the "Poema Morale"[1]—the "Luve Ron" (Love Song) of Thomas de Hales deserves special mention for its richness of imagery and beauty of language. Into this department of poetry, as elsewhere, the complex musical measures of France were finding their way. Closely

[1] *Cf.* Morris's "Old English Miscellany," pp. 192f, 195f.

allied with the religious poetry is the proverbial. This kind of literature was naturally more conservative in form. Collections of proverbs under the name of Alfred and an imaginary wise man Hendyng were made and copied frequently during this reign, though the former can be traced back to the previous century. The "Owl and the Nightingale," written about 1220 in the South on the model of the Provençal "jeux partis," abounds with this proverbial philosophy. Although the poem is full of wisdom, the moral is not obtruded, as is the rule in medieval work. The contending sides are balanced with wonderful skill, and the verse, which is the French short rimed couplet, is as smooth as any that Chaucer wrote. The owl is a humorous Puritan who represents old-fashioned manners and morals, and will know nothing of love and women, the themes which interest the graceful gay-hearted Philomel, who would like to refer the quarrel to a certain Nicholas of Guildford, one of the King's confidants. His decision is left to our imagination, though we may guess that it was not in the owl's favour.

In imitation of the "Owl and the Nightingale," a series of these "disputacions" sprang up, especially in the South, *e.g.* "The Thrush and the Nightingale" in tail-rime.[1] At the same time the taste for secular as opposed to religious erotic poetry grew, though the latter continued to be popular. The famous "Cuckoo's Song,"[2] written in rimed septenars with refrain, and frequent alliteration and middle-rime, is an example of this growing fashion. The English were fast beginning to take an interest in other things than the Church, and it was therefore no accident that the ballad written on the Victory of Lewes was in English instead of French or Latin, as such poems had always been hitherto. Remembering this we shall not be surprised to find shortly before the middle of the century the reappearance of national epic. Truly "King Horn" and "Havelok the Dane" are in many ways better to be described as "Romans d'aventures" than as epic, and they have little enough in common with the dignified high heroic style of the Old English national

---

[1] Or *rime couée* (also called tailed rime) : a stanza where some lines, usually the third and sixth, are shorter (*e.g.* Chaucer's "Rime of Sir Thopas").

[2] E. E. T. S., vii. 419.

epos. But the stories are native and based on historical fact, and their very plebeian tone, the truth with which they reflect the stubborn spirit of the downtrodden but unconquered English, makes them worthy of the higher title. Both Horn and Havelok are sons of kings, who suffer exile, and gradually work their way, after many trials and adventures, to their own again, with the reward of a royal and beautiful bride. But the story of Havelok is much more coarsely and realistically drawn, as befitted the hard-handed men of Lincolnshire for whom it was written. Were it not for its evident seriousness (its humour notwithstanding) it might be taken for a parody of " King Horn."[1] The hero grows up as a fisher and scullery-boy instead of at the Court, and shows his worth by throwing a huge stone instead of splintering lances. Banishment and ultimate return was a favourite theme with medieval romances, and similar legends wove themselves round the names of Hereward the Wake, Fulk Fitz-Warin, and others. The romances of Guy of Warwick, written in Kent, and Bevis of Hampton, a West Saxon poem, can only be mentioned by name. But the stories of every land were laid under contribution quite as eagerly as native legend.

"Amis and Amiloun," the Orestes and Pylades of Western romance, "Floris and Blancheflor," and "Sir Tristrem" are all taken from the French, the last being of Celtic origin. Both the latter are stories of love—but there all similarity ceases, the first being a tale of tender and innocent affection, the second of an all-mastering destroying passion. The English " Sir Tristrem " is chiefly interesting as showing the line of transition from the romance to the ballad, for the story is greatly compressed, and the verse consists of a stanza made up of four Alexandrines with middle and end rime, followed by a fifth of like construction connected with them by a line of one accent. But British and English stories were just as popular as Celtic or Oriental, and the romances of " Arthur

---

[1] " King Horn " was written before 1250, was intended to be sung, as its opening lines show, and is the only romance written in the same metre as Layamon's " Brut " and the " Proverbs of Alfred," " Havelok the Dane," on the other hand, is in rimed couplets of the French type, like the Anglo-Norman " Lai de Havelok " on which it is founded, and was meant to be recited, not sung.

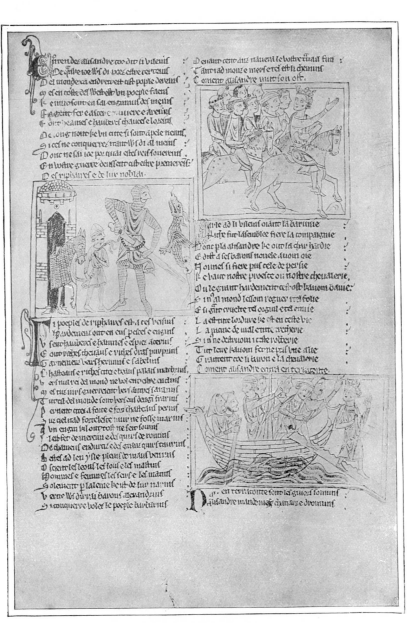

PAGE FROM THE ROMANCE OF ALEXANDER.
(*Trinity College, Cambridge.*)

and Merlin" and "Richard Cœur de Lion" were scarcely less popular than those of "Alisaunder," his Eastern prototype, or Tristan and Isolde. Not only romances, but fabliaux were borrowed from France, stories in which the chief interest lay in the action, not in the characters of the persons. In a romance the art lies in the method of presentation, in a fabliau the plot is in itself a work of art. Examples of this kind of art are "Dame Siriz" and "Reneuard and Sigrim" (taken from the Reynard Saga), the author of which is one of the finest of Chaucer's forerunners in the art of telling a tale. Others, such as "Orpheo," came originally from the East, but are deeply tinged with Celtic elements.

W. J. CORBETT. Agri- culture. THE two most noticeable features of the agricultural history of the hundred and forty years of which the first portion is now to be described are the increasing pains which most landowners about the reign of Henry III. began to take in superintending and developing their estates, and the silent but steady change during the whole period in the position of the actual cultivators of the soil. The former of these is the easier to trace, but the latter the more important: for by it the great mass of the peasantry, from being serfs owing compulsory services to the lords of the manors where they had been born, became converted into free labourers, earning daily wages, with power to work for whom and where they pleased. In the wake of this great revolution came eventually an entire change in the methods by which English agriculture was carried on, and the tenant-farmer for the first time comes upon the scene as an important and ordinary factor in village life. But though there are several instances of manors being let to farm in the thirteenth century, it cannot be said that lease-holding as a system had been generally adopted even at the beginning of the reign of Edward III. For in many places the older system of communal farming under capitalist land-lords, though it showed signs of breaking down, never actually became obsolete until the whole country had been devastated and every economic relation disarranged by the Great Plague which first broke out in 1348, and which of necessity forms the starting-point for a completely new period.

Up to this year very little outward alteration occurred, men being apparently contented with their prospects and surroundings, and only a gradual improvement of agriculture on the old lines is observable. This state of things would seem to be due to the comparatively peaceful nature of the reigns of Henry III. and his two successors, and to the fact that, with the exception of the ten years 1311–1321, the time, as a whole, was one of prosperous seasons and plenteous harvests, during which everyone devoted his best energies to improving his material condition, and so had little inducement to grumble or think about making fundamental alterations. The ten excepted years, however, show a general rise in prices and must be admitted to have been years of scarcity, while it is known from many independent sources that in 1316 and 1317 there was an absolute and perhaps unexampled famine. This was caused by the exceptionally wet summers which, not in one district only, but all over the country, were experienced both in 1315 and in 1316, and which in both years brought about an almost total failure of the grain crops. The famine, in fact, was so bad and so general that in some places it raised the price of corn in the first year to nearly 27s. a quarter, or about five times the amount it ordinarily sold for, and to very little under four times the amount in the second year; while at the same time the prices of all other commodities rose in proportion. What an amount of misery and even of starvation this must have meant to the great bulk of the people can perhaps best be indicated by stating that never in the 300 years that have elapsed since 1582 has the English farmer been able to sell his corn at much more than double the ordinary price current before a dearth, and certainly never for two years in succession. One other misfortune must also be mentioned which overtook the agriculturist in this period, and that was the outbreak of a new disease among the sheep just as they were beginning to be kept in large numbers and to assume an important place in the economy of English farms. This was the scab, which seems first to have appeared in 1288, and which has remained a common disease ever since.

Of the more general characteristics of agriculture at this time it may be remarked that, as in the preceding centuries

Periods of Dearth.

41

so in the thirteenth and fourteenth, the vast majority of the
population of the country must have been continuously
engaged in farming. The proof of this is simply a matter of
arithmetic; for the rate of production during all this period
was so low (on the average not more than eight bushels an
acre for wheat, or four times the amount sown, and not more
than $3\frac{1}{2}$ times for barley) that otherwise it would have been
impossible to keep alive even the modest population of between

MILKING EWES.
(*Luttrell Psalter.*)

1,500,000 and 2,000,000, which it is estimated England then
possessed. In consequence, the inhabitants of the towns, though
they were now rising rapidly in wealth and importance, still
remained to a large extent agriculturists, and in any case went
out into the fields during the harvest time. It is said, too,
that the students at the Universities, which first begin to attract
our attention at this time, were expressly given the long vacation
in the summer, with which we are still acquainted, in order
that they might return home at this season and share in the
labour of reaping and carrying with the rest of their relations;
and the same is perhaps true of the lawyers. The con-
siderations, too, which lead us to suppose that nearly everyone in England took some share in the production of the
annual food supply also compel us to believe that in the
more thickly populated districts of the country not much less
land was regularly under plough and used especially for

wheat cultivation in the thirteenth and fourteenth centuries than at present. For otherwise not enough acres could have been sown to produce for each man the quarter of wheat which, on the average, he must yearly have consumed; and at this time wheaten bread was an almost universal article of diet, even among the poorest classes. At first sight this seems improbable, but it must be remembered that in many places throughout England, as, for instance, on the South Downs, there are unmistakable traces of former cultivation still existing in the ridges and furrows on lands that have not been ploughed up for centuries; that at this early date hardly any land was set aside for either parks or pleasure grounds, and none used permanently for dairy-farming; and lastly, that wheat seems to have been cultivated with comparative success during these centuries even in the northern counties of Northumberland and Durham, whereas only a century ago it was popularly supposed that such a thing was impossible anywhere north of the Humber. In fact, one of the general characteristics of this period is that the processes of cultivation varied very little throughout the country, and that the same kinds of grain were sown, the same kinds of stock kept, and the same sort of labour was required both in the north and in the south. Nor is the reason for this far to seek; for the object of every landowner was to make each manor as self-supporting as possible. A few articles, such as iron for tools and horseshoes, or salt for curing, had, of course, in most localities, to be obtained from outside; but this was avoided wherever possible, and no effort was spared which could possibly make the home production sufficient to meet all the requirements of the simple style of living then customary. In a word, the advantages of a division of labour were hardly appreciated; and so, though some localities must have been best adapted for pasturage, and others for rye and oat-growing, yet there were hardly any parts of the country used for farming on which some amount of wheat and barley was not produced, and where all kinds of stock were not kept. From an agricultural point of view, that is to say, England was not, as now, split up into several districts, each practising more especially some particular branch of farming, but only into two main divisions—the lowlands, where every-

Mixed Farming.

one farmed on a uniform plan, and the highlands, moors, and mountains, where no agriculture at all was attempted, and which were still almost uninhabited, except, indeed, in some parts of Yorkshire, where the Cistercians and other orders of monks had introduced sheep-farming and made a beginning at reclaiming the wilderness.

The Distribution of Population. In keeping also with this state of things was the distribution of the population, which, instead of being thickest in the hilly districts of the north and west, at at present, was chiefly confined to the south and east, the area of greatest density being approximately marked by a line drawn from Norfolk through Reading to Dorsetshire. The general distribution of wealth in the agricultural districts during this period, if we exclude the towns, is naturally in the main similar. Thus in 1341, a year in which Edward III. laid a wool tax on all England for the purposes of his French war, the details of which have been accurately preserved, we find that Norfolk was by far the richest county; for in this district every 610 acres was expected to furnish a sack of wool or its money value to the Exchequer, whereas in the average county only one sack was demanded from every 1,570 acres. It must, however, be admitted that this great comparative prosperity was not wholly due to any marked superiority in the agriculture of the Norfolk landowners, but rather to the fact that their county happened at this time to be the site of the woollen trade, and consequently was largely inhabited by wealthy Flemish weavers and other foreign craftsmen, the majority of whom resided and worked in the villages. Of purely agricultural districts, Middlesex—excluding London— and Oxfordshire seem to have been the wealthiest, each of these counties having to furnish one sack of wool to every 760 acres; and then come Bedfordshire, Kent, and Berkshire. Instances of counties far below the average in wealth, and yet not particularly mountainous, are furnished by Shropshire and Herefordshire, in each of which only one sack was demanded from every 3,500 acres; while poorest of all were the modern manufacturing districts of Lancashire and the West Riding of Yorkshire.

The evidence that has come down to us of greater attention having been paid by the landowners to agriculture during the thirteenth century than in preceding years is twofold, and consists firstly in the fact that in this century there appeared in England for the first time systematic treatises and manuals dealing with estate-management in its various forms as an art, and designed so as to be of practical assistance both to the landowners and their servants when in difficulties; and secondly in the great mass of written documents still existing in our public libraries and in the muniment rooms of colleges and other landed corporations, which deal in detail with the actual working of particular manors during the reigns of Henry III. and Edward I., and which are either non-existent or practically so for any earlier period. Both these novelties in their origin are no doubt to be ascribed to the example and influence of the great monastic houses, which at all periods bestowed a good deal of attention on their estates, and can in most instances be shown to have been the pioneers in any substantial improvements that were introduced into medieval farming; but it is certain that by 1259 their example had also been followed by the greater lay landowners, and that written documents such as we have just referred to had by this time begun to be regularly kept on the majority of their estates.

The earliest treatise on estate-management that can be dated with certainty is a little book written in Norman-French between 1240 and 1241 by Robert Grosseteste, the celebrated Bishop of Lincoln, for Margaret, the Dowager Countess of Lincoln, and known by the name of "The Rules of St. Robert." This, however, does not appear to have had a very large circulation—perhaps because it was originally written for a woman, and chiefly dealt with the management of the household. More popular but undated and anonymous works of this period are those called "Husbandry" and "Seneschaucie" (stewardship), both also written in Norman-French. The first of these deals more particularly with the methods of keeping farming accounts, while the second describes the duties of the various manorial officers, beginning with the seneschal or steward, and so on down through the various grades to the dairymaid. By far the most popular, however, and also the most practical of all these early treatises was that written by Sir Walter de Henley some time before the

Books on Agriculture.

year 1250, and entitled " Le dite de Hosebondrie," or by some
" Du Gaignage des Terres." In this the author, who had himself
been a farmer, and perhaps the bailiff of an estate belonging
to Canterbury Cathedral, surveys each of the departments of
rural economy—such as ploughing and harrowing—in turn,
and shows how a prudent owner will set about supervising
everything if he wishes to manage his estates thriftily. This
treatise, indeed, obtained such a reputation that it remained
the standard English work on farming for more than 200
years, and even then was only supplanted by Sir Anthony
Fitzherbert's work, which embodied a good deal of its contents.
Another class of treatises which may be noted as dating first
of all from this period, and which also bear to a certain extent
on estate management, though more indirectly, is formed by
the numerous formularies and precedents for holding manorial
courts, which were drawn up at any rate not later than the
reign of Edward II.—for these legal handbooks, equally with
the more strictly economic manuals, all tend to show that
the men of these times felt a desire to regulate their affairs
better, and wished to set up a standard for their subordinates
to work by, so that each might readily judge whether the
most was being made out of his individual property.

**Manorial
Records.**

Of the documents dealing with particular estates — or
manorial records, as they may most properly be called—there
are three distinct kinds, which all came into vogue in the
reign of Henry III. These are—(1) The Extent, or detailed
survey of each manor, made on the pattern of the returns in
Domesday, but at much greater length; (2) the Manorial
Court Rolls, imitated from the records kept in the King's
Courts; and (3) the " Compotus," or annual profit-and-loss
account rendered by the bailiff to the non-resident landlord,
much in the same way as the sheriffs yearly accounted for
the firm[1] of their counties to the Exchequer. The first of
these, which was compiled from the sworn testimony of the
villagers themselves, and only revised at long intervals,
presents us with a minute description of the capabilities and
acreage of all the land in the manor to which it relates,
together with an accurate enumeration of all the tenants,

[1] The " firm," ferme, or farm (Lat. *firmus*) was the fixed sum which the
sheriff of each county paid yearly as composition for its taxes.]

both free and in villeinage, who either held land of the lord
or in any way owed him services, ending finally with a list
of what these services were and what they were worth in
money.   In the second we have a record of all the petty
business transacted in the manor court, showing how from
time to time the various tenements changed hands, how the
homagers shared the burdens that were laid on them, how
frequently they attempted to evade their services, and by
what penalties they had to be enforced.   From the third we
can see what kind of expenses a Plantagenet landlord annually
incurred, how far he depended on the honesty of his bailiff,
how he rewarded his labourers, and how much income he
might reasonably expect to receive from the manor in average
years.   Of course, it is only in comparatively rare instances
that the records now extant of any one manor furnish information on anything like all the points just enumerated, or
even contain contemporaneous specimens of all the three
kinds of documents.   The records, however, of one kind or
another that have survived are so numerous, and relate to so
many localities, that were space available it would be possible
to reconstruct an almost complete picture of the farming
practised in England until the Black Death.   As it is, a mere
outline, such as is given in the next chapter, must suffice :
an outline, too, which in strictness only applies to the larger
estates.   For it should be remembered that it was only on
the estates of large landowners that records were kept, and
we ought not, therefore, to assume that the small squires and
under-tenants always cultivated their holdings in the same
way, though the assumption in itself is not at all improbable.

To trace the development of British trade in the thirteenth
century would seem at first sight a comparatively simple and
at the same time a somewhat unprofitable task.   Not only
are the data available exceedingly scanty, but the historical
interest of the period does not consist in these material con-
siderations, but rather in the study of certain political and
social phenomena of a very distinct character.   On the one
hand we have to trace the struggle for the Charters—confirmed a hundred times during the century—and on the

**HUBERT
HALL.
Trade and
Industry.**

other the steps by which the fusion of the races and the vindication of the native literature were accomplished. Moreover, the king and his council were not so much engaged in discussing the balance of trade or the distribution of wealth as in useless attempts to solve the great problem of a disjointed empire which could no longer be reclaimed or defended with the aid of obsolete feudal services.

Sources of Information.   In fact, however, the opening years of the thirteenth century do form an important epoch in the history of trade and commerce, if only that we now have access for the first time to a new and somewhat neglected source of information. The statistics available for this subject can hitherto be sparsely gleaned from the rolls and registers of the Exchequer, from isolated Charters, and from the vague and metaphorical descriptions of contemporary historians. From the close of the thirteenth century onwards the commercial progress of the nation is fairly illustrated by the rolls of Parliament, and by the elaborate enrolled accounts of the collectors of customs and subsidies which were subsidiary to the making of the Budget. For the intervening period which is now under our notice invaluable evidence is furnished by the great series of the rolls of the Chancery. These records not only supply much information respecting the extent of trade, as gauged by payments or fines for licences, safe-conducts, and other privileges of the merchants, but they also afford indirect evidence as to the growing importance of this trade in the shape of precedents for its control and regulation by the Crown. From this new source, as well as from sources which already existed, from municipal or manorial accounts and precedent books, and from reasonable analogy, we may formulate the conditions under which English trade and commerce were pursued from the death of King John to the accession of Edward I. on the following lines.

Products of the Soil.   In the thirteenth century, and down to a much later date, the classification of trade corresponds very nearly with a division under the heads of exports and imports, although we have also to consider that certain branches of native industry were practically in the hands of foreigners through the inexperience of native traders and the odium which attached to the pursuit of sordid gains. Nevertheless, native traders can at least be recognised in this period as a typical class of the community. In a country whose products are not absolutely self-sufficing—that is to say, which imports foreign wares as necessaries or luxuries of life—there must be some channel for disposing of native products in exchange for those imports. In the same way one district must exchange its peculiar products with those of another, and each producer must furnish himself with what he needs for maintaining the rate of production. It would be difficult to

A COUNTRY CART.
(*Luttrell Psalter.*)

imagine any period of our history in which some such system of barter or trade did not exist, and in the thirteenth century it had attained very definite proportions.

The English at this period being essentially an agricultural nation, it follows that the staple trade consisted mainly in products of the soil, such as corn, flesh, and dairy produce. These products—or, rather, the surplus which remained after the wants of the family had been satisfied and the land stocked for the ensuing year—were sold at the local market or at one of the great annual fairs, and the proceeds, after the purchase of a number of necessaries, went to swell the credit side of the landowner's account.

The abundant illustrations of the manorial economy which exist from the middle of the thirteenth century enable us to realise the whole process of this familiar traffic—the steward and the foreman [1] tallying the corn out of the grange into the carts for market, after the seed-corn required for the autumn and spring sowing had been set apart; the thinning-out of the flocks at Martinmas, both of those bred on the

[1] His Latin name is *messor*, reaper.]

farm and those bought last Hock-tide[1] to be fattened and sold at a profit (with due regard to the requirements of the salting-house for victualling the household until Easter), and the summer output of the dairy-house in the form of "weighs" of thin cheeses, greatly reduced in bulk after the harvest-rations supplied to the lord's "boon-men."[2]

PEWTER SPOONS (GUILDHALL MUSEUM).
(By permission of the Library Committee to the Corporation of the City of London.)

The above products of the soil were not, however, the only ones employed as marketable commodities. From a very early period it had been discovered that flocks and herds were scarcely less valuable for their pelts and hides than for their flesh, and thus the sale of wool, and wool-fells and hides, is a very important item in the manorial accounts. As a minor profit may be reckoned also the animal fats produced from the operations of the slaughter-house. Other products of the soil, as iron, lead, tin, stone, and wood, though equally the fruits of rural industry, may be enumerated under a separate head. At the same time they are to be included with the former among the staple products of this country.

Imports.   The same sources of information furnish us indirectly with a list of the chief imports employed by the agricultural community. The steward, in rendering his account of the profits of the estate, was allowed for certain articles purchased for the purpose of its suitable cultivation, among which tar, canvas, and mill-stones are most frequently mentioned. This list is further supplemented by the household and revenue accounts of the Crown or of some great lord, until it assumes very formidable proportions, including in the thirteenth century

[1 The second or third week after Easter.]
[2 Men doing unpaid services due to the lord as part of their rent.]

such articles as cloths of fine texture (especially those which were dyed in grain or self-coloured), silks, furs, jewels, groceries of all kinds, wax (in great request for candles and seals in the court and monastery), wine (for the hall or tavern), and salt.

These various imports reached the English seaports by several recognised trade-routes. The produce of the north-eastern countries of Europe, representing what may be called the Baltic trade, was, from the middle of the thirteenth century, almost entirely in the hands of the great federation known as the Hanse (p. 523), and by the enterprise of this body

The Hanse League.

MEDIÆVAL JUGS (GUILDHALL MUSEUM).
(By permission of the Library Committee to the Corporation of the City of London.)

England was plentifully supplied with furs, tar, and fish—especially herring. Naturally this trade was directed to the north-eastern ports of this country. Indirectly also there was a communication with the East through this channel, the connecting link being the great Russian fair of Novgorod.

Besides this general trade with the Hanse, there was also a considerable trade with Flanders and with the North of France; but the Hanse practically held sway from Antwerp in the north to Cologne in the south, its members being better known at a slightly later date as the Easterlings.

In another direction Southampton was the recognised emporium for the Mediterranean trade, already almost exclusively in the hands of the great Italian republics, whose citizens monopolised the carrying trade of the highly valued products of the East. These, which consisted for the most

The Mediterranean Trade.

part in spices, reached the Mediterranean either by the Asiatic
route to the ports of Antioch and Trebizond, or through
Egypt to Alexandria, and the difficulties of transport entailed
almost prohibitive prices. Silks, however, were the staple
wares of the Italian cities, which probably exported also, like
those of Flanders, a considerable quantity of fine cloths. It
is needless to enlarge upon the impetus which this Mediterranean trade received from the Crusades during the thirteenth
century, or on the opportunities thus offered for independent
observation and invaluable
experience to the Northern
nations until the spirit of
adventure led them in turn
to follow new trade-routes to
the far East.

A SPANISH TINAJA (GUILDHALL MUSEUM).
(*By permission of the Library Committee to the Corporation of the City of London.*)

After all, however, furs,
silks, and spices formed but a
small proportion of our staple
imports. The demand for
these luxuries, though steady
and always increasing, was
almost exclusively confined
to the Court and to the
wealthy classes, whilst the demand for wine and salt was of
an almost national character.

The proportion between the several classes of imports may
be most easily realised from the fact that at a slightly later
date the collective proceeds of the taxation of merchandise by
the name of poundage barely exceeded that of the tunnage
and prisage (p. 664) of wines. Indeed, the arrival of the wine
fleet from the centre and south of France, and from the Rhine
districts, was an event almost as important as the safe
despatch of the English wool fleet to the Flemish ports.

Native products and foreign imports being thus available
for sale, we have next to ascertain the usual means by which
this was effected. From a very early period markets had
been established in convenient situations. In Domesday Book
the market appears as the natural complement of the manorial
economy, and in the thirteenth century few considerable

franchises could be found without this profitable seigniorial appanage. Three things were necessary for the holding of a market—a suitable position in connection with some highway; the grant of the privilege in question by the Crown to the lord of the soil; and the regulation of the market and the receipt of the dues by the lord. The ordinary market held on a certain week-day is one of those episodes which have continued to be enacted with little change during the lapse of centuries.

A far more important event in this century was one of the great annual fairs, at which the entire produce of the county, and the typical imports also, were exposed for sale. These too, like the local markets, were held under the protection and subject to the jurisdiction of some lord. The risk and cost of attending these meetings must, however, have been considerable.

In the middle of the previous century, we are told, the rents of the king's farms payable in kind—that is, in oxen, sheep, and grain—were commuted for money-rents, owing to the insupportable expense of conveyance to the Court. The roads were inconceivably bad, and even carriage by water was sadly hindered by the weirs and other engines of riparian owners, against which a long string of denouncements, from the Great Charter onwards, have been vainly directed, whilst the apparatus employed was also exceedingly rudimentary. It has even been asserted, with some probability, that the usual excellence of imported wines was merely owing to the fact that only a superior quality would pass the ordeal of the journey. It is true that travelling on certain roads had attained something of the excellence of the later posting system: for instance, the recognised stages from London to Dover *en route* for Paris and Rome, as they were known to Matthew Paris and his contemporaries; but although horse-flesh was cheap, this procedure entailed considerable expense where strangers were compelled to occupy appointed lodgings, and where tolls and ferries could not be circumvented. Once off the beaten track, there was almost a certainty of surprise by the outlaws or robbers who infested the wooded gorges and lonely heaths in the vicinity of the great cities and fairs.

The periodical markets of the villages and smaller towns

were chiefly employed for local traffic of the same nature as that which prevails to the present day. The markets of the larger towns also resembled those of our own time, except that the nature of the wares and the nationality of the sellers were somewhat sharply distinguished. In the case of Smithfield Market, for instance, a thoroughly representative stock of cattle and horses was collected every six weeks. Besides these permanent markets, with their fixed or movable stalls, goods were exposed in the ordinary way beneath the projecting pent-houses of the shops, while some kinds, and especially fuel and water, were hawked about the streets in carts, as they are even to the present day. The fair, though naturally of less antiquity than the market, was, however, a far more distinctive feature of the commercial life of the thirteenth century. This, like the market, was the perquisite of some lord; it was also held at certain dates, but usually only once a year, on some appropriate feast-day. Several of the English fairs enjoyed a European reputation, but two stand out from among the rest as the natural centres of English commerce in the east and south.

Stourbridge Fair was most conveniently situated for the exchange or export of the products of the eastern counties and for the sale of the foreign commodities of the Baltic trade. The fair was opened on the 18th of September and lasted for three weeks, being held under the authority of the Corporation of Cambridge. It was situated in the open country, and temporary booths were erected every year, forming streets which covered a total area of half a square mile. The chief business done seems to have been the sale of wool and cloth for exportation and the purchase of the wares of Hanse merchants, but every trade and every nationality was represented in its numerous streets.

Winchester Fair was of even greater importance in the thirteenth century, since it was connected with the great emporium of the south-eastern trade, Southampton, and the linked ports of London and Sandwich. Here the fair was under the immediate control of the Bishop, by whose officers it was proclaimed on the Eve of St. Giles, to last for sixteen days. The site of the fair was the hill overlooking the city, which was covered with stalls, forming distinct streets, allotted

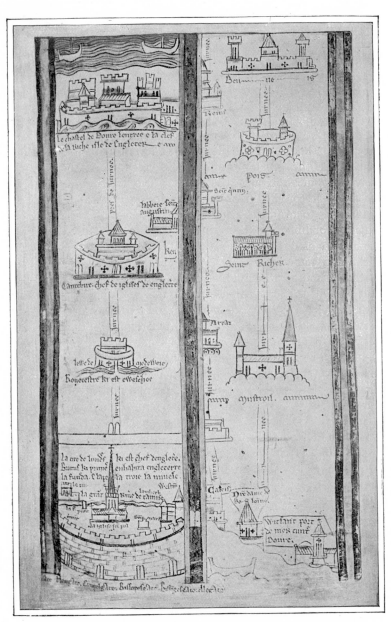

THE FIRST STAGES ON THE ROAD TO ROME (MS. Roy. 14, C. vii.).

in the usual manner to the several trades and nationalities. Since it was an essential condition of the holding of a fair that it should enjoy a monopoly of trade in the vicinity for the time being, the greatest precautions were taken for putting a stop to unlicensed trade within certain limits, in order that the profits of the lord might not be diminished. It was at the same time to the advantage of the mercantile community that a strict police and a close supervision over weights and measures should be maintained, and in return for these advantages the greater number of merchants gladly paid the heavy entrance-toll and the fees at the wool-beam, although cases are recorded in which certain penurious traders endeavoured to evade these payments by burrowing under the palisades or lingering after the fair was at an end to conclude their bargains free of registration dues. In this, as in every other fair, there was a Court of Pie-powder, so called because the several disputes which arose were adjudged with a dispatch that suited the convenience of transitory suitors—the men with " dusty feet " (*pieds poudrés*). From the fact, however, that the cases which arose were mostly trade disputes and outside the narrow purview of the common law, a good deal of interest attaches to their decision by a jury of experts. In this aspect the merchants made their own law, but there was also a large number of cases which did not involve a consideration of " tallies " and " God's-pennies," but merely proof of fraud or violence. Thus we read in the Court-Roll of St. Ives of a defendant charged with selling a ring of brass for 5½d., saying " that the ring was of the purest gold, and that he and a one-eyed man found it on the last Sunday in the church of St. Ives, near the Cross." We gather, however, that in most cases the bargain was satisfactorily concluded by a drink.

Besides Stourbridge and Winchester, there were important fairs held at Boston, St. Ives (Hunts), Stamford, Oxford, Abingdon, St. Edmundsbury, Nottingham, and other places.

Crowth of Industry. The industrial progress of the thirteenth century cannot on the whole be regarded as very considerable. The national wealth was still measured by the welfare of the landed interest. The gap between the artistic feeling of the Romanised Briton and the engrafted skill of the fourteenth-century artisan is a very wide one, but in some aspects the thirteenth century may be regarded as a typical era in the history of English industry. If the industrial reforms of the fourteenth

A LOOM.
(Trinity College, Cambridge.

century are regarded as a new and momentous departure, it cannot be too carefully remembered that almost the whole of English trade was at this time in the hands of aliens, and that native enterprise and adventure toiled painfully in the wake of the Free Cities of the Continent, as the small " cog " was outstripped by the great " carrack " in the Mediterranean trade. Nay, down to the very eve of the industrial revolution in the eighteenth century, the textile fabrics for which this country had long enjoyed the highest reputation were petty industries, supplementing the national occupation of agriculture, the gathering of that other harvest of the sea, and the feverish quest of hidden treasures of the earth. But although we should seek in vain in the thirteenth century, or long afterwards, for any English industry to compare with the great factories of Florence, we cannot doubt that there was sufficient skill in the textile arts to render the industry self - sufficing. The clothing of every lowly and most middle-class households was manufactured at home, and this might be supplemented on rare occasions by the purchase, at any one of the great fairs, of the fine cloth imported from Flanders and Italy, or of that substantial product of the

FOLDING THE WOVEN FABRIC.
(Trinity College, Cambridge.)

Anglo-Flemish looms, the cloth of assize, manufactured by the weavers' guilds in nearly all the great cities of England.

For the most part, however, the village crafts were self-

42

**Manu-
facture.**

sufficing. In every village wool and hemp were ready to hand
for a score of spindles, and the stout yarn produced could be
woven into coats and shirts, which needed not, in the eyes of
their simple wearers, the embellishments of scarlet grain or
Flemish madder. The great nobles hung these coarse friezes
on their chamber walls; the king's officers stretched them on
benches or on their Exchequer table; but the churl and
villein, the monk and sometimes the franklin, wore them as

ROPEMAKING.
(*Luttrell Psalter.*)

their common habit. The village tanner and bootmaker supplied long gaskins[1] of soft leather for such as needed more
protection than home-made sandals. The professional hunter
of wolves, cats, or otters, and even the humble molecatcher,
supplied a head-covering for those who did not go bare-headed
by choice; and the second great want of Nature was provided
for the village resident. For other than the textile arts the
smith was a recognised institution in every village, and possibly
a carpenter for the construction of ploughs and carts. Even
the ropes of hair or hemp which formed the chief part of
their harness were home-made; but the manufacture of
baskets and barrels was somewhat more local. For the
building of a church or castle, carpenters and masons were

[1 A sort of loose leather trousers.]

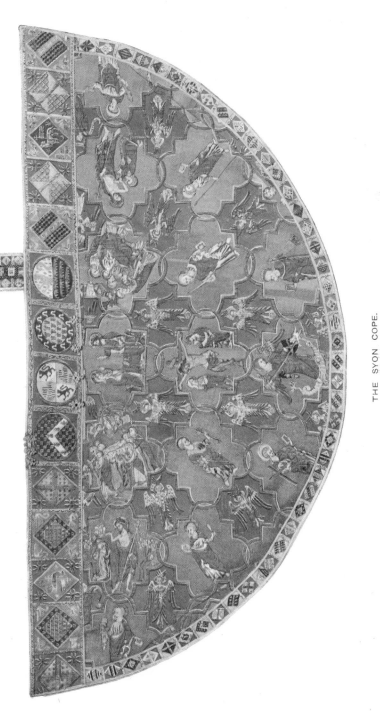

THE SYON COPE.

(*Victoria and Albert Museum, South Kensington.*)

[*To face p.* 658.

imported from a distance, like the stone and shingles and lead with which they worked; but the peasant erected his own wattled cabin, just as the sheriff's men could build the local gaol with saplings from the king's forest. Finally, the mill under the lord's control is another instance of a self-sufficing industry. Here all the tenants were virtually compelled to grind their corn, and the mill was consequently a paying concern from the date of Domesday survey down to

A WINDMILL.
(*Luttrell Psalter.*)

comparatively modern times. At the same time we may recognise a growing regard for the value of even home-made cloth as an article of sale at the local markets and fairs, for, as we have seen, the native supply of this article was rather the surplus of a domestic manufacture than the regular output of the trade communities in the towns.

The thirteenth century saw the position of the English **The** towns assured. Their prosperity had been already guaranteed **Towns.** by the acquisition of their charters in the twelfth. The town was naturally the industrial centre of a district and a unit of the industrial trade of the nation. In England, as in other countries of Europe, the bulk of trade as we now understand the term, was carried on in the towns. These, from the early part of the twelfth century, had obtained in certain favoured instances very necessary and advantageous privileges for the purpose, which were expressed in charters enabling them to render an account of their own farms or assessments payable at the Exchequer. In addition to this concession, which secured them in the enjoyment of the fruits of their enterprise, the citizens obtained at several times the virtual privilege of self-government and also a general exemption from vexatious suits and arbitrary tolls outside their own cities. For example, the citizens of London were free of toll at the fair of Winchester if they availed themselves of this privilege within a reasonable date. Still more important for the welfare of the civic community was the recognition of the status of the guild-merchant.

The Merchant Guilds. In very early times societies had existed for social and religious intercourse, and for the ensurance of mutual responsibility in the police system of the country. These were gradually enlarged for the purposes of trade; and having thus obtained, perhaps, a kind of legal status on the strength of their conformity with the laws of Church and State, they collectively assumed the general control of trade as the Guild-Merchant. This body possessed a central establishment or guildhall, with officers and bye-laws, while outside the influence of the guild itself the machinery of municipal government was available for the common interests of the whole body of citizens. The trade of the country was, therefore, not only essentially municipal in character, but, more than this, it was inter-municipal—that is to say, the guild-brethren of one city were admitted on a common footing to the trade privileges of another city, and they were presumably responsible for the behaviour and liabilities of each other, as they certainly relieved the necessities of their poorer members. The inhabitants of the towns may thus be regarded somewhat in the light of a great family of traders with a common policy and objects; but as the family increased, the poor relations and strangers forming the great class of the artisans who had long enjoyed a more or less independent recognition in the craft-guilds, legalised by the Crown since the middle of the twelfth century, were induced at length to adopt a system of government amongst themselves with the object of regulating their own work—not necessarily with the intention of wresting a monopoly of trade and government from the hands of an exclusive municipality, but merely that their interests might no longer be overlooked in the government of a greater city.

It is not very evident, however, that the industries even of the towns were very extensive or flourishing during this period. It is true that these townsmen were presumably the descendants of those who had flocked together at some convenient site for purposes of trade from a very early time; but of these some might be merchants, or even landed proprietors, and others were mere salesmen of imported wares, who lived chiefly by the custom of the Court or of the civic aristocracy. The most successful and

Photo: T. W. Phillips, Wells.

THE COBBLER, WELLS CATHEDRAL.

enterprising of any were the Jews, and the most skilful of the true artisans were of Flemish extraction. However, we do find here a considerable population of artisans representing every known trade, though only such craft-guilds as are returned in the Pipe Rolls need be considered as of much importance. These include the weavers, who were established in most of the principal towns, the fullers,[1] the bakers, with others—such as the loriners[2] and the cordwainers.[3] The goldsmiths were in high repute, but artistic metal work like armour seems to have been usually imported. A very large provision of warlike gear, together with silks, trappings, pavilions, girdles, and fine cloths, was, however, made for the king's use every year by the sheriffs of London and Middlesex; and these at least may have been manufactured in the city, since they figure indiscriminately in the Pipe Rolls with undoubted native products. We certainly read of a shield-maker (at York) and of a saddler who were fined for selling arms to the king's

[1 Cloth-finishers, who pressed and faced the cloth. 2 Saddlers. 3 Bootmakers.]

enemies as early as the great rebellion of 1173–4; and slightly earlier, merchants of Gloucester were forbidden to equip the English adventurers for the conquest of Ireland. In the reign of John we have a list of nearly thirty towns in which a trade in dyed cloths had been carried on for half a century. Indeed, the very arrangements of the medieval shop were made with a view to manufacture on the premises, the dwelling-chamber being in the upper storey, over an apartment used as a workshop, the goods being exposed for sale on a bench beneath the overhanging porch. It was a feature of these urban industries that the respective crafts were brought together each in a distinct quarter of the city, just as we have seen them grouped in the temporary stalls of the great provincial fairs, and this arrangement much facilitated the close supervision that was exercised by the guild officers over the quality and workmanship of the wares.

Foreign
Inter-
course.
The Norman Conquest effected no more momentous change in the social condition of this country than by opening English ports to the commerce of the west and south of Europe. Hitherto English commerce had been of the north, piratical, until the civilisation of the Scandinavian kingdoms and the humanising influence of the Roman Church caused a temporary depression in barbarian enterprise. The beneficial effect of Continental influences was ultimately attained in the thirteenth century, when the intermunicipal trade of the great Free Cities of Europe had begun to have full play. Then the natural wealth of the land, formerly the tempting prey of northern freebooters and for long past the vaunt of native chroniclers, began to be gradually realised by the intelligent nations of the south. However, it was not between nations that the new conditions of commerce were established, but among cities. The Germans were merchants of Cologne or of Hamburg, and they were not only the Emperor's men but also members of the German guild, which had its Hansehouses in several of the chief English cities. It was the same with the citizen merchants of the great Italian republics or the States of Flanders. Such a title as "merchant of France" was never heard of at the time, but there were merchants of Gascony, and a swarm of hardy fishermen from the Norman and Breton seaports, with whom the men of the

Cinque Ports waged deadly war for the sovereignty of the narrow seas, from the days of Hubert de Burgh to those of Stephen de Penchester. On the whole, however, the amenities of commercial intercourse were faithfully observed, Germans, Northmen, Gascons, and Lombards receiving valuable privileges in their English factories, and English citizens claiming equal protection for their own guild-brethren in foreign ports. In one aspect we observe the renovation of the earlier trade with northern lands which centred in the elaborate organisation of the Hanse towns; in another aspect intercourse with Rome and the Crusading movement brought England into commerce with the Mediterranean states. In both directions we benefited by inexhaustible markets for our wool and other exported products, and perhaps equally by the well-earned comfort afforded by soft raiment and fragrant spices. Again, there was another sort of commerce imparted to us from the Continent—namely, that which was invidiously conducted by the Jewish and Flemish residents.

From a period antecedent to the Conquest itself commerce had been—nominally, at least—under the control of the Crown. This we can gather from the Saxon laws, and this still continued to be no less necessary in the thirteenth century in the real or fancied interests of law and order and generally for the national welfare. Traders might be at this date, as they were invariably in later times, classified according to their respective status as natives, aliens, and denizens—all of whom were subject, in the first place, to certain exactions, and secondly to certain restraints imposed by the Crown. This may be regarded as the imperial side of the subject, as distinct from the municipal or local, which has hitherto engaged our attention. The origin of the royal prerogative herein may perhaps be traced from the tribal contributions in support of the kingly state, which took the later forms of purveyance, pre-emption, prisage and butlerage, dismes, and finally Customs.[1] But however this may be, we find that

Regulation of Trade.

[1 Purveyance was the right to impress carriages and horses for the conveyance of the king's household or goods; pre-emption, the right to purchase provisions, etc., for his household at an appraised price. Dìsmes (*dixièmes*, tenths) were an early form of customs. On prisage and butlerage *see* the text. Dowell, "History of Taxes and Taxation," gives much valuable information on these taxes.]

from the middle of the twelfth century onwards a regular scale of dues was levied at the outports. Similar dues were also exacted by seigniorial and municipal franchises, but these depended in turn upon a grant from the Crown. London, Sandwich, Southampton, and Boston were early centres for the collection of the king's Customs, which were usually accounted for by the Chamberlains until the appointment of collectors and controllers under Edward I. Wine was an especial subject of taxation, native merchants being liable to supply one or two tuns from before and behind the mast, according to the size of the vessel, at a low price to the king's purveyors. In the same way aliens paid a toll of two shillings on every tun, known as the butlerage; this and the above toll in kind—or prisage, as it was called—being collected by the King's Butler. As the average wholesale price of wine during this period was very low, the native trader was more favourably treated than the alien, who was often liable to arbitrary purveyance. But when the value of wine was trebled in the next century, the former was a loser by the composition which he obstinately clung to, while the latter benefited largely by the old rate of butlerage as finally settled in 1303. During three years of the middle of the thirteenth century we learn that 1,455 tuns of prise wines were taken at London and Sandwich alone. As each tun may be taken to represent an average cargo of twenty casks, the average annual importation to these linked ports was about 10,000 tuns.

The Customs or duties on other articles of merchandise usually took, at the close of the twelfth and beginning of the thirteenth centuries, the form of a tenth or fifteenth. In the reign of John we find a fifteenth regularly levied at all the outports of England, of which as many as from thirty to forty make returns, the total amounting to about £5,000. But considerable as is the revenue which is thus accounted for in the Exchequer Rolls of the period, it is possible that a still larger profit was realised by the exercise of the king's prerogative in the restraint of trade.

The nature of these exactions may be gathered from the Chancery Rolls, from which it appears that large fines were paid by divers merchants for licences to trade—namely, to export woad, wool, and leather, as well as corn and other provisions from England, or for safe-conducts and protection for themselves and their merchandise throughout the king's dominions, free of arbitrary prises and tolls. These fines were naturally most frequently paid by foreign merchants, and they varied from a sum of four thousand marks to a present of a palfrey or hawk. In spite of the well-known article of Magna Charta, the restraint of trade and the exactions which accompanied it were continued with little intermission down to the reign of Edward I., when a fixed tariff at the outports, coupled with a vigorous foreign policy, gave a new stimulus to English commerce.

THERE are no signs of the continued residence of Jews in England before the Conquest. The only references to them in Anglo-Saxon literature are in the Church codes, in which they may have been inserted by mere process of copying from the Continental codes. If the Jews came here at all it was for purposes of the slave trade, of which they held the monopoly at the time. It is thus possible that England owes indirectly to these Gallo-Jewish visitors the re-introduction of Christianity, owing to the celebrated incident in the market-place of Rome. But apart from such visits there is no trace of any Jews in Anglo-Saxon England, and it is difficult to see what they could have done here, considering their position.

JOSEPH JACOBS. The Jews in England.

The position of the Jew in a medieval State was entirely determined by the position taken up by the Church towards the Jews on the one hand and towards all capitalism on the other. As soon as the Church began to influence the legislation of the State, it took efficient measures to exclude Jews, and indeed all heretics, from the exercise of any public office by associating the reception to office with oaths of a distinctly Christian, and indeed orthodox, character. The right of holding public office granted to Jews by the Pagan Empire was taken away by the Justinian code, and by the time of the formation of the Holy Roman Empire they had gradually been excluded from every reputable sphere of life. Industry was in the hands of the guilds, which were religious

Forced into Finance.

confraternities as well as trades-unions; agriculture was connected with the Feudal System, which involved making homage with Christian oaths on taking a farm, and the higher functions of the State in municipalities and governments were equally connected with Christian inauguration oaths. It would have been impossible for the Jews to exist in any Christian State except for the attitude of the Church towards capitalism.

Usury.

Basing itself on the Vulgate mistranslation of Luke vi. 35, the Church regarded all addition of interest in the repayment of loans as directly prohibited by the Gospel, and therefore unworthy of a Christian. By this means all support of enterprise by capital was rendered disreputable. But the Jews were not affected by this view of the Church, and were thus enabled to perform an important function in the various medieval States of Christendom, as they emerged economically from the stage of barter. It is accordingly with the emergence of England from this stage that we first find certain evidence of the domicile of Jews in this country. William of Malmesbury states that Jews were brought over by the Conqueror from Rouen, and there is no reason to distrust his assertion. We have, however, only a few references to them before the country became settled under Henry II. A friendly disputation of a Jew from the Rhine Provinces with Gilbert Crispin, Abbot of Westminster, and the alleged martyrdom of St. William of Norwich in 1144, to which we shall refer later, are the chief events of interest of which we have any trace. But it is probable that the rulers of England had already begun to make use of their Jews as sponges to collect money for the Royal Treasury, since we find both Maud and Stephen squeezing financial support out of the Oxford Jews. It is also extremely improbable that the large building activity of the Norman nobles during the disturbed reign of Stephen, which is said to have resulted in the erection of over 1,100 castles, was effected without resort to Jewish "usury" (p. 474).

The Jews and the Crown.

But it was under Henry II. that the operations of the Jews first became extensive. His biographers noticed that he had "favoured more than was right a people treacherous and unfriendly to Christians, namely, the Jewish usurers, because of the great advantages which he saw were to be had from their usuries." The advantages he was enabled to draw from the Jews were due to the adoption by the State of the Church doctrine of "usury." The personalty of every usurer as such reverted or "became escheat to" the king on his death. This principle was equally applied to such Christians as braved public opinion by lending money on interest. But with the Jews it was in perpetual application, for the reason that their property could only be acquired by usury. Hence arose a general presumption, which was even inserted into the so-called laws of Edward the Confessor, that "the Jews

CARICATURE OF ISAAC OF NORWICH, FROM AN EXCHEQUER ROLL.
(*Record Office.*)

themselves, and all theirs, belong to the king." And this seems justified by the fact that the king demanded money from the Jews on almost every possible occasion. Fines were claimed from the Jews for wardship or marriage, for law proceedings, for the right to recover debts, to have residence with the good-will of the king, to have partnership, or, indeed, for any act which involved contract or conflict with others. But in all these cases the king claimed fines from his Christian subjects, who might equally, therefore, be termed his "chattels" as much as the Jews. There was, indeed, a special reason why the king would be more chary in entering upon possession of a deceased Jew's goods than in the case of those of a deceased Christian usurer. While the capital was in the possession of the Jew, it could be multiplied indefinitely by being lent out on interest, whereas the king as a good Christian could not make this use of the

money. Hence it was customary for the king to allow a
Jew's estate to pass to his heirs, merely exacting a fine for
the privilege, amounting as a rule to a third of the estate.

Meanwhile Jews, with the favour of the king, had begun
to organise themselves into what was substantially a great
banking association. As soon as the country became settled
after the disorders of Stephen's reign, we find them spreading
into the eastern and southern counties, then the most populous parts of England. A few of the most prominent Jewish
financiers in the centres of industry, as Jurnet of Norwich,
Isaac of London, and especially
Aaron of Lincoln, began to advance money to the king on the
security of the firms (p. 646) of
the different counties in which
Jews lived, the sheriffs doubtless
paying the amounts to the local
Jews acting as the agents of the
larger capitalists. At least we
have evidence of such agencies
being employed in the case of
private debtors.

Owing to this concentration
of Jewish capital and its dis-
semination through the counties
by means of agents, the higher
clergy and the lesser barons—
who were the only persons in
the kingdom who made much

A JEW OF COLCHESTER, FROM A
FOREST ROLL.
(Record Office.)

use of actual cash—were enabled to obtain money for building
operations or legal charges; but they had to pay a heavy price
for the accommodation. The least that Richard of Anesty paid
was 2d. a week in the pound—that is, about 43 per cent. per
annum; while a groat in the pound per week—that is, about
86 per cent. per annum—was by no means uncommon. We
can easily understand how oppressive even a small debt might
become after a few years' accumulation at this enormous
interest. Jocelyn of Bracelonde gives an interesting example
of the process as it applied to the Abbey of St. Edmunds,
though, curiously enough, the largest creditor of the Abbey was

a Christian, William Fitz Isabel, who does not, however, appear to have claimed interest; but Jocelyn explains how a debt of £26 13s. 4d. to Benedict the Jew, of Norwich, had grown in a few years to £880. Yet, to a certain extent, it was to the debtor's interest to let the debt mount up rather than to pay it off; for, if the Jew died, his estate as that of a usurer fell into the hands of the king, who might be induced to cancel the debt for a much smaller sum. From this point of view usury was in the nature of a bet on the Jew's life.

An interesting example of this occurs among the operations of Aaron of Lincoln, who seems to have been the chief financier among the English Jews of the twelfth century. He appears to have made a speciality of advancing moneys to abbeys; he boasted, for example, that but for him St. Alban would have had no roof over his head. When he died, in 1186, nine Cistercian monasteries of Yorkshire were indebted to him to the enormous extent of over 6,400 marks. But, though Aaron left several sons, the king seized the whole of his estate, both treasure and debts. The treasure was lost as it was being carried over to Dieppe, but the debts remained in the hands of the king, and were so extensive as to need a special branch of the Treasury called "Aaron's Exchequer" for many years to come. Sixteen years after his death the outstanding debts of Aaron's Exchequer amounted to £15,000, so that we may conjecture that his whole estate amounted to at least the king's annual income, which may be put down at about £35,000 at this period. Among the debts which fell into the king's hands was that of the Cistercian monasteries just mentioned, and the deed is still extant in which Richard I. releases them for a fine of only 1,000 marks, scarcely more than a seventh of the debt.

This windfall must have opened the eyes of the Treasury officials to the potentialities of Jewish usury as a reserve fund. The massacres which occurred on the accession of Richard I. showed them on what a precarious tenure the Jews held their wealth. These *émeutes* at London, Lynn, Bury, Stamford, and York were due to some extent to the rise of the Crusading spirit in England, which would naturally lead the crowd to attack the enemies of Christ at home before fighting them abroad. But at York we have evidence that the attack on

The Persecutions and their Grounds.

the Jews was organised by a set of nobles deeply in debt to the Jews, and the final act of the tragedy was to burn the proofs of their indebtedness in York Minster. As the holders of the debts had been slain, the debts themselves had become the property of the king, and to prevent any recurrence of such large losses Richard, on his return in 1194, organised the English Jewry in such a way as to keep a record of all its transactions. The Ordinances of the Jewry made arrangements by which all the property of the Jews, including their debts, should be registered, and provided that a transcript of all their transactions in future should be kept by royal officials. Further, two Wardens or Justiciars of the Jews were appointed, before whom all disputes about Jewish debts should be heard; while in the beginning of the thirteenth century the whole English Jewry was organised in its relation to the Crown in a special branch of the Treasury known as the Exchequer of the Jews. Henceforth they were entirely at the king's mercy, since he kept their business books for them.

Royal Control.

Other circumstances besides this helped to make their condition quite different in the thirteenth century from what it had been in the twelfth. In the twelfth century they had formed part of the upper classes and spoke the same language, Norman French. Their transactions were mainly with the barons and the abbots, and only indirectly affected the common people, who lived almost entirely by barter, and had no reason to resort to Jews for money. During the reign of Henry II., London was the chief French-speaking city in West Europe, and was the capital of the extensive Angevin Empire. Jewish capital had, therefore, a very large field for its operations. Henry II. was, besides, no friend of the Church, the chief and inveterate enemy of the Jews, and their position under him was an exceptionally favourable one.

Jewish Literature in Mediæval England.

We find this favourable condition of affairs reflected, strange to say, in the Hebrew literature of English Jews. Whereas in the thirteenth century we know only of an insignificant poet, Meir of Norwich; a codifier of Jewish ritual, Jacob ben Jehuda of London; and a legal authority, Moses of London; in the twelfth century, recent research has revealed the names of over twenty Jewish authors, some of considerable merit and importance. In particular, the study of the Massora, or text of the Scriptures, was especially prevalent among the English Jews, and led to the compilation of an important Hebrew Grammar by Samuel of Bristol, which was followed by a still more extensive work on the subject, entitled "The Onyx Book," by Moses ben Isaac of London. The chief Anglo-Jewish writer of the twelfth century, however, was Berachyah Nakdan, known as Benedict le Puncteur of Oxford, whose "Fox Fables" resemble those of Marie de France, and were probably derived from the same source. He was also the translator into Hebrew

MOYSES HALL, BURY ST. EDMUNDS
From an old Print.)

of Adelard's "Quæstiones Naturales" (p. 500), and a French work on Mineralogy, and a "Commentary on Job" by him is still extant in manuscript at Cambridge. Outside Spain no such important works were produced by any European Jews at this period, and it is, therefore, not to be wondered at that Abraham Ibn Ezra, the most distinguished author of his time and the original of Browning's *Rabbi Ben Ezra*, visited England in 1158.

But with the opening of the thirteenth century the con- The Jews dition of the Jews in England changed considerably for the in the Thirteenth worse. Throughout their history, Jews have always suffered Century. the most where and when the central authority was weakest. John and Henry III. had less power to protect their Jews than Henry II., and more reason to squeeze them. John had himself been a debtor to the Jews, and was, perhaps, influenced by personal feelings in the harsh attitude he took towards them, while Henry III. added religious antipathy to his pressing need of money during the latter part of his reign.   Both were enabled to work their will on English Jewry by means of the Exchequer of the Jews, which placed all Jewish transactions under the royal control, and practically made the English king the arch-usurer of his kingdom.   This was recognised both by the barons, who inserted a clause in Magna Charta to restrict it, and by the Church dignitaries, who from time to time remonstrated with the king for his participation in the unholy gain.

The Exchequer of the Jews was the visible and constitu-

A JEWISH STARR (MS. Aug. II. 107A).

tional sign of this partnership of king and Jewry. This had its headquarters at Westminster, where were stored up the Jewish deeds or "Starrs," which are said to have given its name to the Star Chamber.   The enrolment of Jewish indebtedness took place at certain specified towns throughout the southern and western counties, where "archae," or chests, were kept.   These were guarded by two Jewish and two Christian secretaries,[1] who kept charge of a third copy of all the deeds of the Jews, the other two being kept by the Jewish creditor and the Christian debtor.   No debt was recognised by the Law Courts the record of which was not kept in one of these chests.   Whenever the king desired to obtain a tallage[2] from his Jews, a list of the contents of these

[1 Technically called chirographers (writers), because they engrossed the requisite copies of the deeds on parchment.]

[2 Tallage (French, *taillage*, "cutting"), a tax or tribute, more especially imposed by the kings on their own tenants or dependants.]

chests was sent out from the twenty-six local depositaries, and at once he was enabled to estimate what resources the whole Jewry possessed to meet his demands. The amounts thus obtained were often very large: for the Saladin tribute, Henry II. obtained £60,000 as a quarter of Jewish chattels, against £70,000 yielded as a tenth by the rest of England. From this, it appears that at that time the Jews possessed no less than a quarter of the whole movable property of the

INTERIOR OF MOYSES HALL, BURY ST. EDMUNDS.

kingdom. In 1210, John imposed a tallage of no less than 60,000 marks, and imprisoned all the Jews of England until they had paid it. It was on this occasion that he used the novel torture of tooth-drawing to extract his quota from a recalcitrant Jew of Bristol. It has been calculated that, on the average, John and Henry III. obtained at least £5,000 per annum from tallages alone, not to mention the fines and escheats, which came from the Jews, as from the rest of his subjects, though, probably, in larger proportions. Altogether, it is probable the Royal Treasury obtained about one-tenth of its income from the Jews, or rather from their debtors,

43

who were, of course, mainly the barons and their retainers, since land was almost the only security which could be offered to the Jew. It was for this reason that the Jews had against them, throughout the thirteenth century, the whole power of the baronage. The barons claimed in 1244 the right to appoint one of the two Justiciars of the Jews, so that they might share with the king the control of the Jewry; and one of the complaints which led to the Barons' War was that the Jews handed over their bonds and the lands pledged for them to some of the greater barons, who thus imitated the king in becoming sleeping partners in the Jewish usury. During the Barons' War, the Jewries of London, Cambridge, Canterbury, Lincoln, Southampton, and Worcester were destroyed in order to get rid of the intolerable pressure of indebtedness. So, too, the towns, when obtaining their charters, endeavoured to minimise the royal influence by stipulating that no Jew could henceforth reside within their precincts, and in 1245 a general decree was issued confining the Jews to those towns in which "archae" were kept.

Owing to this strict supervision on the part of the Exchequer, and the restrictions on their business by the loss of free domicile in the cities, the Jews became rapidly impoverished towards the middle of the thirteenth century. In 1253, Elyas, their Presbyter, or Chief Rabbi, declared in impassioned terms that their life was no longer tolerable, and begged for permission for the whole Jewry to leave England and seek the protection of some prince who had bowels of compassion. He mentioned the fact that the king had now other resources from which he could extract money: he was referring to the important competitors in money-lending who existed in the Italian financiers, at that time extending their business in North Europe, with the connivance and often the protection of the Papal Court.

The Jews and the Church. Meanwhile the Church had been doing everything in its power to embitter the relations of the Jews with the whole population. We can observe a distinct increase of bitterness in the tone of the Church towards the Jews throughout the twelfth century, which was due partly to despair of converting them, and partly to increasing signs of the attraction of Jewish rites for the common people. Several instances are on record in which monks actually became converted to Judaism. The Church, accordingly, did everything in its power to prevent intercourse between Jew and Christian. Christians were not allowed to act as servants or nurses to Jews, under pain of excommunication, and the erection of new synagogues was forbidden. The anti-Jewish policy of the Church reached its culminating point at the Lateran Council of 1215, in which Innocent III. placed a permanent barrier between the Jewish and Christian populations of Europe, by ordering all Jews to wear a distinctive badge. This took the form in England of a patch of yellow taffety on the outer garment in the shape of the two Tables of the Law. When this was adopted in England, Stephen Langton even went so far as to forbid, under pain of excommunication, any intercourse with Jews, or the sale to them of the necessaries of life.

But, above all, the Church had helped to embitter the peace of the Jews by encouraging the myth of the "blood accusation," or the suspicion that Jews sacrificed Christian children on their Passover, which took its origin in England in connection with the case of the disappearance of the boy William, at Norwich, in 1144 (p. 579). The evidence on which this was twisted into the accusation against the whole of Jewry has recently been discovered and published, and proves to be of the most flimsy character. But the myth was encouraged by the local churches, since it brought pilgrims to any cathedral or church which could lay claim to possess the remains of such martyrs. Already in the twelfth century the example of Norwich was followed by Gloucester and Edmondsbury, and in the next century the leading case of Hugh of Lincoln served to confirm the popular belief. No more ingenious means of setting Jew and Christian apart could have been devised than this accusation, which would by itself prevent natural links of common friendship from being formed in early youth. It is but fair to add that several Popes formally declared their disbelief in the myth; but, when once started, it lived on among the common people, among whom it still exists on the Continent to the present day.

It was thus mainly owing to the action of the Church that the Christian and the Jewish population of England were kept apart. It is usual to attribute this aloofness to the fact that

Jews were aliens, spoke a strange language, and so on. But they were not more so than the rest of the Normans and Italians that formed the majority of the upper classes at the time. To take a concrete example—it is absurd to call Jacob fil Mosse, an Oxford Jew, whose ancestors we can trace in London and Bristol for seven preceding generations, more of an alien or foreigner than Simon de Montfort, whose ancestors

MARTYRDOM OF ST. WILLIAM OF NORWICH.
(By permission of Rev. C. B. Mayhew.)

were, indeed, Earls of Leicester, but only visited England occasionally. But for the action of the Church there was every sign that the Jewish population was assimilating itself with the English commonalty. We find Jews joining with Christians in the chase of a doe outside Colchester, and a very instructive incident of *rapprochement* occurred at Hereford under Bishop Swinfield. A marriage was about to take place in the family of some rich Jews at Hereford, who invited

many of their Christian friends to attend the festivity, which
was to be carried out on an unusual scale of magnificence.
The bishop, on hearing this, threatened excommunication upon
any Christian who would attend the Jewish ceremonies, and on
his threats being disregarded carried them out in all their
rigour.   The incident is characteristic of the part played by
the Church.

There is no doubt that the Jews themselves contributed to **Jewish**
the enmity with which they were regarded by the Church **Offence to Chris-**
by the open contempt they expressed for the more assailable **tians.**
sides of Catholicism—miracle-mongering and image-worship.
A Jew at Oxford openly boasted that he could perform the
same miracles as St. Frideswide.   He pretended to become
lame and then to walk straight again, contending that that
was as good a miracle as the saint had done.   Fanaticism was
opposed by fanaticism, and another Oxford Jew is stated to
have snatched a cross that was being carried in a procession
and to have trampled it under foot.   The Jews were only too
ready to meet their theological opponents in private and
public disputation, and on the evidence of Peter of Blois rarely
got the worst of the encounter.   All the chief heresies of the
twelfth and thirteenth centuries were tinged with Judaic
doctrine, and both Franciscans and Dominicans regarded it
as one of their chief aims to counteract Judaic influences.   It
is necessary to insist upon this clerical influence, as without
it it would be difficult to understand the action taken by
Edward I. in the expulsion of the Jews.

Of the internal organisation of the English Jewry during **Internal**
its stay in England something remains to be said.   By a charter **Organisa-**
of Henry II., confirmed by his successors, they were allowed to **tion of the Jewry.**
have Jurisdiction among themselves, according to Rabbinic
Law, in all cases except for the greater felonies.   Such cases
came before the *Beth Din*, consisting of three Dayanim, who
seem to have been called "bishops," and the senior of the
judges was termed Presbyter, and an Arch-presbyter for all
the Jews of England was appointed for life by the king.   He
may be said to correspond to the Chief Rabbi of modern
times; he seems to have had a semi-official connection with
the Exchequer of the Jews, where his advice was doubtless
taken on points of Jewish Law.   Each congregation had a

president (*Parnas*) and treasurer (*Gabbai*), among whose duties was, doubtless, that of collecting funds for the poor. Much attention was paid to education, at least to that of the boys. These were educated in local schools in the Bible and Talmud; and the most promising of them, who were willing to devote their life to the study of the Law, were sent up to the great school of the Jews in Ironmonger Lane. By this means all Jews knew, at any rate, enough Hebrew to write receipts in that language, hundreds of which are still extant, and have been recently published. In the twelfth century, at least, English Jews showed considerable activity as authors, and during the Expulsion of the French Jews, from 1182 to 1196, they received a large accession of learned French Jews. Their vernacular language remained French up to the Expulsion, as we know from letters written by them in that language, and from French glosses in their Hebrew commentaries. Except during periods of commotion, they lived on friendly terms with their neighbours, and even with clerics. Their deeds and valuables were often received for security in abbeys and monasteries. Their wealth enabled them to live in houses more solidly built than the rest of the population, possibly for purposes of protection; and the earliest private house of stone, still extant in England, is that of Aaron of Lincoln, already referred to as the chief Jewish financier of the twelfth century.

C. CREIGH-
TON.
Public
Health.

ONE great event of the reign of Henry III. was the famine with pestilence in the years 1257 to 1259. It appears to have helped, along with one or two other notorious famines, to give England a wholly undeserved repute among foreigners as being a country in which famine was habitual. But the famine and pestilence of 1257–9 was a solitary instance in a whole generation, and there was nothing like it again until 1315–16 Like other great famines in England, it was due to a succession of bad harvests, following either cold and backward springs or wet autumns; but the scarcity and dearness of corn would hardly have had so disastrous effects had it not been that the country was drained of its circulating coin, partly by levies for the Roman See, and partly by king's taxes, which somehow were in pawn to the king's brother, the Earl of Cornwall, candidate for the crown of the Holy Roman Empire, and were used by him to pay his German troops and to buy the votes of the electoral princes. The scarcity, began to be felt in the winter of 1256–7, and was followed by many deaths from hunger in 1257. There was little harvest that year, partly from neglect to till and sow the ground; and in May, 1258, a pestilence followed, which must have been one of the greater kind if the mortality in London had been only a fraction of the numbers alleged—namely, fifteen thousand, mostly of the poorer class. This is perhaps the earliest occasion on which large quantities of grain were imported to the Thames from Germany and Holland, the Earl of Cornwall having sent over sixty shiploads which were sold to his account to the starving Londoners. According to Matthew Paris, who was then living at St. Albans, the quantity of grain imported was more than three English counties had produced in the harvest before. But calamities did not come singly. Although the harvest of 1258 was an unusually rich one, the hopes of the husbandmen were blighted by cruel rains throughout the whole end of the year, which left the heavy crops rotting on the ground, so that the fields were like so many dung-heaps. Whatever corn was saved turned mouldy; the people struggled through the winter and spring (1259) with sacrifice of their cattle and with much sickness and mortality. This had been a characteristic English famine, due to a succession of bad seasons, and aggravated by economic or fiscal troubles. The first bad harvest had caused a smaller breadth to be sown for the year following, that had likewise turned out ill; the third harvest had been spoiled by incessant rain, and the whole calamitous episode had been made infinitely harder to bear by the heavy taxes and the consequent dearth of money. The English famines of that degree had not been many—one happened in the last year of the Conqueror's reign (1086–7), another in 1195–7, after the return of Richard I. from the Crusade; a third as above related; a fourth during the weak government of Edward II. in 1315–16; and, not to mention various local famines, one more in the fifteenth century (1439) as the climax of two or more bad seasons, which were even more disastrous in Scotland and in France. The price of corn was far from steady in the intermediate years; two or three years of very low prices would be followed by years when corn was twice, thrice, or four times as dear. But great fluctuations were normal, if one may so speak, in the medieval period; it needed a rise of eight or ten times from the lowest price to produce the true effects of famine, probably because in an ordinary dear year the poorer classes fell back upon oats, barley, and beans, instead of wheat, which was the staple bread-corn of England. These great fluctuations enabled the rich to grow richer; thus it is on record that the Archbishop of York, in the rather sharp scarcity of 1234, had his granaries at Ripon stored with the corn of four harvests, two or three of which had been hard for the poor. Even in the sharp famine of London in the summer of 1258, when the Earl of Cornwall's sixty cargoes of grain arrived, the first thing that the king had to do was to issue an ordinance against the middlemen's greed.

D. J. MEDLEY. Social Life.

AMONG the questions connected with the development of social life in any country none is more curious than the history of its people's dress. In modern times the costume of civil life would alone concern us; but at a period when every gentleman was perforce a soldier, no description of the costume of the upper classes at any rate would be complete unless it included an account of the military accoutrements. In treating of the costumes of the twelfth and thirteenth centuries in England, it will be well for clearness' sake to take from the head downwards the figures which we are to clothe. The first effect of the Norman Conquest seems to have been to develop extravagant if not vulgar tastes in the conquering race. Against this there was a slight reaction, at least in certain directions, under Henry II.; but the check was only momentary, and before the end of his reign the old love of outward magnificence had reasserted itself, though not perhaps to the same extravagant degree. The Anglo-Saxons, men as well as women, wore their hair long; the Normans, on the other hand, after an Aquitanian fashion, shaved the backs of their heads, so

that Harold's spies are said to have reported that the invaders
were an army of priests. But the long hair of the English
excited their admiration, and already under William II. a
writer complains that the men let their hair grow like women,
parted it in the middle to fall on each side, curled it with
hot irons, and, instead of a cap, bound their heads with fillets.
From time to time the protests of reforming clergy and
other influences of a semi-religious character caused a slight
compunction, as when, in 1104, Henry I. and all his Court

MEN'S HAIR AND BEARDS IN THE TWELFTH CENTURY (MS. Nero C. iv.).

submitted their long locks to the shears of a persuasive and
practical bishop. Even long beards did not escape censure, and
at the beginning of the twelfth century more than one writer
stigmatises his contemporaries of his own sex as "filthy
goats." To judge from the monumental effigies of the
thirteenth century there was a reform in beards. It was not
uncommon to wear none at all, and those that were worn were
of comparatively modest proportions. On the other hand, the
hair was, and for some time remained, as long as ever it had
been, and the beaux of the period curled it with irons and
only subjected their heads to the modest restraint of a fillet or
a ribbon. The Norman ladies, on the other hand, wore their

hair in two long plaits, which were sometimes confined in embroidered silken cases. But in the middle of the thirteenth century these tails were unplaited; married ladies turned up their hair and confined it in a net or caul of golden thread, while unmarried girls and the women-folk in the humbler ranks let it flow down their backs. In the case of the men the more elaborate arrangements of the hair often did not permit of any head-dress. But for those who desired to shelter their heads from cold or heat the choice lay between hats and

A NORMAN LADY'S HAIR
(Nero C. iv.).

caps and hoods. The only hat of which we have a record has been likened to the Greek petasus, and may find its modern descendant in the hard clerical hat of the present day. It was broad-brimmed and made of felt or of some substance covered with skin, and when not on the head could apparently be carried slung at the owner's back. The choice among caps was large; but they seem to have fallen into two classes, according as they resembled the peaked caps of Phrygian shape which had been worn before the Norman Conquest, or rested flat upon the head after the manner of a Scots blue bonnet or a modern smoking-cap. Towards the middle of the thirteenth century, convenience seems to have popularised among all ranks and all professions the ugly fashion of a white linen coif, which was tied under the chin like a night-cap. Hoods, both attached to and apart from cloaks, were used by men and women travellers alike. Otherwise, the women wore a veil or headcloth, called a couvrechef, whence our word kerchief; and this was succeeded by a wimple, a close-fitting covering for the head and throat, and the gorget, which was a fuller wimple—in fact, a kind of copious neckcloth. But the plain wimple was not enough, and before long it came to be artificially raised off the head and adorned with horns and other fanciful shapes.

The rest of the costume went through fewer changes than the manipulation of the head and hair. The substratum of

the dress of a Norman was the same as that of the English- **Men's Dress.**
man; a short tunic covered by a cloak, drawers and chausses
—that is, long stockings or tights, over which would be worn
bandages rolled round the leg, and shoes or short boots.
Here, too, the extravagance of the Normans led to an early
development of the tunic, and the sleeves were increased in
both length and breadth. In fact, in State dresses the long
linen undergarment and tunic over it were worn so long that
they trailed upon the ground. Similarly, the cloaks or mantles

ANGLO-NORMAN LADIES' DRESS (MS. Roy. 2 B. vi.).

were made of the richest cloth and lined with the finest fur.
Robert Bloet, Bishop of Lincoln, is said to have given Henry I.
a mantle of sable which cost £100 in the money of the time.
Henry II. owed his name Court Mantle to his supposed introduction of a shorter cloak. But this did not mean a simpler
costume. The number and kind of garments remained the
same, but the extravagance of their pattern increased, and an
edict of the end of Henry's reign was aimed against the pre-
vailing fashion of cutting the borders of both tunics and
mantles into fancy shapes. In the thirteenth century we meet
with two new garments—a cyclas or cointise, an upper tunic
of fine material worked in a fanciful pattern, supposed to have

been invented in the Cyclades; while over their mantles travellers wore a more ample hooded garment with sleeves,

COSTUME, LATE THIRTEENTH CENTURY (MS. Roy. 2 B. vii.).

called a supertotus or overall, which in 1226, under the name of balandrana, is forbidden to the monks of St. Benedict. Meanwhile the shoes had been prolonged into peaks, and being stuffed with tow were twisted into all kinds of fanciful shapes; while the leg bandages, under the name of sandals, were unrolled, and were worn crossing each other all up the leg. The Norman desire to lengthen every part of the costume affected the

Women's Dress. women as well as the men. The ordinary lady's dress consisted of a long tunic under a gown called a robe. Soon after the Conquest the sleeves and the veils became so long that they had to be tied up in knots to avoid treading upon them. At the same time the tight-lacing in which the ladies indulged caused so much scandal to onlookers that a satirist did not hesitate even to depict the Devil tight-laced and otherwise attired as a fashionable lady of the period. The general appearance of a lady of the twelfth century has been described as Oriental, or at least Byzantine, and in it may be traced the connection of the Normans with Sicily and the Crusades. In the latter half of the twelfth century the long sleeves were discarded. Otherwise, the chief changes to

THE DEVIL TIGHT-LACED (MS. Nero C. iv.).

the end of the thirteenth century consisted in the addition of two garments—the supertunic or surcoat, at first a shorter tunic of a fancy pattern, but ultimately lengthened until its skirt rivalled that of the robe itself; and the pelisse, a richly furred garment fitting close. to the body and worn in winter under the mantle or cloak. Mention is also made of a bliaus, but it is probable that this only describes another form of supertunic.

But after all, except for the incidental light it may shed **Military** upon the manners of the people, there is no department of **Dress.**

A LADY HUNTING (MS. Add. 24,686).

history which passes so soon into pure antiquarianism as that which seeks to trace the changes of fashion in costume. Far otherwise is it with the development of military dress. The constant adaptation of means to ends in what for a long time was, and for an equally long time seems destined to remain, the most serious business in life of a large portion of the human race, is fraught with interest of a peculiar kind. However futile may be the result, and even in the most unworthy cause, the matching of wit against wit will always form a fascinating and even profitable study to thoughtful minds. Under modern conditions the weapons of offence have become so powerful that, as far as the individual human body is concerned, we have practically given over any attempt to protect it. But the invention of gunpowder was preceded by a long duel between the armour of defence and the weapons of offence, for every improvement in the latter necessitated modifications in the means of protecting the body of the warrior. It was not until these means became so cumbersome as to defeat their own purpose that their inventors acknowledged the failure of their aims, and that the prowess of the individual soldier gave place to the skilful ordering of battalions.

The body armour of the Normans was of the kind technically known as *single mail.* The foundation of it was a leathern tunic, called a hauberk, on which were fastened small iron rings or small plates of steel. The most common variant was composed of iron rings sewn flat upon the leather. The head was protected either with a capuchon or cowl which formed part of the tunic, or by a conical-shaped helmet with a nasal, or dependent piece of iron to protect the nose. In the reign of William II. the collar of the tunic was lengthened upwards so as to protect the chin and mouth, and not only was it joined on to the nasal, but steel cheek-pieces were introduced. The legs were protected by leathern chausses corresponding to the tunic, but despite the illustrations of the Bayeux tapestry, it seems improbable that they should have formed one piece with the tunic. The Crusades wrought many important changes in the mode of armament. Thus in Richard I.'s day the warrior wore a long tunic under his coat of mail, and an elaborately embroidered surcoat over it. This last garment served a twofold object; for it was a means by which the various leaders of the Christian host could be distinguished from each other, while it protected the iron armour from the scorching rays of the Eastern sun. Moreover, in addition to the ringed or plated hauberk, mention is now made of quilted tunics of various kinds, of which the gambeson is a type. These were of a simple kind for those who could not afford the hauberk, but were also worn highly ornamented as an additional means of defence. In the middle of the thirteenth century this quilted armour became common for both the body and the legs.

But the greatest revolution was the introduction from Asia of the shirt of *chain mail.* The old iron rings sewn flat on the leathern tunic had gradually been displaced by a tunic in which the rings were set up edgeways. Now, however, the leather foundation altogether disappeared, and the rings were so linked together as to form a complete garment of themselves. This would be worn loose over the gambeson, and was itself covered by a surcoat emblazoned with the warrior's coat of arms. Nor did the lines of defence stop here; for already to hauberk or gambeson had been added a plastron de fer, an iron plate to prevent the pressure of the tunic on the chest,

Brass from Stoke d'Abernoun,
Surrey, 1277.

Brass from Trumpington,
Cambridgeshire, 1289.

ARMOUR AT THE CLOSE OF THE THIRTEENTH CENTURY.

and better known under its later names of gorget or habergeon.
More important, however, is it to notice that at the end of the
thirteenth century small plates of steel were added to the
defences of the shoulders, elbows and knees, thus beginning
the "last great change which cased in complete steel the
chivalry of Europe."

Finally, the protecting armour for the head had also
changed its form. Stephen's capture at the battle of Lincoln
(p. 369) was attributed to the hold which his captor had

KNIGHT IN ARMOUR
(MS. Roy. 2 A. xxii.).

obtained upon the nasal of his
helmet, and the advantage which
such a piece of armour conferred upon an adversary at close
quarters caused it to be abandoned. The helmet had become
a flat-topped steel cap held by
a hoop of iron under the chin.
To this, in place of the nasal,
was fitted a movable grating
which could be unfastened from
the side, so that it was only
necessary to close it when in
actual combat. But as the body
armour became more elaborate
this was not deemed sufficient
protection for the head, and at
the end of the thirteenth century the form of helmet is one
that covers the whole head, and rests upon the shoulders.

Military Exercises.　　It must have been only by constant practice that a
medieval knight could acquire sufficient familiarity with the
weapons wielded in actual warfare under such disadvantageous
circumstances. This practice was obtained in a variety of
military exercises, which are all included under the compre-
hensive name of tournament. More strictly we may distinguish
between four kinds of such pastimes—tilting at the quintain,
running at the ring, tournaments and jousts. In its origin
the quintain must have been merely a dummy adversary,
the chief object being to teach the young warrior to
strike straight and true. As a final development, upon

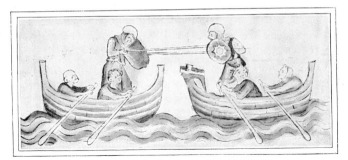

WATER TILTING (MS. Roy. 2 B. vii.).

ARMOURED KNIGHTS (Harley Roll Y. 6).

TILTING.
(*Luttrell Psalter.*)

44

a post was hung a cross-arm turned on a pivot; at one end was placed the shield to be struck, at the other end a bag of sand or some offensive weapon which would swing round and hit the dilatory or awkward tilter on head or back. The quintain was a common means of diversion among all classes of society, and it took many curious forms both on land and water. But as a knightly exercise, demanding the highest skill in the performer, it reached its utmost development in tilting or running at the ring, in which a ring hung from a post had to be carried off on the end of the rider's lance. Tournaments and jousts were strictly military exercises: the tournament being a conflict of many knights divided into two parties; the joust the trial of strength and skill between two knights riding at each other with a lance in rest. Despite the outward trappings of the tournament, it was a cruel and a dangerous sport, and the kings were generally concerned to limit its occasions by insisting on the necessity of their licence. But the feudal instinct was too strong for the royal edicts, and after all it may be questioned whether the tournaments or jousts were more senseless or more fatal to life and limb than the duel of honour which took their place.

THE FAVERSHAM HELMET.

AUTHORITIES.—1216–1273.

GENERAL.

For the long reign of Henry III. there is a good supply of contemporary writers. The important St. Albans Chronicles, compiled successively by Wendover, Matthew Paris, and Rishanger, go down to 1306. The monastic annals of Waverley, Dunstable, Osney, etc., are full and important. A valuable series of royal letters, selected and edited in the Rolls Series, covers the reign. In the same series are Grosseteste's *Letters*, the *Monumenta Franciscana*, and Roger Bacon's works. Thomas Wykes gives the royalist view; the important *Carmen de Bello Lewensi* (ed. Kingsford) and the mass of contemporary political songs give the reformers' ideas. Constitutional documents are very fully given in Stubbs' *Charters*. Modern authorities as for chap. iii., also Blaauw, *Barons' War*, and Prothero's *Simon de Montfort*.

SPECIAL SUBJECTS.

Religion (*see also* above).—The Chronicles of Robert of Gloucester and Matthew Paris (Rolls Series); political songs of the period; and the works of Roger Bacon; *Monumenta Franciscana* (ed. J. S. Brewer); Eccleston's *Coming of the Friars*.

Law.—The best text of the statutes is in the edition issued by the Record Commission. Stubbs's select *Charters* and Bémont's *Chartes* are useful. Various judicial rolls have been published by the Selden Society and the Surtees Society. The best of the three editions of Bracton's *Law of England* is that of 1569. Bracton's *Note Book* (ed. Maitland) contains many of the cases on which he based his text. The best sketch of the material is given by Brunner in Holtzendorff's *Encyklopädie der Rechtswissenschaft*. Reeves's *History of English Law* begins to be useful in this period. *See also* J. F. Stephen's *History of Criminal Law*; Pike's *History of Crime*; and Blackstone's *Commentaries*.

Naval matters, as for chap. iii.

Agriculture (for period 1216-1348).—Thorold Rogers, *History of Agriculture and Prices* and *Six Centuries of Work and Wages*; Nasse, *Zur Geschichte der Mittelalterlichen Feldgemeinschaft in England*; Vinogradoff, *Villainage in England*; Maitland, *Select Pleas in Manorial Courts* (Selden Society); Seebohm, *English Village Community*; Gomme, *Village Community*.

Commerce, etc.—Cunningham, *History of Industry and Commerce*, i.; Ashley, *Economic History*; Thorold Rogers, *Agriculture and Prices*, i., ii.; Hall, *History of the Customs Revenue*, i., ii.; Madox, *History of the Exchequer*; Gross, *The Gild Merchant*: *Monumenta Gildhallae* (ed. Riley, Rolls Series); Jacobs, *Jews in Angevin England*.

Art and Architecture.—As for chap. iii., omitting Freeman's *History of the Norman Conquest*, and adding Kenyon, *Gold Coins of England*.

Learning and Science.—Besides the works of Hampden, Bass Mullinger, Maxwell Lyte, and Poole, referred to in chap. iii., mention may be made of J. S. Brewer's prefaces to his edition of *Monumenta Franciscana*, 1858, and of Roger Bacon's *Opera Inedita*, 1869; H. R. Luard, preface to *Roberti Grosseteste Epistolæ*, 1861; T. M. Lindsay, *Occam* (*Encycl. Brit.*, 9th ed., xvii.); A. Seth, *Scholasticism* (*Encycl. Brit.*, 9th ed., xxi.); Rashdall, *Origin of the University of Oxford* (*Church Quarterly Review*, No. 46, Jan., 1887), and introduction to *The Friars Preachers* v. *the University*, 1311-1313 (in Oxford Historical Society's *Collectanea*, 2nd series, 1890); A. G. Little, *The Grey Friars in Oxford*, 1892; Brodrick, *Memorials of Merton College*, 1885.

Language and Literature (*see also* list appended to chap. iii.).—Skeat, *Principles of English Etymology* (two series, Clarendon Press, 1887-91); Sweet, H., *New English Grammar*, part i. (Clarendon Press, 1892); B. Ten Brink, *Chaucer's Sprache und Verskunst*, Leipzig, 1884; Kluge, *Gesch. d. Englischen Sprache* (in Paul's *Grundriss der Germanischen Philologie*, i.); H. G. Hewlett, *Cronica Rogeri de Wendover, sive Flores Historiarium* (3 vols., 1886, etc., Rolls Series); Sir F. Madden, *Matthaei Parisiensis Historia Anglorum sive . . . . Historia Minor* (3 vols., 1886-9, Rolls Series); H. R. Luard, *Matthaei Parisiensis Cronica Majora* (1872-82, 7 vols., Rolls

Series), and the other chroniclers edited in the Rolls Series ; *Encyclopædia Britannica*, Art. "Romance." H. Ward, Introduction to *Romance Catalogue*, British Museum.

The Jews in England.—Jacobs, *Jews in Angevin England* (up to 1206) ; Tovey, *Anglia Judaica* (mainly derived from Prynne's *Short Demurrer*) ; Madox, *History of the Exchequer*, chap. vi.) ; B. L. Abrahams, *Expulsion of the Jews from England ;* Publications of the Anglo-Jewish Historical Exhibition, and of the Jewish Historical Society of England.

Social Life.—As in Chap. III. with the addition of Strutt, *Sports and Pastimes of the English People.*

THE QUINTAIN, OFFHAM, KENT.

INDEX.

COLSTONS LIMITED, PRINTERS, EDINBURGH.